# INTRODUCTION TO THE
# WORLD'S MAJOR RELIGIONS

Introduction to the World's Major Religions

# ISLAM

## Volume 5

## Zayn R. Kassam

### Lee W. Bailey, General Editor

GREENWOOD PRESS
Westport, Connecticut • London

**Library of Congress Cataloging-in-Publication Data**
available on request from the Library of Congress.

British Library Cataloguing in Publication Data is available.

ISBN 0–313–33634–2 (set)
    0–313–33327–0 (vol. 1)
    0–313–32724–6 (vol. 2)
    0–313–33251–7 (vol. 3)
    0–313–32683–5 (vol. 4)
    0–313–32846–3 (vol. 5)
    0–313–33590–7 (vol. 6)

First published in 2006

Greenwood Press, 88 Post Road West, Westport, CT 06881
An imprint of Greenwood Publishing Group, Inc.
www.greenwood.com

Printed in the United States of America

The paper used in this book complies with the
Permanent Paper Standard issued by the National
Information Standards Organization (Z39.48–1984).

10   9   8   7   6   5   4   3   2   1

**Introduction to the World's Major Religions**
**Lee W. Bailey, General Editor**

Judaism, Volume 1
*Emily Taitz*

Confucianism and Taoism, Volume 2
*Randall L. Nadeau*

Buddhism, Volume 3
*John M. Thompson*

Christianity, Volume 4
*Lee W. Bailey*

Islam, Volume 5
*Zayn R. Kassam*

Hinduism, Volume 6
*Steven J. Rosen*

*For J. William Whedbee (1938–2004)*
*friend, colleague, and mentor*
*"Wisdom is better than weapons of war" Eccles. 9.18*
*and*
*Sebastian, Zara, and Rowena*
*"Invite to the Way of thy Lord with Wisdom" Qur. 16:125*

# CONTENTS

# SET FOREWORD

This set, *Introduction to the World's Major Religions,* was developed to fill a niche between sophisticated texts for adults and the less in-depth references for middle schoolers. It includes six volumes on religions from both Eastern and Western traditions: Judaism, Christianity, Islam, Hinduism, Confucianism and Taoism, and Buddhism. Each volume gives a balanced, accessible introduction to the religion.

Each volume follows a set format so readers can easily find parallel information in each religion. After a Timeline and Introduction, narrative chapters are as follows: the "History of Foundation" chapter describes the founding people, the major events, and the most important decisions made in the faith's early history. The "Texts and Major Tenets" chapter explains the central canon, or sacred texts, and the core beliefs, doctrines, or tenets, such as the nature of deities, the meaning of life, and the theories of the afterlife. The chapter on "Branches" outlines the major divisions of the religion, their reasons for being, their distinctive doctrines, their historical background, and structures today. The chapter on "Practice Worldwide" describes the weekly worship practices, the demographic statistics indicating the sizes of various branches of religions, the global locations, and historical turning points. The chapter on "Rituals and Holidays" describes the ritual practices of the religions in all their varieties and the holidays worldwide, such as the Birth of the Buddha, as they have developed historically. The chapter on "Major Figures" covers selected notable people in the history of each religion and their important influence. A glossary provides

definitions for major special terms, and the index gives an alphabetic lo-
cator for major themes. A set index is included in volume 6 (to facilitate
comparison).

In a world of about 6 billion people, today the religion with the greatest
number of adherents is Christianity, with about 2 billion members, comprising 33 percent of the globe's population. Next largest is Islam, with about
1.3 billion members, (about 22 percent). Hindus number about 900 million
(about 15 percent). Those who follow traditional Chinese religions number
about 225 million (4 percent). Although China has the world's largest population, it is officially Communist, and Buddhism has been blended with
traditional Confucianism and Taoism, so numbers in China are difficult
to verify. Buddhism claims about 360 million members (about 6 percent
of the world's population). Judaism, although historically influential, has
a small number of adherents—about 14 million (0.2 percent of the world's
population). These numbers are constantly shifting, because religions are
always changing and various surveys define groups differently.[1]

Religions are important elements of the worldview of a culture. They
express, for example, the cultural beliefs about cosmology, or picture of the
universe (e.g., created by God or spontaneous), and the origin of humanity (e.g., purposeful or random), its social norms (e.g., monogamy or polygamy), its ways of relating to ultimate reality (e.g., sacrifice or obedience
to law), the historical destiny (e.g., linear or cyclical), life after death (e.g.,
none or judgment), and ethics (e.g., tribal or universal).

As the world gets smaller with modern communications and global
travel, people come in contact with those of other religions far more fre-
quently than in the past. This can cause conflicts or lead to cooperation, but
the potential for hostile misunderstanding is so great that it is important
to foster knowledge and understanding. Noting parallels in world religions
can help readers understand each religion better. Religions can provide
ethical guidance that can help solve serious cultural problems. During war
the political question "why do they hate us?" may have serious religious
aspects in the answer. New answers to the question of how science and
religion in one culture can be reconciled may come from another religion's
approach. Scientists are increasingly analyzing the ecological crisis, but the
solutions will require more than new technologies. They will also require
ethical restraint, the motivation to change the destructive ecological habits
of industrial societies, and some radical revisioning of worldviews. Other
contemporary issues, such as women's rights, will also require patriarchal
religions to undertake self-examination. Personal faith is regularly called

into consideration with daily news of human destructiveness or in times of crisis, when the very meaning of life comes into question. Is life basically good? Will goodness in the big picture overcome immediate evil? Should horrendous behavior be forgiven? Are people alone in a huge, indifferent universe, or is the ultimate reality a caring, just power behind the scenes of human and cosmic history? Religions offer various approaches, ethics, and motivations to deal with such issues. Readers can use the books in this set to rethink their own beliefs and practices.

## NOTE

1. United Nations, "Worldwide Adherents of All Religions by Six Continental Areas, Mid-2002," *World Population Prospects: The 1998 Revision* (New York: United Nations, 1999).

# INTRODUCTION

Islam claims more than a billion followers worldwide; its presence is felt in almost every nation. Muslims are found in a multitude of cultures and ethnicities. There are myriad ways of defining what it means to be Muslim. In more than 1,400 years, its adherents have made invaluable contributions in music, painting, architecture, poetry, philosophy, mathematics, literature, and medicine. As Islam has spread through conquest, trade, and migration, the religion has produced a creative blend of cultures, expressing itself in ever new ways as it adapted to new conditions. It has much in common with the other monotheisms of Judaism and Christianity, and Muslims subscribe to the belief in the same God of Noah, Abraham, Moses, and Jesus. Yet Islam also shares much with Hinduism, Buddhism, and African religions. The study of religions, therefore, brings into focus the many similarities *and* differences across religious traditions, resonating with us even as we recognize the unique characteristics of each faith.

Long before I was invited to write this volume, my friend and colleague, J. William (Bill) Whedbee, professor of biblical studies at Pomona College, observed that the changing politics of the modern world now demanded that every educated person come to terms with Islam, an assertion that has since been underscored by the tragedy of September 11, 2001. There are no easy answers to the painful questions that have since ensued, and, in the aftermath, Muslims, whether in North America or elsewhere, have questioned whether the events of 9/11 represented a legitimate use of their faith. They have reexamined their relationship with Americans, whether those Americans are neighbors and coworkers or the face of a menacing global superpower. Americans have questions of their own: Is Islam hope-lessly backward? Does it predispose one to kill? Clearly, this volume cannot provide all the answers, for no faith calls upon its members to slay the inno-cent, although violence may be condoned or even endorsed under certain conditions. As the Crusades and many subsequent conflicts have shown, religious and civic leaders of virtually all faiths are not above manipulat-ing theology to further wars whose stated goals seem to justify the loss of human life. This short volume is offered in the hope that readers will learn to speak in more informed ways about Muslims, while embracing shared values and appreciating Islam's remarkable history.

# ACKNOWLEDGMENTS

I would like to express my deepest thanks to Wendi Schnaufer for her perceptive feedback (and her patience!); to Lee Bailey, series editor, for giving me the opportunity to write this book; to Peter Losh for his thorough and painstaking editing of portions of the book, turning some of my unwieldy prose into readable pages; and to Tazim Kassam, my intellectual companion and erstwhile editor, to whom the depth of my gratitude is inexpressible. And to Bill, for his encouragement and friendship.

# TIMELINE

| | |
|---|---|
| **570** | Birth of the Prophet Muhammad. |
| **610** | Muhammad receives first revelation. |
| **620** | Death of Muhammad's wife, Khadija, and his uncle and protector, Abu Talib. |
| **622** | Muhammad's emigration to Medina, called the *hijra*; beginning of the Muslim calendar. |
| **624** | Battle of Badr, the first significant battle fought between the Meccan army and the Prophet's Medinan army. |
| **625** | Battle of Uhud, the second battle fought between Meccan and Medinan forces. |
| **627** | Battle of the Trench, the third battle fought between Medinan forces, entailing an unsuccessful siege of Medina. |
| **628** | Treaty of Hudaybiyah, a truce declared between the Meccans and Muhammad. |
| **629** | Muhammad's first attempted pilgrimage to Mecca. |
| **630** | Mecca's surrender to Muhammad. |
| **632** | Muhammad's final pilgrimage to Mecca, followed by his death in June. |
| **634** | Death of first caliph, Abu Bakr; Byzantines defeated in Palestine. |
| **636** | Conquest of Syria, a Byzantine territory captured by the Sassanids. |

637      Conquest of Iraq, a Sassanid territory.

638      Conquest of Jerusalem, a Byzantine territory held by the Sassanids.

644      Death of second caliph, 'Umar.

656      Assassination of third caliph, 'Uthman.

661      Assassination of fourth caliph, 'Ali; beginning of Umayyad dynasty.

680      Massacre of Husayn and his supporters at Karbala.

711      Conquest of parts of Spain and Sind (India) by the Umayyads.

712      Control established over parts of Central Asia.

732      Charles Martel, the de facto ruler of the Franks, defeats Muslims at Tours and Poitiers, France.

749      End of Umayyad dynasty; beginning of 'Abbasid dynasty.

762      Founding of Baghdad.

765      Death of Shi'ite Imam Ja'far al-Sadiq, causing split between Ithna 'Ashari and Isma'ili Shi'ah.

767      Death of Abu Hanifah, founder of Hanafi school of law.

795      Death of Malik ibn Anas, founder of Maliki school of law.

820      Death of Muhammad. Birth of Idris al-Shafi'i, founder of Shafi'i school of law.

855      Death of Ahmed ibn Hanbal, founder of Hanbali school of law.

873      Death of 11th Shi'i Imam (introducing the period of the 12th "Hidden" Imam).

909      Establishment of Fatimid state in North Africa.

969      Founding of al-Azhar in Cairo, an institution of higher learning.

1009     Establishment of Muslim dynasty in West Africa.

1021     Emergence of the Druze movement.

1030     Death of Mahmud of Ghazna, who extended Muslim rule over Central and South Asia.

1038     Founding of Saljuq Sunni Turkish dynasty in Iraq.

1071     Extension of Saljuq dynastic rule over Asia Minor.

1095     Pope Urban II launches First Crusade.

1099     Crusaders conquer Jerusalem.

| | |
|---|---|
| 1143 | First translation of the Qur'an (Islam's holy book) into Latin. |
| 1171 | Saladin, vizier and deposer of the last Fatimid caliph, establishes Ayyubid dynasty in Egypt. |
| 1187 | Saladin recaptures Jerusalem. |
| 1200 | Muslims establish presence in Southeast Asia. |
| 1254 | Mamluk dynasty established in Egypt. |
| 1258 | Mongol leader Hulagu Khan burns Baghdad; Mongol Ilkhanid dynasty established. |
| 1281 | Establishment of Ottoman Empire, founded by Osman I in Anatolia. |
| 1333 | Construction begins of Alhambra Palace and citadel in Granada, Spain, the first example of Moorish architecture in that country. |
| 1399 | Delhi sultanate ends in India by Timur, also known as Tamerlane (d. 1405), Mongol conqueror; Timurid dynasty formed. |
| 1453 | Ottomans take Constantinople and rename it Istanbul. |
| 1492 | Muslim rule in Granada (Spain) brought to an end by rulers Ferdinand and Isabella; Christopher Columbus sets sail for the New World. |
| 1497 | Babur (d. 1530), descendant of Timur and founder of the Mughal Empire in India, captures Samarkand, Timur's capital. |
| 1498 | Portuguese explorer Vasco da Gama sets sail to India, guided by Ibn Majid from East Africa. |
| 1521 | Belgrade captured by Muslims. |
| 1526 | Babur founds Mughal dynasty in India; Ottomans take Hungary. |
| 1530 | Muslim kingdom established in Aceh, Indonesia. |
| 1600 | Beginning of slave trade across the Atlantic, including Muslims from West Africa. |
| 1641 | Dutch conquer parts of Southeast Asia. |
| 1694 | French gain territories in North Africa. |
| 1770 | Ottoman fleet destroyed by Russians. |
| 1783 | Catherine II establishes Russian rule over Crimean Muslim Tatars. |
| 1798 | French under Napoleon Bonaparte enter Egypt. |
| 1799 | French forced out of Egypt by Muhammad Ali. |

1800    Dutch assume control over Java and Sumatra (Indonesia).

1803    English gain control over Delhi.

1818    British rule (Raj) established in India.

1830    France gains control of Algeria.

1857    Indian mutiny; Muslim rule ends, overtaken by the British.

1881    France gains control of Tunisia.

1891    British gain control of Muscat and Oman.

1900    British gain control over Nigeria and the Sokoto empire to the north.

1905    Revolution in Iran; British gain control of the Sinai Peninsula.

1914    Egypt is made a British protectorate.

1922    Ottoman sultanate ended by Mustafa Kemal Ataturk.

1923    Turkish Republic established by Mustafa Kemal Ataturk.

1925    Reza Shah ends Qajar dynasty in Iran and establishes Pahlavi dynasty.

1926    Abd al-Aziz ibn Said proclaimed king of Saudi Arabia.

1941    Syria removed from French and British control.

1942    Japanese occupy Indonesia.

1946    Jordan, Lebanon, and Syria become independent from Britain and France.

1947    Formation of Pakistan and India as independent states.

1949    United Nations sanctions establishment of the State of Israel.

1949    Indonesia gains independence.

1951    Kingdom of Libya gains independence.

1952    Constitutional monarchy established in Jordan.

1953    Democratically elected Mohammed Mosaddeq in Iran deposed, returning the Shah to power; Egypt is declared a republic through a military coup mounted by Gamal Abdul Nasser.

1955    Xinjian Uighur Autonomous region established in the People's Republic of China.

1956    Morocco and Tunisia gain independence.

1957    Malaysia gains independence.

1962    Algeria gains independence; Yemen Arab Republic established.

1971    Establishment of Bangladesh.

1979    Iranian revolution, bringing an end to the Pahlavi dynasty. The Islamic Republic of Iran is formed under the leadership of the Ayatollah Khomeini.

1988    Khomeini issues legal ruling (*fatwa*) calling for death of British Indian writer Salman Rushdie, author of the novel, *Satanic Verses*.

1991    First Gulf War, in response to Saddam Hussein's (Iraq's) annexation of Kuwait.

1991    Soviet Union fragmented into Azerbaijan, Kazakhstan, Kyrghistan, Tajikistan, Turkmenistan, and Uzbekistan.

1992    Bosnia-Herzegovina created from the former Yugoslavia, leading to a campaign of ethnic cleansing mounted by Serbian forces.

2001    Al-Qaida attacks targets in the United States.

2001    United States invades Afghanistan in pursuit of Osama bin Laden, head of al-Qaida.

2003    United States invades Iraq to depose leader Saddam Hussein.

2003    Shirin Ebadi, Iranian human rights lawyer, becomes first Muslim woman to win the Nobel Peace Prize.

2004    Yasser Arafat, Palestinian leader, joint winner of the 1994 Nobel Peace Prize with Shimon Peres and Yitzhak Rabin, dies.

2005    Saudi Arabia's King Fahd dies and is succeeded by his brother, Crown Prince Abdullah bin Abdul-Aziz.

2005    Israel closes settlements in the Gaza strip.

# 1

# HISTORY OF FOUNDATION

The Islamic religion came to an Arab named Muhammad b. Abdallah (ca. 570–632 C.E.) in a series of revelations that began when he was about 40 years old. His revelations are collected in a book called the Qur'an, which is the sacred text for all Muslims. Arabian society at the time of Muhammad was organized around tribal groupings comprised of clans. Each clan was headed by a *shaykh* and was associated with a specific town or city. Muhammad belonged to the powerful Quraysh tribe located near Mecca, one of Arabia's key trading and pilgrimage cities. His clan, the Banu Hashim, was somewhat impoverished but highly respected. It survives to this day in the Hashemite Kingdom of Jordan.

## THE ARABS

### Origins

Arabs are Semites. Their language shares characteristics with other Semitic languages such as Hebrew, Aramaic, Syriac, Akkadian, and Assyrian. The Semitic languages belong to a larger group of Afro-Asiatic languages, which include the languages of the ancient Egyptians, the Berbers, and the Babylonians. The people of the southern Arabian Peninsula are thought to be the aboriginal Arabs, whereas people in the north migrated to the peninsula and became Arabized over time. Both groups see themselves as descendants of biblical forebears. Southerners trace their lineage from the grandson of Shem, son of Noah (Gen. 10:25–26), and northerners believe they are descended from Abraham and his wife Ketura (Gen. 25:1–4), as well as 'Adnan, a descendant of Ishmael, son of Abraham through Hagar.

### Tribal Religious Beliefs

From pre-Islamic poetry (which was transmitted orally and only written down in the 8th century), it is known that the Arabs worshipped multiple deities, many of whom were linked to nature and sacred sites. Allah, which means "the god," was a high god responsible for creation. He kept himself somewhat remote from human affairs, except during crises. Three of the chief divinities were the goddesses al-Lat, Manat, and al-'Uzza, known collectively as "the daughters of Allah." Al-Lat's sacred grounds near Ta'if (slightly east of Mecca in present-day Saudi Arabia) were off limits to human sacrifice, hunting, and tree felling. The Quraysh worshipped al-'Uzza, or Venus, the morning star, and offered human sacrifices to her. Manat was the goddess of fate or destiny.

In Mecca (in present-day Saudi Arabia) stood the Ka'aba, a shrine with divining rods used by seers (*kahins*) who spoke in rhyme and, it was believed, could predict the future and heal. They would enter into trances or states of ecstasy and had ties to the supernatural. A *kahin* could also be a *sha'ir*, or poet. The word *sha'ir* means "one who knows," and a poet received special insights, either from demonic powers or from the invisible beings created from fire (*jinn*). The *jinn* could be either helpful or harmful to humans, and so poets and seers were courted, as their words made them powerful allies or foes. Each year a poetry festival and competition was held at 'Ukaz, for which poets composed odes. Although the Qur'an is considered prophecy inspired by God and not poetry (which is deemed to be from sources other than God), it is held up as a matchless example of inspired verse.

Once a year, Arabs from all over the peninsula would make a pilgrimage to the Ka'aba, around and within which were shrines to 360 major deities. Pilgrims made sacrifices at these shrines and engaged in ritual circumambulation, a practice still seen today in the rituals of the Muslim pilgrimage to Mecca (the *hajj*). The importance of Mecca as a place of pilgrimage and as an economic and cultural center made its guardians, the Quraysh, a powerful tribe in the Arabian Peninsula.

### Cultural Life

Arab nomads raised livestock and the townspeople engaged in trade, but both groups raided for camels, livestock, women, jewelry, cloth, and other items. These planned raids were occasions of sport that gave tribes the opportunity to increase their wealth (or change ownership temporarily). All raids were called off for three months of the year—declared the months of truce—during which the poetry festival in 'Ukaz and the annual pilgrimage to Mecca took place.

Raiding was associated with virility and tribal loyalty. Pre-Islamic poetry depicted the honor of the tribe in elaborate genealogies that traced the daring exploits, bravery, and manliness of one's forefathers. The killing of a tribal member demanded retribution, and sometimes the ill-will between clans lasted for generations. Anyone from another tribe was considered an enemy, but if an outsider sought protection, the tribe would offer the utmost generosity, hospitality, and security.

## Values

All tribal members were imbued with a sense of personal honor, and any challenge to one's honor was grounds for retaliation. As in other patriarchal societies, a man could be dishonored by the compromising behavior of any woman to whom he was bound by blood or marriage or by insults directed at her. Another important virtue was manliness, expressed in displays of courage, generosity, loyalty, and forbearance. Life was to be lived with honor, manliness, and pleasure (this last idea is apparent in the many odes to wine). Impersonal, random fate ruled the day—one of the many concepts that would change with the arrival of Islam.

At the time of Muhammad's revelations, the Arabian Peninsula contained a mixture of religious practices. There were Jewish and Nestorian Christian communities in southern Arabia and around Yathrib, the oasis later renamed Medina. Christian communities lived around Najran in southern Arabia, and the caravan trade brought the Arabs into contact with Zoroastrians, followers of the Iranian prophet Zarathustra, as well. Certainly, enough was already known about biblical figures and ideas that the many subsequent Qur'anic references to them found an audience. Within the Ka'aba there were representations of Abraham, Mary, Jesus, and some unnamed prophets. According to the Qur'an, monotheists called *hanifs*, who were neither Jewish nor Christian, also populated Arabia. The term *hanif* is used in the Qur'an to describe Abraham, who is considered neither Jew nor Christian, being the progenitor of both, but rather *muslim*, or one who surrenders to God. Thus, the central message of Muhammad and the Qur'an is to call Arabs back to the faith of Abraham, the original monotheist or *hanif*.

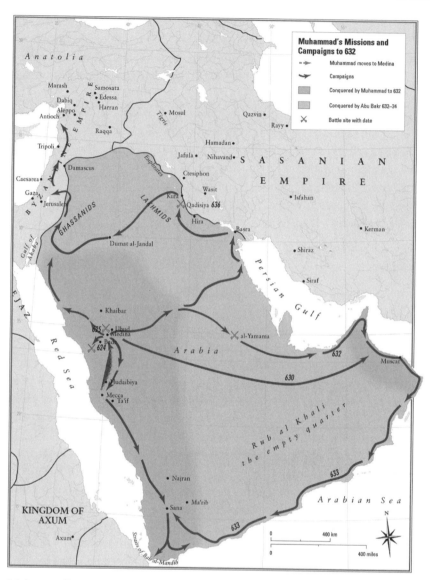

Muhammad's missions and campaigns to 632.


Muhammad was born around 570. His father died before Muhammad was born, and his mother died when he was only six years old. After his mother's death, his grandfather, leader of the Banu Hashim, took over as his guardian. His grandfather, too, died within a couple of years, and guardianship passed to his uncle Abu Talib.

History has left few details of Muhammad's early life. By the time he was a young man, he appears to have earned a reputation for honesty. When he was 25, a wealthy businesswoman named Khadija, 15 years his senior, proposed marriage to him. It was Khadija's third marriage and Muhammad's first, and by all indications it was a happy one. Khadija bore him four daughters and one or two sons (accounts vary). Only the daughters survived beyond infancy. Muhammad remained monogamous until Khadija's death in 620 but ultimately took 11 more wives.

Muhammad's leadership and peacemaking abilities were evident during the rebuilding of the Ka'aba, around 609. While the various tribes in Mecca were vying for the honor of lifting the black stone of the Ka'aba into position, Muhammad devised the strategy of placing the stone on a mantle. Representatives of several tribes carried the mantle into position and hoisted it up while Muhammad lodged the black stone in place.

## REVELATION

Muhammad was in the practice of retiring for a few days at a time to a cave on nearby Mount Hira to engage in reflection, meditation, and spiritual cultivation. Around 610, according to reports, Muhammad was on one of these retreats when the angel Gabriel approached him as he was sleeping and laid a brocaded cover over him.[1] Pressing down on the cover, Gabriel exhorted Muhammad to recite. "I am unable to recite," protested Muhammad. Once again, the angel commanded, "Recite!" and was met by another protest. Upon the third command, Muhammad asked, "What shall I recite?" and Gabriel responded:

> Recite: In the Name of your Lord who created
> Created the human from a blood clot.
> Recite: And your Lord is the Most Generous
> Who taught by the Pen
> Taught the human that which it knew not.   (Qur'an 96:1–5)

These lines are the first verses of the Qur'an, a collection of revelations made to Muhammad over the remaining 20 years of his life. The earliest biography of Muhammad reports that, when he awoke from this experience, the words were indelibly inscribed on his heart. Muhammad feared that he was possessed, and he left the place with the intention of throwing himself over a precipice, when he heard a voice say: "O Muhammad, you are the

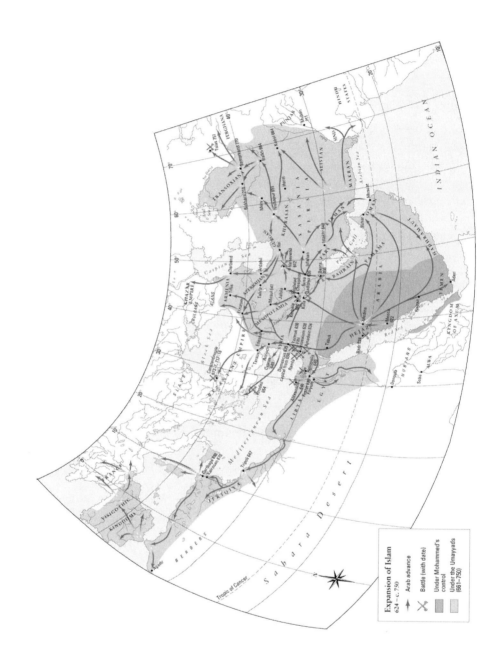

Expansion of Islam
624–c.750

→ Arab advance

✕ Battle (with date)

Under Mohammed's
control

Under the Umayyads
(661–750)

Messenger of God." Looking up, he saw a figure straddling the horizon. Later, refuting the idea that Muhammad had erred or deceived his people, the Qur'an describes the vision thus:

> Your comrade errs not, nor is [he] deceived;
> Nor does he speak of [his own] desire.
> It is nothing but an inspiration that is inspired,
> Which one awesome in power has taught him,
> One vigorous; and he drew clear to view
> When he was on the uppermost horizon.
> Then he drew near and came down
> Till he was two bows' length or even nearer. (Qur'an 53:2–9)

Muhammad stood transfixed long enough for messengers, dispatched by his anxious wife to bring him home, to report that they could not find him. When he finally did return, Muhammad sought the moral and psychological support of his wife Khadija as he struggled with the meaning of the revelations. In the days that followed, Muhammad was plagued by doubt, exhaustion, and fear, and no further revelations occurred. It may have been during this difficult period, known as the *fatra*, that Khadija took Muhammad to visit her learned cousin, Waraqa ibn Nawfal. Waraqa declared that Muhammad's encounter with the angel was nothing other than the *namus* or angelic messenger that had previously descended upon Moses. He also predicted that Muhammad would be facing more hard times.

## ESTABLISHING ISLAM ON THE ARABIAN PENINSULA

### Early Preaching in Mecca

When the revelations recommenced, Muhammad's destiny as a prophet was revealed:

> Deliver what has been revealed to you from your Lord.
> If you do not do so, then you have not delivered his [God's] message,
> and God will protect you from the people. (Qur'an 5:67)

He delivered his message to close family members, garnering the support of his cousin 'Ali, son of his uncle Abu Talib; his adopted son Zayd, freed from slavery by Muhammad; and his friend Abu Bakr, later to become the first leader of the Arabs (caliph) after Muhammad's death. Emboldened to preach publicly, Muhammad called on the Arabs to abandon their worship of multiple traditional deities and to surrender to Allah, Creator and Lord of the heavens and the earth, who had filled the earth with bounty. He admonished them that, on their deaths, God would hold them accountable for whether they had distinguished right from wrong; aided the poor and needy; exercised compassion for widows, orphans, and the disadvantaged; and lived righteously.

Muhammad's message was not well received. In calling for the worship of one God, his message struck at the heart of the Meccan economy that relied heavily on pilgrimages to the Ka'aba, the sacred site of many Arab deities. The idea that people ought to share their wealth and show compassion for the disadvantaged ran counter to the Meccan culture of materialism and individual wealth (most of the initial converts to Islam were slaves and members of the lesser clans). The notion that humans would be judged on the Last Day by a deity who ruled all creation was alien to the Arab worldview that propounded that nothing existed beyond death. It was therefore not surprising that Meccans in general, and in particular the ruling merchant tribe, the Quraysh, responded with alarm. At first, they ostracized the converts to Islam. Ostracism then escalated into persecution and attempts to harm converts, especially converted slaves. Muhammad himself belonged to the Quraysh through his clan, the Banu Hashim, and the Quraysh attempted to dissuade him from preaching by offering incentives through his uncle and clan leader, Abu Talib. Abu Talib never converted to Islam, but he always offered his nephew full security and support.

In the fifth year of Muhammad's ministry, the situation in Mecca had deteriorated to the point where he urged some of his followers to seek refuge across the Red Sea in Abyssinia. King Negus, a Christian, graciously extended his protection. Meanwhile in Mecca, the Quraysh stepped up their efforts against Muhammad, calling him a liar, a *kahin*, a sorcerer, and a madman. With the conversion of a prominent member of the Quraysh, the persecutions hardened into a declaration—later lifted—forbidding marriage or commerce with Muhammad's familial clans. This led to economic difficulty for the Muslims and made them fear for their personal safety. Muhammad's despair only deepened when, in 619, both his wife Khadija and his uncle Abu Talib died. Muhammad's wife had been his first convert and an ardent supporter, and his uncle had shielded him from Meccan persecution. A revelation from this period declares:

By the radiance of morning and the hush of night,
your Lord has neither forsaken you nor left you forlorn.
The end shall be better for you than the beginning.
Your Lord shall provide and you shall be satisfied.
Did he not find you an orphan and shelter you?
Did he not find you erring and guide you?
As for the orphan, do not oppress him,
and as for the one in need, do not spurn him,
and as for your Lord's blessing,
declare it without fear.   (Qur'an 93:1–11)

## The Emigration (Hijra)

Muhammad began to search for support and converts in other tribes near Mecca. He was unsuccessful until 620, when, at the pilgrimage site of al-'Aqaba, he met six members of a tribe from Yathrib, a town some two hundred miles from Mecca. They accepted Muhammad as the prophet whose imminent arrival had been predicted by local Jews, and they converted to Islam in the hope that God would unite their warring tribes. The next year, 12 tribesmen from Yathrib returned and made the first pledge ("first 'Aqaba"), later known as "the pledge of women" because those who took it were not expected to participate in war (this expectation was reversed the following year). The men vowed to ascribe divinity to no one but God and to refrain from stealing, fornication, killing their offspring, slander, and disobedience to the prophet. In reward, they would attain paradise after death, but if they erred, God would judge them accordingly. In 622, a group of 75 Muslims (including 2 women), converts from nearly all the tribes in Yathrib, went to 'Aqaba and pledged to accept Muhammad as prophet, to avoid all sins, and to wage war against God's enemies. This came to be called the Second Pledge of al-'Aqaba. The earliest account of the life of Muhammad notes that, in the beginning, despite the hostility of the Meccans, God had not granted him permission to fight. Although scholars cannot date exactly the various revelations to Muhammad, it is likely that the following verses were revealed prior to the Second Pledge of al-'Aqaba:

Sanction is given unto those who fight because they have been wronged
And Allah is indeed able to give them victory
Those who have been driven from their homes unjustly

only because they said: Our Lord is Allah
For had it not been for Allah's repelling some men by means of others,
cloisters and churches and oratories and mosques,
wherein the name of Allah is oft mentioned,
would assuredly have been pulled down.
Verily, Allah helps one who helps Him.
Lo! Allah is Strong, Almighty—.   (Qur'an 22:39–40)

After receiving this revelation, Muhammad ordered all Muslims in Mecca to emigrate to Yathrib. The people of Yathrib would henceforth be called "the Helpers," and are remembered to this day as men and women of courage who converted early to Islam and stood by the prophet. Muhammad's followers embarked in small groups until only Muhammad, Abu Bakr, and 'Ali remained behind. The Meccans, fearing that Muhammad would raise an army against them upon reaching Yathrib, plotted to kill him and collectively share the responsibility for his death. But Muhammad foiled the plot and rejoined his followers. Yathrib was henceforth called Medina, from *madinat al-nabi*, "city of the prophet." Muhammad's emigration to Medina marks the beginning of the Muslim calendar. The year 622 is the first year of the *hijra*, or emigration (signified in the Muslim calendar as A.H., *anno hijri*).

Now free of persecution, the Muslims in Medina organized, translated the revelations into rituals and prayers, and built a community. Muhammad built a house around a courtyard where he could pray. He also wrote the Constitution of Medina, a document establishing law and order and cementing a pact among all the tribes and inhabitants of Medina, including Jews and Christians, who accepted Muhammad's authority. This confirmed Muhammad as the leader and judge who would henceforth settle all disputes and committed Muslims to refrain from infighting so they could present a united front against their enemies. Eighteen months later, the Muslims, who had previously faced Jerusalem during prayer, turned their prayers to Mecca (to the east). Jews and Christians were free to practice their faiths in a collective community termed the *ummah*. To this day, Muslims consider themselves to be part of one *ummah*, despite their racial, cultural, theological, and geographical diversity. Increasingly, the revelations made to Muhammad during the Medinan period related to specific rituals and practices of the community. The new revelations established not only the ritual expression of the faith, but the means and manner by which that faith would be translated into commercial, social, and legal activity, while reinforcing each Muslim's accountability to God.

In the raiding tradition of the time, Muhammad prepared to attack a caravan laden with goods destined for the Quraysh. His army of 300 men camped at Badr on the coastal road from Syria to Mecca, near some wells. Learning of Muhammad's plans, the Quraysh sent an army of 950 Meccan tribesmen to intercept him, and they also camped close to Badr. In the meantime, the leader of Muhammad's caravan had changed his route to avoid being attacked and sent a message instructing the Meccan army to return home. Although there was no longer a reason to fight, and two Meccan clans left immediately, most of the Meccan army remained—their commander may have thought that an opportunity to rout the Medinan forces was too good to be missed. In any case, when Muhammad realized that the Meccan army was nearby, he blocked up all the wells in the area except for the well closest to Mecca, which he surrounded with his men. Running out of water, the Meccan army attacked the Medinans. In March of 624, the Battle of Badr began, as was the custom, with single combat between the champions of the opposing sides, followed by arrows and general fighting. Once it became obvious that the much smaller Muslim army had gained the upper hand, the Meccan army fled. This victory, seen as divinely ordained, consolidated the Muslims' faith in Muhammad as a prophet and leader. In 625, however, the Meccans again waged war on Medina and nearly defeated their foes. During this Battle of Uhud, which ended in a standoff, some of the Medinan Jews who had conspired with the Meccans were expelled or killed for breaking the agreement set forth in the Constitution of Medina. In 627, a Meccan army of 10,000 men again laid siege to Medina but could not advance past a trench that had been excavated around the city. This Medinan victory is appropriately remembered as the Battle of the Trench.

In 628, Muhammad and the Meccans agreed to a truce, and the Meccans promised to let the Muslims make a pilgrimage to the Ka'aba shrine the following year. Eight months after Muhammad and 200 men performed their pilgrimage, a series of events led to the dissolution of the truce. A Meccan tribe loyal to Muhammad killed a man from another Meccan tribe who had written inflammatory verses against the prophet. When the tribe of the killed man retaliated, a few Muslims were slain, breaking the terms of the truce. A prominent leader of the Quraysh, Abu Sufyan (who was Muhammad's father-in-law), was sent to Medina to protest. Abu Sufyan and Muhammad settled the dispute by deciding that any Meccan who wished to convert to Islam could do so under Abu Sufyan's protection. However, Abu Sufyan's visit was also a signal to Muhammad that the Meccans, whose administrative skills and support would be important assets to the growing Muslim community, no longer strongly opposed his leadership and mission. Muhammad therefore plotted to overwhelm the Meccans with a force large enough to discourage active resistance. On the eighth of Ramadan, eight years after the *hijra* (December 30, 629), Muhammad appeared with a formidable army on the outskirts of Mecca, and the Meccans surrendered peacefully. Muhammad proceeded to destroy the deities in and around the Ka'aba and established the Ka'aba as a focal point of the annual Muslim pilgrimage, the *hajj*.

Upon the fall of Mecca, two tribes that had been enemies of the Meccans gathered a force of some 20,000 men to march on the city. In January 630, Muhammad met them with a much smaller force and won decisively. Muhammad was now a leader to be reckoned with, and later in that "Year of Delegations," many tribes sent emissaries to Medina, seeking alliances. While conversion to Islam was not a condition of alliance, it appears that accepting Muhammad as God's prophet and contributing to the treasury were part of the deal. Before long, all of Arabia was unified under Muhammad. The raiding tradition came to an end, and the confederacy of Arab tribes was now well positioned to turn its attention outward. Muhammad had already sent messages to the rulers of Abyssinia, Yemen, Egypt, Byzantium, and Persia, inviting them to join Islam, although few details of these transactions are known. It is clear that Muhammad was trying to establish political and possibly religious relations with the rulers of the territories surrounding Arabia. In December 630, he raised an army of 30,000 men and began a march to Tabuk near the Gulf of Akaba, on the route to Syria. Muhammad's march toward Syria was intended as a challenge to the Byzantine emperor. Along the way, Muhammad made agreements with Jewish and Christian tribes long associated with the Byzantine Empire, guaranteeing them protection under the growing Islamic state. These agreements set the tone for the future Islamic Empire. In exchange for tribute, non-Muslim groups would be allowed to manage their own internal affairs and receive state protection without the requirement of conversion—a Pax Islamica in which religious minorities would be tolerated. Most of the Islamic expansion into Byzantine territories occurred after Muhammad's death, but Muhammad established the model for subsequent political and economic alliances.

In 632, Muhammad made his final pilgrimage to Mecca, later called "the pilgrimage of farewell." He returned to Medina in March in poor health, although he continued to manage the affairs of state for some time before asking his close friend Abu Bakr to lead prayers. On June 8, suffering from debilitating fever and headaches, Muhammad died with his head on the lap of his youngest wife (Abu Bakr's daughter). He was buried in her apartment rather than in the customary burial ground. Abu Bakr is said to have declared to the assembly of Muslims: "O ye people, if anyone worships Muhammad, Muhammad is dead, but if anyone worships God, He is alive and dies not."

## ISLAM BEYOND THE ARABIAN BORDERS

### The Wars of Conquest

At the time of Muhammad, the Arabian Peninsula was flanked on the west by the Byzantine Empire, with its seat of power in Constantinople (Istanbul in modern Turkey), and on the east by the Sassanid Empire, whose capital was Ctesiphon on the banks of the Tigris River. The Byzantine Empire encompassed portions of the Mediterranean Basin, Asia Minor, and the Nile Valley. Since the fourth century, its state religion had been a form of Christianity known today as Eastern Orthodox Christianity. Zoroastrianism dominated the Sassanid Empire, which included Mesopotamia and Persia. From 613 to 620, the Sassanid Empire made incursions into the Byzantine territories of Syria, Palestine, Egypt, and Anatolia. The Byzantines countered with a brief occupation of Ctesiphon. Continual warfare between the two empires had drained their treasuries and left them both vulnerable to attack.

Soon after Muhammad's death, the Muslims embarked on wars of conquest. Abu Bakr (r. 632–634), the first caliph (or successor, a title for the ruler of Muslim territories after Muhammad), brought all of Arabia under Islamic control before making forays into Palestine and parts of Iraq. The second caliph, Umar ibn al-Khattab (r. 634–644), conquered the Fertile Crescent, Egypt, and western Iran, effectively destroying the Sassanid Empire and forcing the Byzantine Empire to retreat north of the Taurus mountains into what is present-day Turkey. The wars of conquest slowed somewhat after these campaigns, and in 660, 678, and again in 717, the Byzantines repelled Arab armies in Anatolia, a territory they held until 1071. Still, by 670, eastern Iran, Armenia, Libya, and Tunisia had been overtaken in what is known as the third wave of conquests. Internal strife and civil wars during the 680s and 690s temporarily hindered expansion, but conquest resumed once order had been restored. By 712, Muslim armies had reached the Iberian Peninsula, Central Asia, and the Indus Valley. The Islamic Empire now stretched from North Africa in the west to Sind in the east, spanning almost one quarter of the globe and covering an area much larger than any previous empire, including that of Alexander the Great. In 1453, Constantinople fell to the Ottoman Turks and much of the remaining Byzantine territory came under Muslim control.

## Islamic Civilization

The early conquests saw the rapid formation of a vast empire that was geographically, ethnically, culturally, and religiously diverse. But the conquests did not result in immediate, widespread conversion to Islam. Instead, Islam remained a minority religion in the conquered territories for more than two centuries. The reasons for this are several: First, conquered populations were given the choice of either converting to Islam or retaining their religious traditions and paying tribute, in exchange for which they would be protected. For many of these conquered peoples, Arab administration was a relief from the tyrannical Byzantine authority and from heavy taxation under both the Byzantines and Sassanids. Second, prisoners of war were freed if they converted to Islam. Those who did so were considered *mawali,* or clients, and were offered protection along with other non-Arab converts, but the numbers of these converts were relatively small. Third, the Arab Muslim minority lived in their own encampments, forming an aristocracy. Any offspring from the liaisons of an Arab with a non-Arab was deemed inferior.

## The Heartlands

Muhammad was succeeded by four leaders (r. 632–661), called the Rashidun, or "rightly guided" caliphs, all of whom ruled from Medina.[2] They were followed by the Umayyad dynasty (r. 661–750), which ruled from Damascus (in present-day Syria) and which publicly proclaimed Islam in its monuments, coins, and public works. The Umayyads under caliph 'Abd al-Malik (r. 685–705) established Arabic as the official state language; minted a new Arabic coin reinforcing the message of monotheism; and improved the roads to Jerusalem and Damascus with milestones inscribed in Arabic with Qur'anic verses, distance remaining, and the caliph's name and titles. In 692, 'Abd al-Malik ordered the construction of the Dome of the Rock in

Dome of the Rock, 7th century, Jerusalem. © Getty Images/21000054805.

Jerusalem, famous for its mosaics. His son continued to build public monuments, such as mosques in Medina, Jerusalem, and Damascus.

Eventually, the second-class social and economic status of the *mawali* and the non-Muslims (*dhimmis*) incited them to armed revolt under the leadership of a Persian convert. They formed a coalition around Abu'l-ʿAbbas, a descendant of the prophet's uncle ʿAbbas, and their military success led to the formation of the ʿAbbasid dynasty in 750. One of the Umayyads escaped to Spain, unseated the governor, and established a caliphate in Cordova. The ʿAbbasids moved their capital from Damascus in Syria to Iraq, initially to a site near Kufa and later to the village of Baghdad near the ruins of Ctesiphon, capital of the Sassanid Empire. This new capital was officially called Madinat al-Salam, or the City of Peace, but was known simply as Baghdad.

The ʿAbbasids ushered in the Golden Age of Islamic civilization. They adopted Persian courtly ceremony, created private armies, instituted bureaucracies, patronized the arts, and encouraged the translation of Greek, Persian, and Indian philosophical, medical, and scientific treatises into Arabic. During this era Islamic study of the Qur'an, theology, philosophy, mysticism, and law grew into established disciplines, and mathematics, medicine, music, geography, and astronomy were cultivated. Islamic schools (*madrasas*) libraries, courts, and institutions overseeing religious endowments became part of the social fabric. The 'Abbasids allowed the farthest reaches of the empire to be governed by local rulers who set up their own dynasties in exchange for tribute. Islam gradually became the majority faith throughout the empire, as people converted for economic reasons or reasons of conscience, through contact with mystics, or in response to missionary activity. There is scant evidence that conversion was forced.

During this Golden Age, a traveling merchant might speak Arabic, Persian, Greek, and the languages of the Franks, Andalusians, and Slavs. The cities of Cordova, Fez, Cairo, Baghdad, Isfahan, and Samarkand were at their peak culturally. It has been noted that,

> In the Islamic lands, not only Muslims but also Christians and Jews enjoyed the good life. They dressed in fine clothing, had fine houses in splendid cities serviced by paved streets, running water, and sewers, and dined on spiced delicacies served on Chinese porcelains. Seated on luxurious carpets, these sophisticated city dwellers debated such subjects as the nature of God, the intricacies of Greek philosophy, or the latest Indian mathematics.[3]

The 'Abbasids were defeated by the Mongols in 1258, having first witnessed the rise of independent dynasties in their territories. By this time, the 'Abbasids, as well as the Mamluks in Egypt and Syria, were warring with the Crusaders over the control of Syria, Palestine, and Egypt. The Mongols ruled Iraq and Iran until the turn of the sixteenth century, when they were driven out of Iran by the Safavid dynasty and out of Iraq by the Ottoman dynasty, which became the central ruling power over Anatolia, Syria, Iraq, Egypt, Tunisia, and Algeria until the end of World War II, when it was dissolved by the Allies.

### Spain, or al-Andalus

In al-Andalus, as Spain was called after the Arab conquests of 716, 'Abd al-Rahman formed armies of non-Muslim slaves recruited from Europe (called Saqalib, or Slavs, to indicate their origin).[4] These slaves were raised as Muslims and subsequently freed to assume military and government posts. (The 'Abbasids drew their armies from Turkish slaves and other mercenary groups from Central Asia.) Berbers from North Africa, who had entered Spain during the first wars of conquest in 716 and converted to Islam, eventually established the Berber Almoravid kingdom that included territories in North Africa. The Almohads—who ruled from 1130 to 1269 and were finally defeated by the Christian sovereigns of Portugal, Castile, and Aragon—followed them.

As growing numbers of Jews and Christians in Spain converted to Islam, they were granted, as elsewhere, "protected" status (*dhimmi*), and they retained the right to be governed by Visigothic law in the case of Christians or rabbinic law in the case of Jews. The city of Cordova at this time has been described as

> clean and well-paved, well-lit, and abundantly supplied with running water at a time when all other European cities were dirty, dark, and rank with disease. The Umayyad caliph exchanged ambassadors with Byzantium, Baghdad, Cairo, Aachen, and Saxony. The city's power and wealth stretched far and wide. Merchants brought gold and ivory across the Sahara from tropical Africa, and skilled craftsmen transformed these precious metals into coins, jewelry, and luxury goods for the caliph and his courtiers.[5]

By the middle of the thirteenth century, the Christian rulers of Portugal, Castile, and Aragon had reconquered all of Islamic Spain, except for the principality of Granada, which fell to Ferdinand and Isabella in 1492. At this time many Muslims in Spain, or Mudejars, most of whom had lived under Christian rule in an arrangement similar to the *dhimmi* status Muslims had offered to Jews and Christians, were forcibly converted to Christianity and came to be known as the Moriscos—outwardly Christian but privately practicing Islam. They were finally expelled from Spain in 1620. Approximately 275,000 Mudejars resettled in North Africa, some whose families had been in Spain for close to nine centuries.

At first, Spanish-born thinkers traveled to Arabia, Egypt, and Iraq to complete their education. However, the Spanish cities of Cordova and Seville soon became centers of learning in their own right and produced notable legal scholars, philosophers, poets, architects, and musicians whose influence reached far beyond al-Andalus.

Spanish Islam is noted for its creative mix of European and Asian elements, as evidenced in its architecture, music, literature, and art. The religious and cultural pluralism that brought together Jews, Christians, and Muslims contributed to the larger fabric that has been termed "Islamicate" civilization.[6] Maimonides, the celebrated Jewish theologian, philosopher, and physician, expressed himself in both Hebrew and Arabic and was well acquainted with Arabic philosophy, as were other scholars of his time. Arabic philosophy played a significant role in the development of Christian theology, for instance in the writings of St. Thomas Aquinas. Hybridized

forms of poetry emerged, combining Arabic and Romance elements of
verse. Hybrids occurred in Andalusian architecture as well, drawing their
inspiration from both Arabic and Visigothic architectural forms. Mudejar
architecture became a signature Spanish style that was later carried to the
New World and is evident in Spanish mission architecture of the western
United States and Mexico. Arabic works, translated into Latin, had a far-
reaching influence on the development of European philosophy, theology,
mysticism, mathematics, music, medicine, and other arts and sciences,
ultimately contributing to the European Renaissance. The Mudejars and
Moriscos also created a body of literature composed in Romance dialects
but written in Arabic, enriching the Spanish language with Arabic vocabulary that is still used today.

### North Africa and the Mediterranean

Islam in North Africa dates back to 640—eight years after the death of
Muhammad—when Muslim armies crossed into Egypt.[7] This initial incursion was followed by the conquests of Cyrenaica (eastern Libya) and Tripoli
and westward expansion into the Maghrib (literally, "place of sunset" or the
west) across North Africa to modern-day Tunisia. The indigenous tribes of
the Maghrib were mostly pagan Berbers, but Jewish and Christian tribes
also populated the area. According to Berber folklore, an Algerian Jewish
priestess named al-Kahina led a resistance against the Muslim armies. By
and large, non-Jewish and non-Christian Berbers converted to Islam early.
Many of them did not qualify for *dhimmi* status; as pagans, they were not
entitled to the same protections offered to peoples of the Book, i.e., the
Jews and Christians. In converting, Berbers were able to join the army and
would play an important role in the future conquest of Spain. In the eighth
and ninth centuries, Berber groups managed to throw off the political
dominance of their Arab invaders and establish dynasties of their own. But
between the tenth and the fifteenth centuries, Arab tribes from the peninsula migrated to the Maghrib, further diluting the Berber population. All
the same, Berbers in the Maghrib retained a cultural identity distinct from
that of the lands east of North Africa, called Mashriq ("place of sunrise," or
the east) in Muslim historical literature.

During this early period of Islam, several important dynasties arose
in North Africa. The Fatimids claimed direct descent from Muhammad
through his daughter Fatima. Supported by the Kutama Berbers, they expanded westward from Tunisia toward Egypt. Arriving in Cairo in 969, the

Fatimids remained a political rival of the 'Abbasids for two centuries. From Sicily, they launched naval attacks on Mediterranean towns in Italy, France, and islands in the western Mediterranean. Cairo became a great center of civilization and learning: the Fatimids are credited with founding the world's oldest university, al-Azhar, in 970.

The Almoravids rose to power from the southern Moroccan Sahara and made their capital in Marrakesh. They extended their empire into the Western Sahara, Maghrib, and Spain, and their influence reached as far as West Africa, which was Islamized through their efforts. At the end of the twelfth century, the Almoravids gave way to the Almohads, who espoused a puritanical form of Islam opposed to anything they considered contrary to Islamic teachings. The Almohads further Islamized the Maghrib but fell from power during the mid-thirteenth century, giving rise to three successors: the Hafsid dynasty in Tunisia, the Marinid dynasty in Morocco, and the Zayyanid dynasty in Algeria.

Beginning in the fifteenth century, these three dynasties were subjected to European attacks on their North African ports. In the early sixteenth century, the Portuguese managed to gain a foothold on the Atlantic coast of Africa and made forays into Morocco. The Spanish seized several ports along the North African coast of the Mediterranean. These European military successes led the Moroccans, especially the Sufi *shaykhs* of the more mystical schools of Islam, to call for holy war (*jihad*) against the Portuguese and the Spaniards. Prayer halls (*ribats*) organized around charismatic leaders became centers of resistance to Christian incursions into the Maghrib. In south Morocco, the Saadian dynasty expanded its territory to include Fez. By the early sixteenth century, the Ottomans under Sultan Selim I had conquered most of the Middle East and were beginning their campaign in the Maghrib, which brought them into conflict with the Iberians (the Spaniards and the Portuguese). Thus, for the next century, the Ottomans, Iberians, and Saadians vied for power in the Maghrib, with the Spanish gaining control of Tunis in 1571 in the Battle of Lepanto.

In Morocco, the Saadians defeated invading Portuguese armies in the 1578 "Battle of the Three Kings." The Saadians ultimately extended their reach into West Africa, causing the collapse of the indigenous Songhay dynasty. They set up the Arma dynasty in Timbuktu (in present-day Mali) and presided over the region until the French wrested power from them in 1893. In Algiers, the Janissaries, an elite corps of converted war captives and Christian youths, turned on their Ottoman masters and gradually forced them out. The Janissaries ended up ceding power to local governors (*dey*) who were deposed in the French invasion and occupation of 1830.

In 1847, France suppressed the last bit of resistance in Algeria. Morocco lost its independence to France in 1912, while Spain retained control of a zone in the north. In Tunisia, as had been the case in Algeria, the Ottomans were replaced by the Janissaries, who were then replaced by local rulers until they in turn were replaced in the French occupation of 1881. In 1711, local rulers wrested control of Tripoli (and therefore all of Libya) from the Ottomans. The Ottomans regained control of Libya in 1835, but, in 1911, Italy annexed Libya, a move that the Ottomans resisted. Even after the Ottoman Empire was dismantled at the end of World War I, Libya continued to fight for its independence until Italy defeated the country in 1932.

## West Africa

Following ancient trade routes, North African Berber Muslims brought Islamic teachings and culture to West Africa. During the tenth and eleventh centuries, converted Muslims could be found at the court of the Ghana Empire. Under the Almoravid dynasty in North Africa, the influence of Islam spread even further. In the twelfth and thirteenth centuries, West African Muslim states emerged, initiated pilgrimages to Mecca, and used trade to consolidate relationships with Egypt, the Sudan, and Muslim neighbors to the north. One West African ruler of note was Mansa Musa, who undertook the pilgrimage to Mecca in 1324 and enlarged the kingdom of Mali to include the Sahel region and much of the Sudan. Another noteworthy figure is Sonni Ali, ruler of the Kingdom of Songhay, under whom the city of Timbuktu became a center of trade, learning, and culture. His successor incorporated the Hausa region in northern Nigeria, and Nigeria gradually became Islamized over four or five centuries, beginning in the ninth century. Around the eleventh century, Islam took root in Senegal and Gambia (Senegambia). Muslim institutions of learning, mosques, and practices were present throughout the West African region. The region came under French rule in 1891, and the nineteenth century witnessed a number of *jihad* movements in response to calls for a more Islamic society and rule. According to Islamic scholar Sulayman Nyang, these *jihads* developed a Muslim sense of identity and a frame of reference for minorities within the larger culture, a "reorientation" that would dictate the forms of resistance to colonization that swept West and North Africa during the nineteenth and early twentieth centuries.

### Sub-Saharan and South Africa

Trade routes along the Nile River facilitated the introduction of Islam into Ethiopia, Eritrea, the Sudan, Somalia, and the East African coast as far as Madagascar.[8] The gradual process of conversion to Islam began as early as the tenth century and was hastened by the development of immigrant Muslim communities along the horn and eastern coast of Africa, with Arab and South Asian immigrants arriving by way of the triangular trade routes of the Indian Ocean. By the end of the fourteenth century, small Muslim kingdoms were found throughout the largely Christian-ruled Ethiopian territories. By the end of the fifteenth century, most of the Sudan had been wrested from the Nubian Christians, and the Kingdom of Axum and was now under Muslim control. By the sixteenth century, the Ottomans were in Egypt and the Sudan. The later arrival of the Europeans, with their interest in ivory and slavery, led to a revolt in 1881. Britain, which ruled the Sudan until its independence in 1956, suppressed the revolt.

Arab immigrant communities along the East African coast and the island of Zanzibar evolved into Swahili civilization (from the Arabic word *sawahil,* coastal peoples), a unique blend of Arab and indigenous language, culture, architecture, and literature. Islam was introduced to southern Africa by Indonesian Muslims forced into exile by the Dutch, and later spread by Muslim settlers from India during the period of British colonial rule on the subcontinent.

### South Asia

The history of Islam in India and South Asia may be divided into three phases.[9] The first phase began with the conquest of Sind (in India) by 17-year-old commander Muhammad ibn Qasim in 711. Three centuries later, Sultan Mahmud of Ghazna (d. 1030), a Turk who ruled over Afghanistan and Khurasan (northeast Iran), mounted several invasions of India. He established the Ghaznavid dynasty in Lahore (now in Pakistan), which became one of the many cosmopolitan cities of classical Islamic civilization, attracting scholars, poets, travelers, and bureaucrats from Central Asia, Iran, and the Arab world, until the Ghaznavid dynasty ended in 1186.

The second phase began in 1192 with Muizuddin Ghori of Ghazna, Afghanistan, who launched a major invasion of India and extended the borders to include most of northern India, including Bengal. This period, known as the Sultanate period, lasted until 1525. Sultan Ala al-Dhalji (d.

1316) expanded into Central India and parts of South India, and Sultan Muhammad ibn Tughluq (d. 1351) consolidated his rule by going still further into South India and moving his capital to Devagiri, renamed Daulatabad. Apart from the Hindu kingdom of Vijayanagar in the extreme south, all of India now was under Muslim control.

The translation of Arabic and Persian religious texts into local languages, the creation of Urdu—a camp language that blended elements of Turkish, Arabic, Persian and local vernaculars—and the adoption of Persian as a court language helped spread Islamic culture throughout India, as did the promise of social and bureaucratic advancement. Hindus were protected as "people of the Book" (*ahl al-kitab*) and given *dhimmi* status. Sufi houses of worship (or *khanqahs*) were open to all and played a key role in the conversions to Islam. In time, South Asian Muslims, as they made pilgrimages to Mecca and traveled through the region, brought back ideas and texts that were reinterpreted in South Asian culture. Such conceptual imports led to the enrichment of cultural life—in music, the arts, and mysticism—and at times led to its detriment—in the purging of Sufi Muslims from state institutions.

In the third phase, the Mughals established dominance over India through the leadership of Muhammad Zahir al-Din Babur (d. 1530), who, at the beginning of his reign, defeated both the Muslim Afghan ruler Ibrahim Lodi and the Hindu Rajput ruler Rana Sangha. Ushering in a period that led to the high point of Islamic civilization in India, the Mughals left an impressive legacy of miniature paintings inspired by the Persians. They also refined the Islamic (*madrasa*)-based education system with secular schooling whose curriculum included mathematics, geometry, astronomy, physics, philosophy, ethics, logic, theology, and history, along with Persian *belles lettres.* Babur was succeeded by his son Humayun, who lost the empire to an Afghan named Sher Khan Sur, recovering it 15 years later, just one year before his death in 1156. His son Jalal al-Din Muhammad Akbar, known as Akbar the Great, expanded the territory and introduced a centralized system of administration, unifying his ethnically diverse subjects under a common bond to the emperor. He also attempted to form, with little success, a universal religion that borrowed the best elements of each religious tradition and combined them in the worship of one God. His successors Shah Jahan, Jehangir, and Aurangzeb continued his cultural legacy and left behind monuments of incredible skill and beauty, including the Taj Mahal. Internecine struggles and weakening leadership led to the defeat of Muslim armies by Lord Clive of Britain in 1757. In 1803, Lord Lake took control of Delhi, the administrative heart of the Mughals, and in 1857 the remaining Muslim provinces of Sind, Awadh, and the Deccan succumbed to British rule and the British East India Company. The British remained in India for 90 more years, their rule ending with the partition of India and independence of India and Pakistan in August, 1947.

## Central Asia and the Caucasus

Muslim armies first crossed the Oxus River and entered the Transoxiana region of Central Asia (present-day Uzbekistan, Tajikistan, and western Kyrgyztan) in the middle of the seventh century.[10] Zoroastrianism, Buddhism, Christianity, and Manicheism were the established faiths of Central Asia, and Islam made slow progress in the region, primarily through traders and mystical orders. Local Muslim dynasties constructed mosques, religious schools, mausoleums, and institutions of higher learning. From the ninth century onward, Islam became more firmly established in Khurasan (eastern Persia), Transoxiana, and Khwarazm (now divided between Uzbekistan and Turkmenistan) and produced a number of key Muslim scholars, such as al-Bukhari, credited with compiling traditions (*hadith*) relating to the words and deeds of the Prophet, and al-Tirmidhi, who similarly compiled a canonical collection of *hadith*.

In the late tenth and early eleventh centuries, military excursions northward from Transoxiana and Khwarazm into the Turkish steppes were followed by the conversion of the largely shamanic Turkic people there. Here, too, Sufi organizations played a key role in conversion. A figure of note is the Turkish Sufi Ahmad Yasawi (d. 1166), who founded the Yasawiyya order and influenced the development of Central Asian Turkish Islam. Traders from Khwarazm crossed the Emba and Ural Rivers to the Volga River and introduced Islam into the region, and tenth-century travelers reported a Muslim king and mosques in Bulghar, in present-day Russia (the city was replaced by New Bulghar, now named Kazan, two centuries later). Kazan remained a religious center for Volga Tatar Muslims, and in the fifteenth and sixteenth centuries it was the capital for the Mongol Khanate under the Golden Horde before falling in 1552 to the Russian Tsar Ivan IV. Meanwhile, Turkish invasions into the Kuban steppes north of the Caucasus Mountains and the South Russian steppes contributed to the conversion to Islam of the many Christians there. The Moroccan traveler Ibn Battuta reported that the city of Machar on the Kuma River north of the Caucasus had become a center of Turkish Muslim culture.

In the mid thirteenth century, the Mongols under Chingiz (Genghis) Khan invaded Islamic lands from southern Siberia and took control of Syria, Turkey, the Caucasus, and Baghdad, the capital of the 'Abbasids. Non-Muslim shamanic rulers governed the Muslims in these regions. However, by the fourteenth century, the Mongol rulers in Persia and Transoxiana had converted to Islam, and by the end of the fourteenth century, the Khans of the Golden Horde and the Chaghatayids had converted as well.

Chingiz's son Chaghatay was given the land between Transoxiana and what is now known as Chinese Turkestan or Sin-kiang (Xinjiang), forming the Chaghatayid Khanate. These lands were controlled by the khanates until the latter third of the nineteenth century, when the khanates became vassals of the Russian state.

Chingiz's grandson Batu Khan assumed control of South Russia and the Qipchaq steppe (the "Blue Horde," later to be the core of the "Golden Horde") and established the capital at Saray on the lower Volga River. The Golden Horde held power for two centuries before it was fragmented into various khanates. Many of the subjects remained Russian Christian Orthodox; the main concentrations of Tatar and Turkish Muslims were found in the middle Volga region and in the Crimea, where Muslims persisted until World War II. Crimea fell to Russia in 1781.

Another grandson of Chingiz, Orda, founded the "White Horde" in western Siberia, where Islam did not take root, in part because of Russian expansion. Ivan the Terrible assumed the title of Emperor of Siberia in 1552, but skirmishes between the khanate and the Russian Empire continued until the Russians gained full control over the area in the late seventeenth century.

### China

Early Muslims came to China when traders crossed the Indian Ocean to such southeastern Chinese ports as Guangzhou, Quanzhou, and Changzhou, but the first evidence of Islam in China is with the Mongol incursions.[11] The annals of Liao emperor Tianzuo (r. 1101–19) report that the Yelu Dashi, founder of the Qarakhitai Western Liao dynasty, accepted the surrender of a Muslim Huihui king. Most Muslims in China are Hui, thought to stem from the Huihui. Ethnically, the Hui are the result of intermarriage among indigenous Han Chinese and Persian, Arabic, or Central Asian Muslim forebears. Other Chinese Muslim ethnic groups include the Uyghur, Kazakh, Uzbek, Tajik, Tatar Khalkhas, Dongxiang, Salar, and Baoan communities. The largest concentrations of Hui are in the Ningxia

Hui Autonomous region, Gansu, Qinghai, Henan, Hebei, Shandong, Yun-nan, and the Xinjiang Uyghur Autonomous region.

The thirteenth-century Mongol invasions of Central Asia caused the migration of Muslims eastward into China. As fighting subsided in Central Asia, traders followed the migrants. In addition, the Mongols are believed to have conscripted as many as two to three million Central Asian Muslims during their conquest of China. By the time of the Mongol Yuan dynasty (r. 1271–1368), Muslim mosques stood in Guangzhou, Quanzhou, Hangzhou, Xian, and Kumming. The close relationship between the Hui and the Mongols led to an elevated political status for the Hui under Mongol rule, resulting in fewer trading restrictions and preferential treatment in many areas, including official appointments. This encouraged the migration of Hui merchants throughout Yuan China in the wake of the conquering armies. Muslim traders specialized in perfumes, spices, pearls, and luxury goods.

Muslim troops accompanied the new Ming dynasty (r. 1368–1644 C.E.) into Hunan, and, as traders followed, Muslims settled in Shaoyang and Changde. During this dynasty, the village of Tianmu in the northern suburbs of Tianjin, a large and important port city, was established under the name Mujiazhuang. Its first mosque dates from the fifteenth century; a second mosque was built in 1854. Intermarriage between the Han Chinese and the Hui increased the Muslim population even more, and the areas of Shaanxi and Gansu, which already had large numbers of Hui, grew substantially. With intermarriage, the influence of Arabic and Persian languages waned, except among those living in "Chinese Turkestan" or Xinjiang, where Turkic languages prevail to this day, as do Tajik Persian and Mongolian. During the Ming dynasty, Chinese was the language used by most Hui outside Xinjiang and was the language of key Islamic texts.

With the conquests of the Qing dynasty (r. 1644–1911 C.E.) came restrictions on foreign trade and intra-Hui tensions as well as tensions between the Hui and the Han. These restrictions were lifted in 1684, allowing Muslims to make the pilgrimage to Mecca. Travel exposed Chinese Muslims to Sufi practices and beliefs, which were then introduced into China. Most of China's Muslims today are Sunni Muslims. Other groups include Sufis, Shi'a, and indigenous Chinese Muslims (see also Chapter 3, Branches).

## Southeast Asia

Indonesia has the largest concentration of Muslims in the world, and approximately 90 percent of its population practice Islam.[12] Buddhism and Hinduism were well established in Indonesia before the arrival of Muslims;

Hinduism was the faith of the powerful Majapahit Empire that lasted until the close of the fifteenth century. There is some evidence that Arabs traded in Indonesia as far back as the fourth century, but it was not until the twelfth century that Middle Eastern and South Asian Muslims carried Islam to the Malay world through commerce, intermarriage, and preaching. Explorer Marco Polo reported that, in the thirteenth century, a sultan ruled over Muslim subjects in Pasai in northern Sumatra. The main incursion of Islam into Indonesia began in the fourteenth century from Gujarat in India and expanded through trade, first in northern Sumatra, in Aceh, and then Java. In 1511, the Portuguese captured Melaka, a major center of Muslim trade due to its strategic location in the straits between Sumatra and the Malay Peninsula, scattering Muslim merchants throughout the Indonesian archipelago (comprising 17,000 islands, not all inhabited). Muslim communities formed in parts of the archipelago free of strong Hindu influence—that is, in North Central and West Java and the Aceh and Minangkabau regions of north and west Sumatra. Meanwhile, the center of Muslim power shifted to Johore, north of Singapore. There were also Muslim communities in southern Thailand, the southern Philippines, and the Sulu Sea. Local Indonesian populations converted to Islam in response to the conversion of their Hindu rulers. Thus, in 1477, Demak in Java became the first city to convert to Islam, followed by Cirebon in 1480. In 1487, the Muslim princes together put an end to the remaining Majapahit strongholds, resulting in the formation of 20 Muslim kingdoms across the archipelago.

Pre-Islamic features of Indonesian religious life were incorporated into Muslim faith and practice. Deceased rulers were worshipped as saints, signal towers were converted into minarets, and meeting halls were transformed into mosques. Gamelans (indigenous orchestras) were placed in the mosques, where they aided conversion to the new faith. Islam's social appeal was its concept of the equality of all human beings before God, in contrast to the feudal system of bondage to the king. Politically, Islam helped to create a common identity, manifested in the resistance to the incursions of Portuguese Christians in the early sixteenth century, and then the Dutch a century later. Economically, it facilitated trade with Muslim nations beyond the archipelago and emphasized the virtues of hard work and prosperity. Islam in Indonesia did not replace existing cultural and religious norms but sought to incorporate them; in addition to the examples given, the calendar retained its Hindu Shaka yearly count but changed from a solar to a lunar system and adapted the Arabic names of the Muslim months to Javanese.

The Santri form of Islam in Indonesia is sometimes identified as "true" Islam, because it is oriented toward Middle Eastern culture, unlike Priyayi and Abangan forms of Islam. However, this devalues the cultural and religious synthesis that made Islam so important in the life of Indonesians. Agama Java (Javanese religion) is a blend of local traditions and Sufism. This melding of cultures and religions is apparent in mosque and cemetery architecture, batik cloth decoration, wayang puppet performances, and doctrinal beliefs.

Indonesia was colonized by the Dutch in the early seventeenth century and remained under Dutch control for approximately 350 years until its independence in 1949. The Malay Peninsula gained independence in 1957, and Malaysia—comprised of the Malay Peninsula, parts of North Borneo, and Singapore—was founded in 1963. Singapore withdrew from the federation in 1965.

### Europe, the Americas, and Australia

Muslims have been in Europe (except Spain) since the Ottoman rule in Bulgaria and parts of the former Yugoslavia for about 400 years. Muslims first arrived in Britain about 300 years ago as sailors with the British East India Company, some of whom remained in Britain to form small communities. In the Americas, Muslims from Africa were among the slave population in the eighteenth century. Some Spanish Muslims are thought to have accompanied Christopher Columbus on his travels to the New World, accounting for the presence of Muslims in Latin America, chiefly Mexico. For the most part, the movement of Muslims into Europe, the Americas, and Australia is a late-nineteenth- and twentieth-century phenomenon, brought about by the search for better opportunities and work, the migrations that came with decolonization, and the desire to escape political and religious persecution.

## NOTES

1. Ibn Hisham, Abd al-Malik, *The Life of Muhammad.* A translation of Ishaq's *Sirat Rasul Allah* (London: Oxford University Press, 1955).

2. Campo, Juan E. "Islam in the Middle East" in Azim A. Nanji, ed., *The Muslim Almanac* (Farmington Hills, MI: Gale Research, 1996), 27–43.

3. Jonathan Bloom and Sheila Blair, *Islam: A Thousand Years of Faith and Power* (Farmington Hills, MI: Gale Research, 1996), 80.

4. Thomas Burman, "Islam in Spain and Western Europe" in Nanji, *The Muslim Almanac*, 107–114.

5. Bloom and Blair, *Islam*, 88.

6. The term Islamicate was coined by the world historian Marshall G. S. Hodgson to refer to the influence of Muslim civilization without requiring the practice of Islam as a religion. See Marshall G. S. Hodgson, *The Venture of Islam* 3 v. (Chicago: University of Chicago Press, 1974).

7. Schroeter, Daniel J. "Islam in North Africa and the Mediterranean" in Nanji, *The Muslim Almanac,* 115–129.

8. Nyang, Sulayman. "Islam in Sub-Saharan Africa" in Nanji, The Muslim Almanac, 45–54.

9. Sajida Alvi, "Islam in South Asia" in Nanji, *The Muslim Almanac,* 55–72.

10. C. E. Bosworth, "Islam in Central Asia and the Caucasus" in Nanji, *The Muslim Almanac,* 83–89.

11. Dillion, Michael. "Islam in China" in Nanji, *The Muslim Almanac,* 91–105.

12. Denny, Frederick M. "Islam in Southeast Asia" in Nanji, *The Muslim Almanac,* 73–81.

# 2

# TEXTS AND MAJOR TENETS

## INTRODUCTION TO THE QUR'AN

The revelations received by Muhammad, the Prophet of Islam (d. 632 C.E.), over the course of 22 years were written down, collated, and compiled into what is called the "Noble" Qur'an (*Qur'an al-Sharif*) or the Book of God (*Kitab Allah*). Muslims consider the Qur'an to be the words or speech of God revealed to Muhammad. In this respect, it is a sacred book. The Qur'an is considered the "Criterion" or "Discernment," because it confirms the scriptures given to earlier biblical peoples and enables humans to distinguish between right and wrong, truth and falsehood, faith and ingratitude. It is also considered to be the "Guide," because it guides humans to walk on the straight path (*sirat al-mustaqim*).

## REVELATION

The word Qur'an is derived from the Arabic verbal root *qara'a*, meaning to recite or to read aloud, and thus may be translated as "The Recitation." During the process of revelation, Muhammad was often subject to powerful experiences. For instance, when Muhammad first received revelation while in solitary retreat in the cave of Hira, he said: "He [Gabriel] came to me while I was asleep, with a coverlet of brocade whereon was some writing and said, 'Recite!' I said, 'What shall I recite?' He pressed me with it so tightly that I thought it was death."[1] Revelations are reported to have begun during the month of Ramadan, on the "night of destiny" or *laylat al-qadr* (literally, "night of power"). A short interruption in revelations left Muham-

Folio from a Qur'an, Arabic, East Persia, 11th century. Ink, color, and gold on paper. Courtesy of the Freer Gallery of Art and Arthur M. Sackler Gallery, Smithsonian Institution, Washington, D.C.: Purchase, F1929.70.

mad in despair and grieving. Revelations eventually resumed with what is termed the Chapter of the Morning Hours. The angel of revelation assured Muhammad that God had not forsaken him and that he should "Speak of the kindness of thy Lord" (Q. 93:11), for had not God found Muhammad an orphan and given him refuge, found him going astray and given him guidance, found him poor and made him rich? Here God gave the command not to oppress the orphan and not to repel the beggar.

Revelation was both aural and visual. The most famous examples of Muhammad's visions are of the angel of revelation, Gabriel, as a man with feet astride the horizon and the account of Muhammad's fabled night journey to Jerusalem and then to heaven into the divine presence, known as the heavenly ascent or *mi'raj* (see also Chapter 5).[2] During this ascent from Jerusalem to heaven, Muhammad met Abraham, Moses, and Jesus assembled with a number of prophets, and he prayed with them. Revelation is often described as that which is brought down or descends, and the angel Gabriel is identified as the one who brought revelation down upon the Prophet's heart (Q. 2:97). God reminded Muhammad that revelation is a form of divine grace: "If God so willed, [God] would seal up your heart, so that no more revelation would come to you" (Q. 42:24). The Qur'an is revealed in Arabic (Q. 12:2) so that the Arabs, to whom a messenger had not previously been sent, could understand it, hence making Muhammad "a prophet for the unlettered." Revelation was sent as guidance for humankind (Q. 2:185), for God sends divine messengers (such as Noah, Abraham, Moses, Jesus, and Muhammad) "as a mercy" (Q. 44:3–6), and every messenger is sent speaking the language of his people (Q. 14:4). According to the Qur'an, all scriptures brought down by divine messengers come from a heavenly prototype known variously as the Preserved Tablet (Q. 85:21–22), the Mother of the Book (Q. 13:39), or a book kept hidden (Q. 56:78). Thus, the Qur'an came from the same divine source as prior biblical scriptures and declares that it is a continuation of these (Q. 2:136; 3:3). Muhammad is considered to be the last prophet (Q. 33:40), and religion, which belongs only to God (Q. 39:3), is declared to have been completed or brought to perfection in the final divine message expressed in the Qur'an. Muslims hold the view that the Qur'an is inimitable—that is, it cannot be produced or replicated by humans (Q. 2:23).

## THE COLLECTION OF THE QUR'AN

For Muslims, the Qur'an is a source of pride because it is one of the earliest of the world's major scriptures to be written down, collected, and organized to form a canonical document closest to the lifetime of the religion's founder or prophet. Some traditions (*hadith*) testify that Muhammad began the process while in Medina of directing scribes to write down the revelations he received and instructed them on the ordering of revelations. His adopted son Zayd is often mentioned as being in charge of this process. Additions or changes sometimes were made to prior revelations, for which an explanation is given in Qur'an 2:106: "For whatever verses We abrogate or cause you [Muhammad] to forget, We bring [another that is] better or like it." Another explanation is offered in 22:52: "We have never sent any messenger or prophet before you, but Satan cast into his thoughts what he was yearning. But God abrogates what Satan casts in, and then God adjusts his verses." An example of these "satanic verses" that were later

abrogated may be found in 53:19, in which the pre-Islamic Arabian goddesses al-Lat, al-'Uzza, and Manat are mentioned, after which Muhammad
is said to have recited the words, "These are the exalted ones, Whose intercession is to be hoped for." According to later commentators on the Qur'an,
Muhammad was informed by Gabriel that these verses were inserted by
Satan, and God then revealed 22:52 (quoted above), followed by verses 53:
21–7, which once again assert that God alone rules over both the life before
and the life after death (and no other deities have this power, including the
pre-Islamic goddesses).

According to some accounts, the collection of the Qur'an into sheets
was begun by the first leader or caliph of the community after the prophet's
death, Abu Bakr. 'Umar, the second caliph, had the sheets compiled into
a book , and Zayd was instrumental in collecting and collating the various copies of revelations that had been written down by scribes, including
himself. However, traditional sources are not in agreement over when the
collation of the Qur'an began after Muhammad's death. Each of the first
four caliphs (Abu Bakr, 'Umar, 'Uthman, and 'Ali) is claimed to have been
the first to begin the process toward a canonized collection of the Qur'an.
Whatever may have been the case, most sources record that, by the latter
half of 'Uthman's reign—that is, within 20 years of the prophet's death—an
official version had been prepared, and it is reported that other collections
in the hands of private individuals were burned by 'Uthman's order.

The 'Uthmanic version was by no means the only authoritative version
to remain in existence. Written Arabic at that time did not use orthographic symbols (vowels and dots) to distinguish certain letters and letter
combinations, so it is possible to read variations depending on how the
vowels and dots are placed. Early Muslim authors were aware that there
could be various readings of the Qur'an, and, indeed, several different versions are reported as having been heard in Medina, Kufa, Damascus, and
Basra. In a few cases, there are variations in synonyms or certain phrases.
Other variations are ascribed to theological or legal differences. Eventually, a text with all the orthographic symbols was established, and, by the
eleventh century, seven official readings were accepted (although at least
ten continued to be used), and several different styles of recitation (*tajwid*)
came to be accepted. Today, two versions are mostly in use, one following
the Egyptian standard version based on the reading of Hafs al-'Asim, and
the other recited in parts of Africa other than Egypt, based on the reading
of Warsh al-Nafi'.

## THE FORMAT OF THE QUR'AN

The Qur'an consists of 114 chapters or *suras,* each of which is divided into verses or *ayat.* Both terms in the Qur'an refer to a revelation being sent from God. The term *ayat* in the Qur'an also refers to a natural phenomena or an extraordinary event or miracle that confirms God's power and beneficence to evoke a response of gratitude and an enlightened knowledge of God's workings. Thus, *ayat* can mean both a verse of the Qur'an and a sign of God's mercy and power. The opening chapter of the Qur'an is the *Fatiha* (the "Opening"), and all chapters following it are arranged in order of descending length rather than chronological order. The Qur'an ends with two short chapters that are incantations to take refuge in God. A chapter does not necessarily have thematic unity, but may instead comprise unrelated segments. Except for accounts of Noah, Joseph, and Solomon, the Qur'an contains very few narratives or stories; much of the Qur'an presumes knowledge of biblical figures and invokes these characters to make a point about God's justice or mercy or about the obedience and faith expected of humans as a response to God's generosity. Sometimes, despite their varying lengths, chapters are kept together for thematic unity—for instance, chapters 10 through 15 all concern prophets. Muslims traditionally refer to the chapters by name and not by number; thus, chapter two is known as "The Cow," because the word occurs within the chapter.

Each chapter (except the ninth chapter) begins with the *basmala,* a shortened version of the phrase *bismi'llah al-rahman al-rahim,* which means "In the Name of God, the Compassionate, the Merciful". In 29 chapters, the *basmala* is followed by a letter or group of letters before the verses of the chapter begin. Scholars do not know the reasons for these letters, and Muslims believe only God knows their meaning and significance. Scholars have suggested that the letters form the initials of the scribes who wrote down the text, or the initial of the owner of the sheet or manuscript used by Zayd to compile the Qur'an, or perhaps the initials of several owners and possibly even the abbreviations of discarded titles. However, evidence suggests that the letters were part of the revelation and were recited as an integral part of the chapter. All together there are 14 letters, which make up the entire Arabic alphabet, with the dots distinguishing one letter from another taken out. For instance, the letters y, b, t, and th all have the same form in Arabic, but dots are used to distinguish one letter from the other. In the mysterious group of letters, only one of these, y, is represented.

Many verses in the Qur'an are responses to Muhammad's historical situation or allude to events occurring in his time. Nonetheless, it is difficult to date the chapters and verses in the Qur'an, because the book is arranged not chronologically but by length. Many of the shorter chapters that appear at the end of the Qur'an were, in fact, early revelations when Muhammad was still in Mecca. These chapters are characterized by their short, rhythmic verses and their poetic power. Rhythmic prose (*saj*, important for sonorous recitation) is the characteristic form of Qur'anic verses, which is true even of the longer, more prosaic revelations made in Medina that are only loosely rhythmic. Western scholars of the Qur'an have divided the chapters/verses into four periods: revelations of the first or early Meccan period; those of the second or Middle Meccan period; those of the third or late Meccan period; and, finally, the verses revealed in Medina. The Qur'an's tone and style, although poetic throughout, become progressively more prosaic and attendant to the historical situation during the course of Muhammad's life. Some scholars have suggested that the Qur'an might be best studied according to a thematic scheme that has six classifications: confirmatory, declamatory, narrative, descriptive, legislative, and verses revealed in Medina.

Early Muslims attempted to link passages in the Qur'an with stories about how and why a particular verse came to be revealed, and these stories came to be called "the occasions of revelation" literature. Some of the stories are hagiographic in nature, and they helped Muslims determine whether a passage was revealed earlier rather than later. The dating of a passage takes on great importance for establishing a law on the matter, for a later verse abrogates or cancels out the earlier verse's ruling. Establishing dates for such purposes created a literature known as the "abrogation" literature. So, for instance, the changing of the direction of prayer from Jerusalem to Mecca is upheld by the date of the latter verse, as is the prohibition on drinking wine, which was once allowed but then abrogated by a later verse.

## THE QUR'AN'S LITERARY FORMS

Classifying passages in the Qur'an according to standard literary types such as myth, legend, short story, and parable does not yield much fruitful analysis. Rather, the Qur'an uses oaths, prophetic utterances, sign-passages, say-passages, and narratives that refer to mythic motifs and include prophet stories, punishment stories, and parables. Many of the verses in the Qur'an concern regulations for rituals, religious duties, and ordinary conduct, and there are passages that are liturgical in form, praising God. The most well known of the praise passages is the Throne verse (Q. 2:255). Some passages may be classified as dramatic scenes, while others are theological, and several passages are intended for Muhammad or are personal in that they address his family problems. Examples of some of the above rubrics are as follows:

*Oath:* "By the fig and olive, / By Mount Sinai, / By this land secure, / Surely We have created the human being most beautifully erect" (Q. 95: 1–4).

*Prophetic utterance:* "When the heaven is cleft asunder, / When the planets are dispersed, / When the seas are poured forth, / And the sepulchres are overturned, / A soul will know what it has sent before [it] and what [it has] left behind" (Q. 82:1–5).

*Sign-passage.* "And of [God's] signs is this: [God] created you of dust, and indeed you are mortal, scattered widely! / And of [God's] signs is this: [God] created for you of your own species spouses that you may dwell with them, and has set love and mercy between you. Surely in that are signs for those who reflect. / And of [God's] signs is the creation of the heavens and the earth and the variety of your languages and colors. Surely here are signs for people of knowledge" (Q. 30:20–22).

*Say-passage.* "Say! We believe in God and what has been revealed to us and what was revealed to Abraham, and Ishmael, and Isaac, and Jacob, and the tribes, and that which Moses and Jesus received, and that which the prophets received from their Lord. We make no distinction between any of them, and unto [God] we have surrendered" (Q. 2:136).

*Mythic motifs.* These include a brief mention rather than a full narrative of creation, God seated on a throne, the trumpet sounding the advent of the Last Day, the flood at the time of Noah, the role of Iblis or Satan in the banishing of the primordial human couple from paradise, and so forth.

*Prophet stories.* The longest narrative concerning prophets is the story of Joseph. There are also accounts of the birth of John the Baptist and Jesus, as well as stories about Abraham, Moses, Solomon, Adam, Noah, Lot, Ishmael, David, Elijah, Jonah, and Job. Nonbiblical prophets such as Luqman, Hud, Salih, and Shu'ayb are also mentioned.

*Punishment stories.* These include the story of Lot, Moses and Pharaoh, Noah, and some others.

*Parables.* "And coin for them the similitude of the life of the world as water which We send down from the sky, and the vegetation of the earth mingles with it and then becomes dry twigs that the winds scatter. God is able to do all things."

*Regulations.* "Establish worship at the two ends of the day and in some watches of the night" (Q. 11:114); "It is prescribed for you, when one of you approaches death, if he leave wealth, that he bequeath it to parents and near relatives in kindness" (Q. 2:190); "O believers, when you stand up for the prayer, wash your faces and your hands up to the elbows, and wipe your heads and your feet up to the ankles" (Q. 5:6); "Fight in the way of God those who fight you, but do not provoke hostility" (Q. 2:190).

*Liturgical passages.* These constitute praise of God and prayers such as found in the chapter on Abraham: "Our Lord! Indeed you know that which we hide and that which we proclaim. Nothing in the earth or in the heaven is hidden from Allah" (Q. 14:38), and "Our Lord! Forgive me and my parents and believers on the day when the account is cast" (Q. 14:41).[3]

## KEY CONCEPTS AND THEMES IN THE QUR'AN

### God and Creation

The most important concept introduced in the Qur'an is that of God as the sole, absolute Creator, Lord, and Sustainer. For humans, this knowledge necessitates the response of surrender (*islam*) to God as the sole deity. The Throne verse, the most famous of the praise passages, declares: "Allah! There is no god (*ilah*) save God (Allah), the Alive, the Eternal. Neither slumber nor sleep overtake [God]. Unto [God] belongs whatever is in the heavens and whatever is in the earth. Who intercedes with [God] save by [God's] permission? [God] knows that which is in front of them and that which is behind them, while they encompass nothing of [God's] knowledge save what [God] wills. [God's] throne includes the heavens and the earth, and [God] is never weary of preserving them. [God] is the Sublime and the Tremendous" (Q. 2:225).[4]

In the Qur'an, there is nothing irrational about the existence of God, for the Qur'an repeatedly mentions that God's signs (*ayat*) are sufficient evidence for "those who reflect" of God's existence as well as God's beneficence to humankind and, indeed, to all life. Everything in creation depends on God for its existence and, hence, all things and beings are connected to each other and to God. All of creation is a sign of God's creative power. God is essentially a God of mercy ("My Mercy comprehends all" Q. 7:156) and justice. God is infinite and everlasting.

There is no god but God; [God] is the Knower of the unseen and the seen, the Merciful, the Compassionate. There is no god but God, the Sovereign, the Holy, the One with peace and integrity, the Keeper of the faith, the Protector, the Mighty, the One Whose Will is Power, the Most Supreme! Glory be to [God] beyond what they [pre-Islamic Arabs] associate with [God]. There is no god but God, the Creator, the Maker, the Fashioner, to Whom belong beautiful names; whatever is in the heavens and the earth sings [God's] glories, [God] is the Mighty One, the Wise One. (Q. 59: 22–24)

Creation in general and of humankind has a purpose and is not done out of a sense of sport or frivolity: "We have not created the heaven and the earth and whatever is between them in vain" (Q. 38:27); "Do you then think that We have created you purposelessly and that you will not be returned to Us? The True Sovereign is too exalted above that" (Q. 23:115). Having created the world in six days—the Qur'an assumes the biblical creation timeline—God sustains creation by placing everything needed for survival into creation itself, so that living things can sustain themselves through the bounties provided by God. Humans are, through God's mercy and beneficence, endowed with the capacity for knowledge and the will to realize God's purpose for humankind—that is, to live in righteousness and distinguish between good and evil and surrender to God's lordship. Hence, divine messengers are sent to humans in order to remind them of their obligations toward God and each other, and revelation guides humans' moral choices and social and religious comportment. Such guidance is ingrained in human nature as the capacity to distinguish between good and evil (Q. 91:8). Humans will be called to account for their deeds, and the human attitude of fearing God, also understood as piety, serves as a rudder to keep humans mindful of being accountable at all times to their Creator, Lord, and Sustainer. Indeed, there is nothing in the universe to be feared other than God, for a Muslim is "not afraid of losing anything but God's support.... God is his only helper, the sole refuge; all other imagined havens are hopeless: 'Those who have taken friends besides God, their likeness is that of the spider which takes for itself a house, but the weakest of all is the spider's house—if only they knew!'" (Q. 29:41).[5]

According to the Qur'an, God creates things according to their measure, not blindly or in a chaotic manner. The Arabic term for power and for measuring out is the same, *qadar*. The Qur'an takes the pre-Islamic idea of fate as a blind and inexorable ruler of human destiny and turns it instead into a God-directed measuring out that flows from God's beneficence and mercy. Thus, all things are created within a framework of orderliness, interconnectedness, and cohesiveness. The power to measure things out implies that it is itself immeasurable, hence God is incomparable in power. To suggest that any entity, mortal or otherwise, could share in that power to is commit the error of ascribing partnership to God, a notion that is firmly rejected by the Qur'an. The principle of being measured out is nowhere more evident than in nature, which obeys the command of God and is therefore called *muslim* ("that which surrenders") in the Qur'an (Q. 3:83).

### The Human Condition

The first, or prototypical human is named *adam* ("from the earth") in the Qur'an. Adam was fashioned out of clay (Q. 15:26), after which God "breathed My own spirit" (Q. 15:29) into him, distinguishing him from other creatures. God created Adam in order to place a vicegerent on earth, at which the angels protested, "Will You put there being who will work mischief on the earth and shed blood, while we sing Your glories and exalt Your utter holiness?" God taught Adam the names of things and asked the angels and the human to name things; when the angels could not, it became clear to the angels that here was a being endowed with the capacity to know things that they did not (Q. 2:30 ff.). God then asked the angels to bow before Adam, and they all complied, with the exception of Iblis or Satan, who asked, "Why should I prostrate before a mortal whom You have created out of altered black mud?" God banished Iblis, and cursed him until the Day of Judgment, the day when all creatures will be "raised" to be judged and meet their fate. Iblis asked for a reprieve from the curse, which he was granted. Iblis then vowed, because God had led him astray (there is much speculation as to why Iblis felt this way; perhaps because in his view God alone was worthy of one's prostration), to lead every human astray except those who were God's devoted servants. God's response was that Iblis would have no power over such servants, and those who followed Iblis would be judged accordingly and sent to hell. Hell is described as a place with seven gates, each of which has an "appointed portion," while heaven, to which God's servants will be sent on the Day of Judgment, is described as filled with gardens and springs (Q. 15:26 ff).

Several narratives in the Qur'an detail the expulsion of the primordial couple from the Garden. Adam's mate is unnamed in the Qur'an, and Muslim tradition calls her Hawwa. The Qur'an does not describe how she was created, but several verses refer to the creation of males and females as having come from a single soul (Q. 4:1) or simply that God made humans in pairs (Q. 35:11). God enjoined the pair to "dwell in the Garden and eat freely of its bountiful fruit" but "not to approach this Tree" (Q. 7:19, 2:35). Iblis whispered his temptation to Adam (Q. 20:120), and Adam disobeyed God and "went astray" (Q. 20:121). In another account, Iblis approaches both Adam and his mate, promising them eternal life if they eat of the tree, and they both disobey (Q. 7:20–22). Various accounts in the Qur'an suggest that the couple asked for forgiveness, which they were granted. God then bestowed them with the garment of righteousness (Q. 7:26), but they were no longer permitted to live in the Garden. God further assured them that whoever followed God's guidance would be free from fear and grief (Q. 2:38). The Qur'anic accounts differ from the accounts in the biblical book of Genesis in that nowhere does the Qur'an mention that Adam's mate was created from his rib; nor does the Qur'an lay the blame for having succumbed to Satan on the woman. The only punishment meted out to both Adam and his mate for disobeying God is banishment from the Garden, not the various punishments that men and women in the biblical narrative are dealt.

Humans in the Qur'anic narratives thenceforth are subject to a legacy in which they continually strive between the call to live in righteousness, and the urgings of Satan or Iblis to fall into error. In addition, humans take on the "trust" that God offered to the heavens and the earth but that they refused to shoulder. Muslims have understood the trust to mean God's exhortation to human beings to create a just social order on earth. Humans have an original, primordial nature through which they can choose to do good or evil and that they can keep intact despite the many temptations that are placed in their way. Those who deny revelation and wrong themselves are described as having been sent astray; they are those who "have hearts but cannot understand, have eyes but cannot see, have ears but cannot hear" (Q 7:179). Although the Qur'an talks of God sealing up the hearts of humans, such sealing is a consequence of human refusal to believe in revelation (Q. 6:111). Thus, humans are free to make their own moral choices, albeit with consequences.

## The Human Response to God

In acknowledging that God is a beneficent Creator and Sustainer who provides for all creatures (Q. 15:19–23), the appropriate response for humans to make to God is one of *islam,* voluntary surrender to God's will through placing one's trust entirely in God. In so doing, the human takes on the attitude of being an *'abd*, one who serves God with the utmost humility in all dimensions of human existence, and reflects this in worship (*'ibadah*, a term that stems from the same root as *'abd*): "Lord of the heavens and the earth and all that is between them! Therefore, worship [God] and be steadfast in service to [God]. Do you know any that can be named along with [God]?" (Q. 19:65). Pride in one's accomplishments that are not properly viewed as having been granted by God's grace and a sense of confidence and power due to one's own efforts are contrary to the Muslim concept of *'abd*. Rather, the attitude of *'abd* entails a profound sense of humility in the recognition that all forms of success are a result of God's kindness and generosity toward humans. Concomitantly, all trials and tribulations are to be borne with steadfast faith and trust in the Lord who provides for all creatures.

Such an attitude of striving to be an *'abd* as a natural outpouring from *islam* contrasts sharply to the attitude of a *jahil* or "ignorant one" that was considered to be people's prior state before they chose to declare themselves *muslim*—that is, one who has surrendered to God. The period before Islam was revealed is known as *jahiliyya*, or the age of ignorance. *Jahili* values consisted of the refusal to submit to the authority of any person and defending with zeal any attacks on one's honor; hence the *jahil* was one who was presumptuous, arrogant, and insolent. An invitation to the attitude of *islam*—surrender to God—struck at the very heart of *jahili* values, as did the attitude of service to God accompanied by a sense of humility. A *jahil* is thus also a *kafir*, one who displays ingratitude for all that God has provided for in the heavens and the earth, and one who remains blind and deaf to God's signs or revelations in both the seen and the unseen worlds. The stubbornness of those who will not believe is expressed in Q. 6:3: "Even if We should send down the angels to them, and the dead should speak to them, and We should gather all things in array before their own eyes, yet they would not be believers, unless God so willed. But most of them are ignorant." The idea is that God could choose, out of divine power, to *make* people into believers, but instead God prefers people to have faith from their own volition or free will.

The notion of *jahil* is further contrasted with the idea of *hilm*, self-control and forbearance. A *halim* can control his or her passions and restrain his or her power and remain calm in the face of provocation. When the term is applied to God, it indicates the divine tendency to show mercy and forgiveness despite God's ability to retaliate and punish. The quality of *hilm* was ascribed to Muhammad, and in the Qur'an, the term is applied almost without exception to God as *Halim,* one who has forbearance, one who forgives. It has been argued that the notion of *hilm* as a laudable human characteristic is retained in the Qur'an as a constellation of characteristics that God encourages humans to embody: kindness, justice (*'adl*), and forbidding of tyranny or injustice (*zulm*)—all of which are concrete manifestations of the pre-Islamic value of *hilm.* The Qur'an sought to replace the values of a *jahil*—refusal to submit, arrogance, and a vengeful defense of one's honor—with an attitude of *hilm*—expressed in the notions of kindness, justice, and a refusal to engage in tyranny—as the appropriate manner for human beings to treat one another.[6] Furthermore, the attitude of a *jahil* toward God is also inappropriate, for religion (*din*) means to worship or serve God, as reflected in the following Qur'anic verse: "Say: O humankind! If you are in doubt about my religion, then [know that] I worship/serve not those whom you worship/serve instead of God, but I worship/serve God" (Q. 10:105). Further, while the term *din* indicates a personal decision to serve and worship God, it is linked to the term *millah,* or religion in its public or communal aspect: "As for me, my Lord has guided me to a straight path (*sirat al-mustaqim*), a right religion (*din*), the religion (*millah*) of Abraham the monotheist" (Q. 6:162).

Thus, a Muslim who wishes to remain on the straight path cultivates a state of attentiveness to the consequences of one's actions and how these might be accounted by God. Such a state is termed *taqwa,* often translated as piety, although the word piety does not fully convey the notion of remaining continually conscious of the consequences of one's actions. This concept is closely related to being in a state of service to God that prevents humans from transgressing moral boundaries. The accounting of all human deeds is said to take place at the end of time, when God will raise all humans in order to call them to account. This day is the Day of Religion, understood as the Day of Judgment. At that time, the righteous will be sent to heaven or the gardens, while the unrighteous will have the veils before their eyes lifted and will be sent to suffer in hell. Although heaven and hell are understood literally by some Muslims, many Muslims construe these as denoting nearness or distance from God's presence.

For its relatively short length, the Qur'an is a rich text evoking many topics, such as prophecy, legal matters, eschatology, mysticism, philosophy, theology, ritual behavior, gender issues, and moral guidance. The book continues to inspire Muslims, as each generation draws guidance from it with respect to what constitutes a moral life, a just society, and a meaningful framework within which to live a life that will be judged laudable by God.

Muslim poets, artists, musicians, and writers continue to draw inspiration from the Qur'an for their interpretations of its relevance to contemporary life.

## THE HADITH LITERATURE

Muslims retain the memory of what Muhammad was thought to have said and done during his lifetime in a collection of narratives known as the Hadith literature, also called the Tradition literature. The *hadith* (literally, narrative, that which is recounted) literature is considered second in authority to the Qur'an. As long as Muhammad was alive, the community turned to him for guidance on all matters, personal as well as social and religious. After his death, the caliphs continued to guide the community through the Qur'an and what the Prophet had taught them. However, as the generation of Muhammad's contemporaries began to die, Muslims increasingly felt the need to record what people remembered of his actions and teachings as a guide for individual and communal behavior. The task of administering a vast new empire over the century after Muhammad's death led to a search for legal principles and guidance to address the new situations encountered by Muslim rulers. The Prophet's importance as a model for a Muslim's behavior was based on the notion that, since God had chosen Muhammad to be a prophet, he did not stop being a prophet when he was not receiving revelation and not in direct communication with God; thus, everything he said and did provided a model for Muslims to follow. Meanwhile, while the Qur'an contained verses of legal importance, it was clear that the Prophet's guidance in communal matters could provide more specific direction in how Qur'anic values were implemented. Thus, in the first century after Muhammad's death, an interest in collecting *hadith* narratives resulted in traditionists, as these collectors were known, traveling Muslim lands in search of people who remembered what the Prophet had said or done in various situations. The annual pilgrimage to Mecca also brought together people from different regions, thereby allowing for the exchange and spread of *hadith.* Some debate was raised by an early group of theologian-jurists called the Mu'tazila regarding whether *hadith* stories, because they were transmitted by individuals, were a true source of knowledge about the Prophet's teaching and hence whether they were important as a source of guidance. The debate was resolved by the legal scholar al-Shafi'i (d. 820 C.E.), who argued that the term "wisdom" in the Qur'an (2:151, 3:164, and others) was a reference to *hadith,* and that the Qur'an and the Prophet's own example were key sources in defining a Muslim life, both individually and in the context of social well-being. Further, he argued on the basis of Qur'an 24:52, which enjoined Muslims to obey God and obey the Prophet, that emulation of the Prophet's actions was incumbent upon Muslims, and that *hadith* narratives were therefore an infallible source of law.

Over time, there was a need to develop authoritative sources for *hadith* to determine the veracity of Tradition reports. In sources as early as the biography of Muhammad written by historian Ibn Ishaq (d. 768) and the writings of legal scholar Malik b. Anas (d. 795), *hadith* were recorded with or without chains of authority. It is unclear whether the Prophet encouraged or forbade his community to write down what he said and did, but there are reports of men who made notes for themselves, which later came to be used as sources for larger, more formal *hadith* collections. The nephew of the Prophet's wife 'A'ishah, 'Urwa b. al-Zubayr (d. ca 717), and al-Zuhri (d. 741) are both widely quoted authorities.

As a result of the need to trace a report concerning the Prophet back to its source, a *hadith* came to comprise two parts: (1) a complete chain of transmission (*isnad*) and (2) the text of the *hadith* (*matn*). Interest in verifying the authenticity of a *hadith* came about as a result of common knowledge that, as the community began to develop different theological and political interpretations of the meaning of Islam, a variety of *hadith* narratives were readily available to support such viewpoints. Muslim scholars of tradition were aware that people were inventing *hadith* narratives as the need arose. Thus, it became essential to develop a method through which a *hadith* narrative could be classified as sound, good, or weak, each with further subcategories. A *hadith* narrative's chain of transmission relied on genealogical investigation of birth and death dates to ascertain that the individuals recorded in the chain lived at times when they could have met and could have been in close proximity to Muhammad. Further, the moral character of the person transmitting the tradition at each point in the chain was investigated. Ideally, a *hadith* would go back to the Prophet himself or to one of his companions or family members. Technical terms were given to each *hadith* according to the criteria of how many transmitters it had, its ultimate source, whether the transmission had special features such as whether all the transmitters came from the same place, and so forth.

The earliest written collections of *hadith* such as those of al-Tayalisi (d. 818) and Ahmad b. Hanbal (d. 855) were organized according to their ultimate source of transmission—that is, according to the name of the Prophet's companion. Such an arrangement, with its emphasis on the transmitter, was inconvenient for someone interested in *hadith* pertaining to a certain subject. Over time, *hadith* narratives came to be organized according to subject matter, in emulation of *al-Muwatta*, the legal text written by the scholar Malik b. Anas (d. 795). For Sunni Muslims, six collections of *hadith* narratives are considered authoritative: the *Sahih* of al-Bukhari (d. 870), the *Sahih* of Muslim (d. 875), and the *Sunan* works of Abu Da'ud (d. 888), al-Tirmidhi (d. 892), al-Nasa'i (d. 916), and Ibn Maja (d. 886). The *Sahih* works are distinguished from the *Sunan* works by their inclusion of biographical materials, Qur'anic commentary, and thematic organization of *hadith* narratives into those pertaining to religious observance, law, commerce, and public and private behavior.[7] The Shi'ites—who accepted *hadith* narratives sourced back only to the Prophet, to Fatima, 'Ali, their progeny, and their companions—developed their own authoritative Tradition collections, most notably *al-Kafi fi'ilm al-din* by al-Kulayni (d. 939), *Kitab man la yahduruhu'l-faqih* by al-Qummi (d. 991), and *Tahdhib al-ahkam* by al-Tusi (d. 1068).

Modern Western historical scholarship has leveled criticism against the veracity of the *hadith*. For instance, referenced in the *hadith* are several biblical phrases; towns either far from Arabia and yet to be conquered or not yet founded; theological groups not yet formed at the time of the Prophet; the Umayyad and 'Abbasid dynasties; and attributions of miracles to the Prophet despite the fact that the Qur'an does not present him as a miracle-worker. Such features raise the possibility that much of the *hadith* literature comes from a date later than Muhammad's lifetime.[8] Indeed, Muslims themselves were aware of the spurious nature of many of the *hadith* they collected, and al-Bukhari—one of the most stringent of the *hadith* collectors—sifted through approximately 600,000 reports, selecting only 2,602 *hadith* (9,082 if repetitions are included) to compile his *Sahih*. Indeed, the *hadith* literature is really the crystallization of what the Muslims of the second century after the Prophet's death believed he had said and done, based on what they thought were accurate oral reports handed down through the generations closest to the Prophet's own time. Moreover, the *hadith* literature, whether Sunni or Shi'a, represents, in part, the collector's understanding of what was correct for the community to uphold in the example of the Prophet and provided continuity for later generations about what was remembered as the Prophet's conduct. Scholars have suggested that *hadith* that conformed more readily to Muslim beliefs and practices at the time may have been privileged in selection, thus making the *hadith* literature a testament not only to what Muslims cherished at the time as they memorialized the Prophet's words and actions, but also a reminder to future generations of Muslims of their understanding of the Prophet's message. Indeed, the *hadith* literature collectively is translated into providing Muslims with a model for their own practice of Islam, as the *hadith* is considered the *sunnah* (practice and hence, irreproachable model) of the Prophet: as God's prophet, Muhammad is a model for all God-fearing and God-loving Muslims to follow.

Feminist studies of the *hadith* have argued that there was a patriarchal mindset at work in the selection of *hadith* that saw the world and the Prophet's teachings from a male point of view. This is nowhere more apparent than in the *hadith* depictions of the wives of the Prophet, who had been named "the Mothers of the Believers" by Muhammad toward the end of his life. The wives were depicted in diverse ways: "On the one hand, they emerge as perfect exemplars of their sex regarding virtue and righteousness. On the other hand, they are portrayed as embodiments of female emotionalism, irrationality, greed, and rebelliousness."[9] It has been argued that the traditionists' recording of the Prophet's wives depicts them simultaneously as the paradigm for all Muslim women to follow regarding their social and religious roles, while at the same time providing symbolic evidence through the reports of their frailties "for all that was wrong with the female sex."[10] The inordinate amount of attention paid to women's weaknesses has been characterized as a reflection of the patriarchal culture and attitude toward women during the time of the *hadith* collectors that devalued women's social rank as well as their access to legal rights, thereby undermining the equality between men and women during the time of Muhammad. Also questioned were the political motivations behind the *hadith* often quoted to prevent women from holding political office: "Those who entrust power to a woman will never know prosperity."[11] This tradition was reported by a freed slave, Abu Bakra, when he opposed the first civil war initiated by the Prophet's wife 'A'ishah. His was the only gender-based reason for opposition to the war, suggesting that its appearance at such an opportune moment was politically motivated. Moreover, despite the *hadith* being considered sound by al-Bukhari, it did not garner unqualified support among legal scholars. The scholar al-Tabari did not consider the *hadith* in question to be weighty enough to justify women's exclusion from politics, but it still hounds every Muslim woman who seeks to enter the political realm.

## HADITH QUDSI

The *hadith qudsi* is a class of sacred traditions that records words spoken by God (distinguished from words spoken by the Prophet). These divine sayings might not necessarily have been revealed through Gabriel and are thought to have come to the Prophet through inspiration. They form part of the required communal prayers, and, when quoted, they are prefaced with the words: "God's messenger said in what he related from Lord" (in contrast to quotations from the Qur'an, which are prefaced with "God said"). Some *hadith qudsi* are quotations from the Bible; for example, "What the eye has not seen, the ear not heard, nor has entered the heart of man" (from Isaiah lxiv, 4; Cor. ii., 9). The *hadith qudsi* were initially compiled along with the larger collections of *hadith,* but scholars later culled the *hadith qudsi* from the larger collections; for example, al-Madyani's (d. 1476 c.e.) compilation of 858 traditions is the largest, followed by the compilation of the noted Spanish mystic Ibn al-'Arabi (d. 1240).

## POST-QUR'ANIC LITERATURES

In addition to the "occasions of revelation" (*asbab al-nuzul*) literature that explained the context in which a verse of the Qur'an had been revealed, there developed an *isra'iliyat* literature. These were Bible-related traditions probably from Jews and Christians, some of whom were converts to Islam, and these traditions provided details of references made in the Qur'an to biblical figures or events. The *qisas al-anbiya'* collections, which contained stories of biblical and Qur'anic prophets, formed yet another kind of literature. All three of these literatures were used in the writing of commentaries on the Qur'an. The commentaries became a source for further discourses on legal issues, theological works, philosophical works, mystical works and the Qur'an and the *hadith.*

## MAJOR TENETS

The major guidelines for a Muslim are understood by Muslim theologians as consisting of two parts—*iman* (expressions of faith) and *ihsan* (doing what is right)—both of which are reinforced by *'ibadat* (acts of worship). According to the Qur'an, *iman* or faith consists of belief in God and the Prophet, previous prophets and revealed scriptures, angels, and the Day of Judgment (Q. 4:136). Shi'ites would additionally include love of and obedience to the family of the Prophet and to his progeny through 'Ali and Fatima (see Chapter 3) as part of *iman*. The following description of faith is found in the *hadith* collection of Muslim (d. 875):

A man asked the Prophet, "What is faith?"

He replied, "Faith consists of belief in God, His angels, the meeting with Him, His Apostles, and the resurrection."

The man said, "What is *islam*?"

He replied, "*Islam* consists of the service of God, the refusal to associate anything with Him, prayer, alms-giving, and fasting during the month of Ramadan."

The man said, "What does it mean to do good?"

He replied, "To serve God as though you see Him. Even though you cannot see Him, He can see you."

The man said, "When is the last hour?"

He replied, "The one who is asked does not know any more than he who asks, but I can tell you about the signs that point to it. When the slave woman gives birth to her master, that is one of the signs [of doom]. When the naked and the barefoot become the chiefs of the people, that is one of the signs. When the shepherds take insolent pride in constructing buildings, that is one of the signs. Then there are five things that only God knows."

After that he recited, "Surely God—He has knowledge of the Hour; He sends down the rain; He knows what is in the wombs. No soul knows what it shall earn tomorrow, and no soul knows in what land it shall die. Surely God is All-knowing, All-aware." (Q. 31:34)

Then the man slipped away. The Apostle of God said, "Send that man back to me." They tried to do so, but they could not find him.

The Apostle of God said, "It was Gabriel who came to teach the people their religion."[12]

From faith come the ethical guidelines a person of faith must strive to uphold. Q. 17:23–38 lays down such ethics as divine injunctions for Muslims:

1. To worship none other than God
2. To show kindness to parents
3. To give kin their due
4. To be charitable toward the needy and the traveler
5. To not squander one's wealth
6. To not be either miserly or wanton in one's spending
7. To not slay one's children
8. To not commit adultery
9. To not slay wrongfully
10. To not rob the orphan
11. To measure and weigh correctly
12. To not follow that of which one has no knowledge
13. To not be full of pride
14. To not set up with Allah any other god.[13]

*Ihsan,* or "right-doing" consists of obligatory and voluntary practices for Muslims. The obligatory practices have come to be termed the "five pillars" of Muslim praxis:

1. Pronouncement of the key article of faith, the *shahadah:* There is no God but God (in Arabic, Allah), and Muhammad is His Messenger, to which Shi'ite Muslims add: and 'Ali is the Master of the Believers;
2. Prayer or *salat,* to be performed five times a day for Sunni Muslims and three times a day for Shi'ite Muslims;
3. Almsgiving or *zakat,* the giving of which is left up to individual conscience, and which consists of a percentage of a person's wealth or earnings and can be remitted in cash or kind according to the guidelines set by the Muslim's particular community;
4. Fasting or *sawm,* during the holy month of Ramadan; and
5. Pilgrimage to Mecca, or *hajj,* to be undertaken by able and solvent Muslims at least once in their lifetime.

Muslims may perform more or fewer acts of *ihsan* than the five pillars as an expression of their faith. For instance, Muslims may participate in acts of worship that go far beyond the obligatory *salat* prayers; they may express their devotion to God and their remembrance of and love for the Prophet in poetry, devotional songs, music, architecture, art, and theatrical performance; they may do good works in charitable ways in addition to *zakat;* many fast on additional days as part of their own discipline, and pilgrimages to shrines of persons considered to be saintly in their teachings, practices, and stature as Muslims are a feature of Muslim life in many lands.

## NOTES

1. Ibn Hisham, Abd al-Malik, *The Life of Muhammad: A Translation of Ishaq's Sirat Rasul Allah* (London: Oxford University Press, 1955), 106. The word "read" in the translation has been changed to "recite" to conform to the contextual meaning of the word *iqra,* which could equally mean to read or to recite.

2. Ibid., 106; Q. 53:5–18; 181–7; Q. 97:1–5.

3. Material for the formal elements of the Qur'an has been culled from A. T. Welch, "al-Kur'an" in the *Encyclopedia of Islam,* CD-ROM Edition v.1.1.

4. The personal pronoun for God, which has usually been translated as "He" is replaced here with God in brackets to indicate the Qur'anic conception that God is beyond gender delineations.

5. Fazlur Rahman, *Major Themes of the Qur'an* (Minneapolis: Bibliotheca Islamica, 1980), 11. See this work for a fuller exposition of the major themes in the Qur'an.

6. See Toshihiko Izutsu, *God and Man in the Koran: Semantics of the Koranic Weltanschauung* (Tokyo: Keio Institute of Cultural and Linguistic Studies, 1964), Chapter 8, "Jahiliyyah and Islam."

7. See "Hadith" in *Encyclopedia of Islam,* CD-ROM Edition, v.1.1.

8. Ibid.

9. Barbara Freyer Stowasser, *Women in the Qur'an, Traditions, and Interpretation* (New York: Oxford University Press, 1994), 106.

10. Ibid.

11. Fatima Mernissi, *Women and Islam: An Historical and Theological Enquiry* (Oxford, England: Basil Blackwell, 1991), 57.

12. Kenneth Craig and Martin Speight, *Islam from Within: Anthology of a Religion* (Belmont, CA: Wadsworth, 1980), 80.

13. Caesar E. Farah, *Islam* (New York: Barron's, 1987), 113–114, where Farah sees these as "commandments."

# 3

# BRANCHES

When the Prophet Muhammad was alive, questions about what it meant to be a Muslim could be referred directly to him for his guidance, and the community was mostly united under his prophetic authority. To be sure, there were challenges to Muhammad's prophetic authority, but it would be some time before communities of interpretation would coalesce into distinct branches of Muslims.

One early challenger to the Prophet was a man named Maslama or Musailima from the tribe of Banu Hanifa in Yamama, who claimed prophetic abilities and preached in the name of Rahman (the Compassionate One). He was killed in battle soon after Muhammad's death. Another challenge to his prophetic authority came from a woman named Sajah from the Banu Tamim, who preached in the name of Rabb al-Sahab ("the Lord of the Clouds"). Accounts vary as to whether she joined and married Musailima or whether she disappeared into obscurity once Musailima was killed in battle.

Tradition reports that, on the way back from his last pilgrimage to the Ka'aba in Mecca, the Prophet stopped at an oasis named Ghadir Khumm and there made the declaration, "O God, be a friend of whomever he ['Ali] befriends, and an enemy of whomever he takes as an enemy."[1] Accounts such as these led to later declarations of 'Ali, the Prophet's cousin and son-in-law, to be the legitimate spiritual and temporal successor to Muhammad.

Discrete communities of interpretation arose among Muslims with respect to questions pertaining to authority, interpretation, and practice: Who has the authority to interpret Islam or, more specifically, the Qur'an?

How is the Qur'an to be read with respect to its teachings about a righteously guided life here and toward the soul's happiness in the hereafter? And, finally, what duties and obligations must a Muslim observe in order to remain true to the teachings of Muhammad and of Islam?

By and large, despite the many distinct communities of interpretation that developed within Islam, all Muslims consider themselves to belong to a single global *ummah,* or community. This *ummah* is united in its acknowledgment of three key beliefs (1) belief in a single divine being, God (Allah in Arabic); (2) the belief that God communicated with humankind through the person of Muhammad, who is considered God's final prophet in a line of biblical prophets; and (3) the belief in the authority of the sacred text, the collection of divine revelations made to Muhammad, which were compiled to form the Qur'an.

However, the notion of a single *ummah* has not precluded Muslims from engaging in intellectual and physical warfare against other Muslims who interpret Islam differently, on the grounds that interpretations other than their own are heretical. While pluralism within the Muslim *ummah* has fared better in some eras than others, differences of interpretation historically have been used during times of political struggle, thereby creating doctrines and writings intended to discredit alternate forms of interpretation and authority. Communities of interpretation develop according to differing responses to historical situations; hence, in what follows, the historical conditions that gave rise to differing Islamic theologies are laid out.

## EARLY BRANCHES: THE KHAWARIJ, MURJI'A, AND SHI'A

After Muhammad's death, while 'Ali was occupied with preparing the Prophet's body for burial, members of the Medinan community (mostly companions of the Prophet) met to determine who would assume leadership of the community. Although later Shi'ites claim that the Prophet's declaration at Ghadir Khumm had clearly established 'Ali's right to rule the community after Muhammad's death, during this meeting, 'Umar ibn al-Khattab proposed that Abu Bakr, who had been assigned the task of leading the prayers during the Prophet's illness, should bear the responsibility for leading the community. Thus, Muhammad's close companion, friend, confidante, and ally, Abu Bakr, father of his youngest wife, 'A'ishah, was named the first caliph. Abu Bakr immediately faced revolts from a few tribes who felt that, with Muhammad's death, their contractual obligation to Islam was over and they could withdraw their support. In one or two cases, such defections were accompanied by the claims of counter-prophets such as Musail-ima. Abu Bakr contested their withdrawal, leading to the apostasy (*riddah*) wars, and he succeeded in uniting all of Arabia under his command. He also sent out armies to Jordan and the Byzantine and Persian territories as well as Palestine. He died two years after assuming the caliphate, to be succeeded by 'Umar ibn al-Khattab, also a close companion of the Prophet. To 'Umar is accorded the honor of founding the Islamic empire through the conquests made during his reign. At 'Ali's suggestion, he adopted the date of the emigration from Mecca (the *hijra*, 622 C.E.) as the start of the Muslim calendar. He is also credited with establishing institutions of governance with respect to taxation, military training, the judiciary, religious behavior, and penal institutions. Stoning as punishment for adultery was introduced in his time, a feature borrowed from Jewish law. Feared rather than loved, in part due to his heavy taxation policies, 'Umar was murdered by a Christian slave belonging to the governor of Basra in 644.

'Umar was succeeded by 'Uthman b. 'Affan, another close companion of the Prophet. 'Ali, who had contested 'Umar's heavy-handed taxation policies, was once again bypassed. 'Uthman's reign continued 'Umar's policies, leading at the end of his reign to a series of civil wars. In order to quell opposition, 'Uthman appointed members of his family to key governorships and instituted a system whereby war spoils were first divided among these members before being distributed to the military. Such practices as well as diminishing war spoils led to an economic crisis that increased opposition to 'Uthman's policies. 'Uthman also had all local copies of the Qur'an destroyed, establishing the government-controlled copy as the only authentic version of the Qur'an. Revolutionary movements began in the provinces, and, in 656, rebels from Iraq, Egypt, and Syria headed toward Medina. 'Ali was chosen by the rebels from the provinces to represent their complaints to 'Uthman, and he negotiated for the caliph with the rebels. Placated by the negotiations, they turned back, only to discover a letter in which 'Uthman purportedly instructed the governor of Egypt to punish or kill the rebels on their return. The rebels turned back and placed 'Uthman's house under siege, a battle during which one of the rebels killed 'Uthman. His death sparked the civil wars that had been brewing. 'Ali was declared caliph and proceeded to suppress the civil wars in Iraq and Syria. At the crucial point of the battle in Syria, 'Amr b. al-'As, an advisor to the Syrian leader Mu'awiya (who was a kinsman of Uthman), ordered pages of the Qur'an to be placed on the swords of the retreating Syrian troops, a maneuver that forced 'Ali's men to fall back. 'Ali was forced to agree to ar-

bitration, during which the arbitrators declared that Mu'awiya was entitled
to avenge his cousin 'Uthman's murder against 'Ali, who was falsely accused
of aiding the rebels in murdering the third caliph. Mu'awiya was declared a
counter-caliph, and thus began the Umayyad dynasty, ending the election
process that had put the first four caliphs in power. The first four caliphs are
known as the Rightly Guided Caliphs (*khulafa al-rashidun*), and the period
of Muhammad and the four Rightly Guided caliphs is idealized by modern
Muslims as the golden age of Islam. However, that characterization belongs
more accurately to a later time, the ninth and tenth centuries, during which
Islamic civilization flourished in creativity and expression in the sciences
and the arts.

A sizeable group among 'Ali's forces refused to agree to arbitration and
rose in arms against him, arguing that one who had been appointed caliph
should not have to agree to arbitration. This group came to be known as
the Kharijites ("those who secede"). Their rallying cry was *"la hukma illa
li'llah"* ("to God alone belongs the decision"). They declared war in Ctesiphon, committing many atrocities there, and 'Ali was persuaded to march
against them, a battle that he won in Nahrawan. Mu'awiya meanwhile
seized the opportunity of 'Ali's weakened army and marched against him.
However, 'Ali was cornered in Kufa by a Kharijite and was murdered in
661.

The murder of 'Uthman and the arbitration between 'Ali and Mu'awiya
led to the formation of three different views of what it meant to be a Muslim, what constituted right belief, and what constituted community. The
Kharijites believed that faith must be expressed in righteous acts, and,
hence, sinful behavior took away one's right to be considered a Muslim.
Judging 'Uthman to be guilty of sinful acts, they argued that he ought to
have been expelled from the Muslim community. They also held that, in
agreeing to arbitration, 'Ali had behaved in a sinful manner and not carried out his obligations to the community in his authority as a caliph. They
thought that any male Muslim who demonstrated his piety publicly in righteous acts was qualified to lead the Muslim community, even if that person
were a slave. The Kharijites withdrew from society to their own encampments and considered the world to be divided into the realms of belief and
unbelief, with themselves as the instruments of God's justice. After their
defeat at the hands of 'Ali in Nahrawan, they continued to practice guerilla
warfare against the Umayyads and later against the 'Abbasid caliphs. One
of the more moderate Kharijites named 'Abd Allah ibn Ibad founded the

Ibadiyya during the eighth century, and these communities are found today in North and East Africa, Yemen, and Oman.

In response to the Kharijites, the Murji'ites argued that no person could judge another Muslim unless such a Muslim's behavior ran contrary to the common good, in which case it ought to be punished. However, with respect to assessing the degree of faith possessed by any Muslim, that was a matter for God to judge, to be postponed to the Day of Judgment. They also held that a Muslim's sins did not warrant exclusion from the community. While the Kharijites resented the power of the Meccan elites from which the first four caliphs and subsequently the Umayyads were drawn, the Murji'ites were strong supporters of 'Uthman and the Umayyads even though they, too, leveled criticism against the Umayyad dynasty's lack of piety.

The Shi'ites or supporters of 'Ali disagreed with the Kharijites and the Murji'ites on one pivotal issue: leadership of the community. For them, the rightful succession to Muhammad belonged to 'Ali and his progeny, whom they considered to have been specially entrusted with the task at Ghadir Khumm, and thereby keeping guidance of the community within the family of the Prophet. They held that the Prophet had communicated to 'Ali the means through which to interpret the Qur'an and guide the community through a special spiritual knowledge or *'ilm* that 'Ali would, in turn, pass on to his progeny—a gift that the Prophet had not made to the first three caliphs. In his capacity as Imam, or leader of the community, 'Ali would interpret the *shari'a* or divine law for Muslims in accordance with the times, providing a guide for what constituted correct belief, community, and what it meant to be a Muslim. Sympathy for the Shi'ite perspective was found largely among non-Arab peoples in Iraq, although, over time, both Arab and non-Arab Shi'ites constituted the opposition to the central caliphate of the Umayyads.

Practical realities and political developments led to differences in interpretation regarding what faith means. Over time, three distinct strands of interpretation emerged as parties or communities of interpretation: the Sunni, the Shi'i, and, as an overlay of both, the Sufi. Within these three groups were many variations. Differences among Sunnis arose regarding the specifics of the theological and legal regulations that a Sunni might follow; among Shi'ites, the differences comprised who might be considered the legitimate spiritual successor to the Prophet; and Sufis disagreed about which Sufi master's teachings were the defining philosophy and practice for a Muslim. A Sufi could be either Shi'a or Sunni with respect to the legal framework followed by the practitioner.

## THREE COMMUNITIES OF INTERPRETATION: SUNNI, SHI'I, SUFI

Islam contains innumerable communities of interpretation. However, most fall under the umbrella of Sunni Islam, and a sizeable minority, close to 20 percent, are categorized as Shi'ah Islam. Alongside these are various orientations depending on emphasis and interpretation: a Sunni or a Shi'i may also be legalistic, theological, philosophical, and/or mystical in outlook. The mystics or Sufis are sufficiently distinctive in their outlook that in this chapter they are treated as a third community of interpretation. All three communities hold within their parameters innumerable distinctive subcommunities. The key difference between Sunni and Shi'i Islam revolves around the question of who may legitimately rule and guide the community, while Sufi Islam denotes an orientation toward a mystical and inner spiritual development that would emulate the Prophet's experience of, and closeness to, the divine being. The difference between the Sunni and Shi'ite notions of legitimate governance of the Muslim polity and community was expressed in the Sunni notion of the caliphate and in the Shi'ite notion of the imamate. For the Sunnis, the caliph was one who was selected or elected to the caliphate after Muhammad's death and who was responsible for political leadership of the community but did not succeed Muhammad as its religious authority. Sunni Muslims placed religious authority in the consensus of the community, expressed in the collective agreement of the *'ulama'* (religious scholars).

The Shi'a, on the other hand, held that the more central aspect of Muhammad's mission—that is, his religious authority from which flowed his political authority—was to be continued in the imamate, bestowed first to 'Ali by the Prophet through a process of spiritual designation known as *nass* and then passed down through each of 'Ali's successors until the end of time. Such successors, designated *Imams,* are distinguished from the Sunni term *imam,* whose primary function is to lead the community in prayer. The Imam for the Shi'a was a figure of paramount authority, who could not be selected by the community or elected to office, but, rather, was to be explicitly designated as such by the previous holder of the Imamate. Such an Imam was, by implication, also the rightful holder of the political office of caliph, although the latter was not central to his mandate of providing the community with guidance on what it meant to be a Muslim. Although the Imam was not a prophet, he was nonetheless considered to be sinless, infallible, and divinely inspired. The Imam also had to be a direct lineal descendant of 'Ali, even though many early Shi'ites argued that the Imam ought to be the descendant of both Muhammad and 'Ali through 'Ali's progeny with Fatima, the daughter of Muhammad.

For the Sufis, regardless of who held political office, spiritual authority resided in the Sufi master, a person known for his piety who was also endowed with spiritual insight or divine inspiration and who understood the inner meaning of the Qur'an and the divine law (*shari'a*). Each Sufi master was appointed by an earlier master who invested him with the mantle of religious authority to take disciples on the spiritual path. Many Sufi lineages trace back to either Imam 'Ali or to one of 'Ali's successors such as his

Prophet's Mosque, al-Madinah. The tomb of the Prophet Muhammad is located within the structure. Courtesy of the Saudi Information Office, Washington, D.C.

great-great-grandson Ja'far al-Sadiq (d. 756), with the idea that the Prophet passed on his special knowledge or *'ilm* to 'Ali.

The term Sunni derives from the phrase *ahl al-sunna wa'l-jama'a*, meaning the people who follow the *sunna* (practice) of the Prophet. Contrary to popular notions, the identifications Sunni, Shi'a, and Sufi did not come about overnight; rather, political factors, theological interpretations, legal regulations, and institutions of governance all played a role in coalescing what later came to be identified as Sunni, Shi'i, and Sufi communities. In the case of Sunni Islam, the development of the Murji'i theological position that left the decision to God regarding the sinfulness of a Muslim was imbedded in a political context in which the Murji'a declared their tacit support for the caliphate. This contrasts with the theologically articulated political position against it as expressed by the Kharijites and the Shi'ites. At the rise of the Umayyads, what has come to be termed Sunni Islam was backed by the state, including its military power, and thus the Sunni interpretation was able to establish its numerical majority and hence its claim to orthodoxy.

To understand the commonalities among and differences between the three communities of interpretation, the development of the key sources of authority held by each, the instrument of social governance or legal regulations subscribed to by each, and the intellectual rationalizations developed by each to support their claims are examined here. Each community practices norms of ritual behavior to express its understanding of the relationship between humans and the divine being. These forms of ritual practice will be discussed in the next two chapters.

## SUNNI ISLAM

### Sources of Authority

For Sunni Muslims, the key sources of authority after Muhammad's demise included the Qur'an and the collections of traditions (*hadith*) recording what Muhammad is alleged to have said and done during his lifetime. Another important source of authority was the body of legal discourse (*shari'a*) or that governs how Muslims should comport themselves with respect to ritual obligations (*'ibadah*) and the well-being of society (*maslaha*)—that is, the common good. The caliph was responsible for upholding the *shari'a*, so he appointed the institutions that governed the regulation of *shari'a* such as the judiciary. In an effort to understand divine will as revealed in the Qur'an, Muslims developed various fields of inquiry that have been called the Arab sciences, among which are the study of the Arabic language; the development of commentaries (*tafsir*) on the Qur'an that relied on exploring the historical and social context in which each of the verses of the Qur'an was revealed; the collection of traditions (*hadith*) to record what the Prophet said or did during his lifetime to reveal what the practice (*sunna*) of the Prophet had been during his lifetime, intended to serve as a guide for Muslim behavior; and the development of the science of drawing out the legal implications of relevant verses in the Qur'an to regulate society. Expertise in these sciences qualified a person (generally male) to be one of the learned (*'ulama'*), through whose efforts were developed the norms and guidelines of Muslim religious and social life.

## Legal Developments

The term *shari'a* derives from the verb *shara'a,* meaning to mark out a path to water. In Islam, God ordains a *shari'a* or path for humans to follow, and following such a path constitutes *din* or religion.[2] The *shari'a* is a practical concept covering all aspects of human behavior—spiritual, mental, and physical—and hence includes both faith and practice. Within the purview of *shari'a* are included all legal and social transactions as well as all personal behavior relating to belief about God and to religious obligations such as prayer and fasting.[3] During the time of the first four caliphs, a distinction was drawn between two complementary sources necessary for determining the *shari'a* or ordained path: *'ilm,* which is knowledge of the Qur'an and the practice (*sunna*) of the Prophet; and *fiqh,* which is jurisprudence or the understanding of how what was given in the Qur'an and the *sunna* could be applied to the specific situation at hand. Thus, jurisprudence was the instrument through which the knowledge of the Qur'an and the Prophet's habits of behavior could be made clear to Muslims. Early books of jurisprudence necessarily included discussions of theology, since legal reasoning required taking into account correct belief to formulate how to be a good Muslim.

Under the Umayyads, while the caliph acted as the supreme authority, different legal practices developed in each of the key centers of the empire, such as Medina, Damascus, Kufa, and Basra. In all of these legal establishments, local custom (*adat*) informed the practice of law. Many of the religiously learned, the *'ulama',* thought that the wealth and power of the caliphs led to corruption and the abuse of power, and at times they took a stand against the caliphate because they thought that Islamic principles should be the foundation of a uniform system of law throughout the empire. They argued that the Qur'an and the *sunna* should be used as the key sources of law and thus permeate every aspect of a Muslim's life.[4]

Over time, writings about legal understanding or *fiqh* accumulated into a substantive body of literature, and *fiqh* itself became a subject of study, just as the Qur'an and the *sunna* were studied; in other words, jurisprudence became an object of *'ilm*. Theological developments from the eighth century onward led to the development of the science or *'ilm* of theology (*kalam*) as distinct from the science of jurisprudence (*fiqh*), and, henceforth, *fiqh* was identified as the science of the law. Under the 'Abbasids, who came to power in 750, the religious scholars found patrons to support their scholarship, build mosques, and establish schools of learning. The 'Abbasids reformulated the concept of the caliphate from that of deputy to the Prophet to that of deputy to God, thereby bringing the implementation of the *shari'a* under their control. Through their patronage of religious scholars and their support of a formidable legal system through which the empire could be governed, the 'Abbasids facilitated the creation of a class of religiously learned, the *'ulama*, from whose ranks were drawn the jurists, theologians, educators, and judges who established the Islamic court system.

Notable jurists who aided in the development of Islamic law were Abu Hanifa (d. 767) in Kufa, Malik b. Anas (d. 795) in Medina, al-Shafi'i (d. 820) in Egypt, Ibn Hanbal (d. 855) in Baghdad, and Dawud b. Khalaf (d. 883) in Baghdad. The purpose of the *shari'a* was to establish for Muslims what it meant to fulfill God's will. Its underlying principles included the idea that all humans were equal before God and could not be privileged by social class; that every Muslim everywhere, regardless of race, gender, or nationality, was subject to the same duties and obligations to God; that the basic duty of a Muslim was "to command the right and forbid the wrong," thereby making it every Muslim's duty to uphold public order. Although every jurist thought that his local tradition best exemplified Islamic practice, the Medinan jurist Malik advanced three principles that formed the basis of all later Islamic law: (1) that the actions of the Prophet were to be become paradigmatic for all Muslims, thereby establishing the *sunna* as practice governing a Muslim's life; (2) that every Muslim was subject to obligatory duties, thereby leading to the establishment of the five pillars as incumbent upon all Muslims; and (3) that the community's mission was to bring knowledge of God's ways to all people.[5]

Al-Shafi'i attempted to construct a comprehensive legal system that would derive all its tenets from the Qur'an and from the practice of the Prophet. It was al-Shafi'i's opinion that such a legal system would reflect the correct interpretation of the Qur'an, since the Prophet was a divinely certified exemplar. Al-Shafi'i recognized that there would be instances when the jurist would be called upon to exercise his own judgment in the application of a law. However, al-Shafi'i minimized the use of independent judgment in an attempt to standardize the legal system; he preferred instead the use of analogical reasoning for determining the applicability of a law in a novel situation. Thus, statements in the Qur'an or actions taken by the Prophet recorded in the *hadith* (narratives of what the Prophet said or did in his lifetime, comprising the *sunna* or practice of the Prophet) could, by analogy, apply to situations that were not specifically addressed by either the Qur'an or the *hadith.* Al-Shafi'i also placed great emphasis on *ijma'* or the consensus of the community as a binding legal ruling. If the *'ulama'* agreed upon how a matter was to be handled according to their reading of the Qur'an and the *hadith,* then their collective view held force. Thus, for al-Shafi'i, the key sources of the law were the Qur'an, the *hadith* corpus, analogy, and consensus of the *'ulama'.*

Ahmad b. Hanbal (Ibn Hanbal) was a *hadith* scholar who trained under al-Shafi'i and is considered to be a purist, literalist, and traditionalist. He received the wrath of the caliphs, because he refused to submit to the dogma initiated by a group of early theologians known as the Mu'tazila, who held that the Qur'an was not eternal, but created by God. The caliph at the time, al-Ma'mun, and his successor, al-Mu'tasim, both subscribed to Mu'tazilite views and had Ibn Hanbal imprisoned and punished. Under the next caliph, al-Mutawakkil, Ibn Hanbal was restored to the court and became well known for his learning and his piety. Ahmad b. Hanbal tried to eliminate individual juridical opinion as much as possible, basing his legal system almost entirely on the Qur'an and the *hadith,* resulting in a strict form of practice. His adherents supported the early Umayyad caliphs Mu'awiyya and his son Yazid as upholders of orthodoxy.

The Hanbali school of law and interpretation is considered the strictest of all the Muslim legal systems, and it inspired the later work of Ibn Taymiya (d. 1328), who rejected the application of rational methods to the examination of the Qur'an and the *hadith.* Ibn Taymiya also condemned practices such as tomb visitations or veneration of persons considered holy by Muslims, such as Prophet Muhammad, members of his family, or the various Sufi *shaykhs* who are considered saints by their adherents. The historical decline of Hanbali views was reversed in the eighteenth century by Muhammad b. 'Abd al-Wahhab (d. 1787) in Saudi Arabia; today the Wahhabi-inspired legal system enjoys official status in Saudi Arabia. Since the eighteenth century, parallel movements have included the Wahhabi-influenced Salafiyya, who advocate a return to pristine Islam (by which they mean the Islam of the Prophet's time), and modernists, who interpret Islam in light of contemporary times.

Another noteworthy but defunct legal school is the Zahiriya, founded by Da'ud b. Khalaf, which spread to Iran and was enunciated in Spain by Ibn Hazm (d. 1064). The Zahirites sought to derive all law from the literal text of the Qur'an and the *hadith*. It rejected all forms of juridical reasoning and restricted consensus or *ijma'* to the opinions of the Muhammad's official companions.

Thus, Sunni Muslims, depending on their geographical location, were subject to the legal school or *madhhab* of either the Hanafi, Maliki, Shafi'i, or Hanbali school, with some adherents who followed the Zahiri school. The legal school defined the rights and responsibilities of a Muslim, including the manner in which Islam was to be practiced. It is for this reason that Islam has often been called an orthopraxy ("correct practice") rather than orthodoxy ("correct belief"), although to suggest that the realm of belief lacked importance to Muslims is erroneous. In fact, the theologians in Sunni Islam spent rivers of ink outlining correct belief, as did their Shi'i and Sufi counterparts. In contemporary times, each nation state with a Muslim majority has government-appointed *muftis* or specialists in legal matters who are qualified to deliver legal rulings (*fatwas*) and who may be consulted by a judge for rulings appropriate to the dispute at hand. Contact with Western nations through trade and colonization resulted in the adoption of Western forms of legal codes and practices, such as the codification of existing *shari'a* laws, as well as the attempt made by modernist lawyers to adapt Islamic law to contemporary conditions—a move that has been met with opposition from conservative clerics. Many nation states, in granting constitutional rights to their citizens, have sought to adapt Islamic law in ways that restore the jurist's right to make decisions based on Islamic principles while negotiating with the clerical establishment on thousand-year-old customs that have taken on the mantle of religious obligations.

## Intellectual Traditions

Among the thinkers who contributed to the development of Sunni views is Hasan al-Basri (d. 728), who declared that humans were responsible for their actions, in contrast to a deterministic view that all actions were foreseen and foreknown by God. The Mu'tazila, a group of theologians who were conversant with Hellenistic methods of reasoning, introduced the idea that human reason should investigate conceptions of God and morals; so, for instance, they declared that something is forbidden by God because it is bad, not that it is bad because God has forbidden it. That is, the moral guidance of the Qur'an is understandable to humans because of their capacity to reason; hence, what is wrong is self-evident. Similarly, when a person is confronted with someone who is dying, it would be clear that helping the dying person would be a good thing to do, regardless of whether that person follows the *shari'a*. The Mu'tazilites emphasized the importance of God's justice and unity and argued that God could not be anything but just; if God did not punish as promised, then God could also be considered a liar.

Such views were not acceptable to other Muslims who believed that God was beyond human conceptions of justice and that humans cannot place God under a humanly construed understanding of justice. In their defense of free will and of justice and unity as the hallmarks of divinity, the Mu'tazilites rejected the idea of any attributes other than justice and unity being essential to God, because they believed that any other attribute applied to God would limit divinity. Similarly, since divine speech was not an eternal attribute, the Qur'an must have been created. Traditionalists such as Ahmed b. Hanbal took exception to the idea that God was not omnipotent, and so he emphasized God's power, will, grace, and determination of human fate in contrast to the Mu'tazilite emphasis on human free will. Furthermore, to protect God from being anthropomorphized or compared with humans, the Mu'tazilites suggested that verses in the Qur'an that spoke of God in human terms should be read allegorically. The Hanbalites thought that it was not for humans to ask about the details of such verses but simply to acknowledge that God understood what was meant. For example, a verse in the Qur'an refers to God sitting on a throne. For the Hanbalites, asking whether this means that God has a body or speculating on the size of the throne is irrelevant and may even be an act of bad faith. The Hanbalites believe that God knows precisely what is meant by the verse in the Qur'an, and humans should be content with that.

Al-Ash'ari (d. 942), a former Mu'tazilite, attempted to reconcile the two viewpoints with the notion that God is the author of all acts, but that humans "acquire" these acts—thus making it appear that they acted of their own volition and hence were responsible for their actions—because God gives them permission to act. Al-Ash'ari was trying to make humans responsible for their actions while maintaining that the power to do all things comes from God. Al-Maturidi (d. 945) agreed with al-Ash'ari on most points, but thought that evil actions do not occur with God's permission or pleasure; for these, humans are solely responsible.

These kinds of theological debates were a science in themselves: the science of disputation or *kalam*. For the traditional and pious-minded such as Ahmad b. Hanbal and Ibn Taymiyya, and those inspired by them, theological speculation with its application of rationality toward such debates and disputations was rejected in favor of a literalist and practice-oriented understanding of what it meant to be a Muslim. Al-Ash'ari's attempt to retain the concerns of the traditionalist Muslims using rational methods became the dominant articulation of Sunni Islam. The theologian al-Ghazali (d. 1111) further attempted to include mystical understandings of Islam but to exclude philosophical understandings. While al-Ghazali defined the broad parameters within which Sunni theology would later develop, some key theologians preceded him with important contributions to disputation. These include Najm al-Din al-Nasafi (d. 1142), whose *Creed* was a standard textbook in theology for several centuries; Fakhr al-Din al-Razi (d. 1209), Hafiz al-Din al-Nasafi (d. early fourteenth century); al-Iji (d. 1355); al-Taftazani (d. 1390), who wrote a commentary on the *Creed;* al-Jurjani (d. 1413); al-Sanusi (d. 1490); al-Dawwani (d. 1501); al-Birqili (d. 1570); al-Laqani (d. 1621); al-Sialkuti (d. 1657); al-Bajuri (d. 1860); Muhammad 'Abduh (d. 1905); Rashid Rida (d. 1935); Hassan al-Banna (d. 1949); Sayyid Qutb (executed 1965), and Mawdudi (d. 1979).

## SHI'I ISLAM

### Sources of Authority

For the Shi'a, the key source of authority is the Imam—literally, "supreme leader." Although the early Muslim community elected to choose the four rightly guided caliphs as holders of political authority and 'Ali chose not to contest the nomination of Abu Bakr as the first caliph, some members of the early Muslim community clearly believed that the spiritual authority of the Prophet was vested by Muhammad in 'Ali, and they turned to him for leadership during the reign of the third caliph, 'Uthman. During the Battle of Siffin, 'Ali's supporters clearly identified themselves as such—hence, the term *shi'a* (literally, "party" or supporters of 'Ali). The Kharijites, who initially supported 'Ali and his temporal and spiritual leadership, broke away from him because he consented to arbitration during his battle with

Mu'awiya. A second civil war led by al-Mukhtar against the Umayyads en-sued after the death of Mu'awiya. At the hands of Mu'awiya's son and suc-cessor Yazid, 'Ali's son Husayn was massacred at Karbala (in present-day Iraq) in 680. The massacre led to the development of a radical Shi'i view articulated by followers of al-Mukhtar that the community had erred in denying 'Ali the divine right to lead the community and that the first three caliphs had usurped the leadership that rightly belonged to 'Ali. This group declared that the imamate belonged to 'Ali's son Muhammad from another wife (not from Fatimah, the daughter of the Prophet). More conservative elements within the Shi'a—such as those from Kufa—upheld the caliphates of the first two caliphs on the basis that 'Ali had not contested their leader-ship. Other Shi'ites rejected the authority of the first three caliphs entirely.

The doctrine of the imamate was developed during the time of Ja'far al-Sadiq (d. 765), 'Ali's great-great-grandson. In his view, the imamate was founded on the notion that humankind could never be devoid of guidance from God and was in need of a divinely guided and infallible leader who was appointed by the Prophet through a designation known as *nass.* While the Prophet's authority was foundational in that he was chosen by God to be a divine messenger who revealed a scripture, the Imam's function was executive in that he was to interpret that scripture as well as establish clear religious guidelines for Muslims; hence, disobedience of the Imam was dis-obedience of the Prophet. The Imam's mandate was to give moral and spiri-tual guidance. He was entitled to political authority, but he did not depend upon it to fulfill his mandate. The office of the imamate was to be held by 'Ali's progeny, first his sons by Fatimah, Hasan and Husayn—thereby re-taining a bloodline to the Prophet and thence by designation (*nass*) from father to son until the advent of the Mahdi (the savior who would appear at the end of time to restore justice). In addition to developing the doctrine of the imamate, Ja'far is credited with founding the Ja'fari legal school, and he was also an authority in the development of a mystical and esoteric un-derstanding of Islam.

Upon Ja'far's death, the question of succession was not clear. His elder son Isma'il, whom he had designated Imam, had died before Ja'far. The Imamiyya, who today form the largest contingent of Shi'ites worldwide, held that Ja'far's younger son, Musa al-Kazim, was thus the rightful heir to the imamate. The Imamiyya line of Imams continued to the eleventh Imam, Hasan al-Askari, who died in 874 C.E. ostensibly without an heir. However, the existence of a son was affirmed, and the doctrine of the oc-cultation or hiddenness of the Imam was proclaimed, according to which the Imam continues to exist in a hidden form and will make himself known

as the Mahdi at the end of time. This group, which came to be called the
Twelver (Ithna 'Ashari) Shi'ah, divided the period of occultation into two
parts: the lesser, during which the hidden Imam was in continual contact
with a series of four guardians who represented him to the community;
and the greater, during which no one remained in contact with the hidden
Imam except those to whom he chose to reveal himself. Religious authority
thus passed to the learned within the community, the *'ulama'*, and today in
Iran the Council of Guardians represents the collective will of the learned
with respect to spiritual and temporal guidance to the community.

The Isma'iliya, who elected to follow Isma'il's son Muhammad after Ja'far's
death, pose a problem for historians for lack of reliable sources. They reap-
pear about a hundred years after Ja'far's death as the Fatimids, also called
the Batiniya or esotericists because of the distinction they made between
the outward or exoteric aspects of religion and its inner or esoteric aspects
that could only be known by the guidance of the Imam and a system of
symbolic interpretation that did not take the words of the Qur'an literally.
The Fatimids, who ruled from Egypt, went on to establish an empire from
Yemen through Bahrain through much of North Africa and briefly to Malta
and Syria. Despite various splinter groups, chief of which was the split between Nizari and Musta'ali branches of Ismailism occurring toward the end
of the Fatimid caliphate at the end of the eleventh century, Ismaili communities exist to this day. The Nizari Ismailis are followers of the Aga Khan IV,
whose efforts are largely directed toward development programs in health,
education, architecture, industry, tourism, and culture. The Musta'alian Ismailis (also known as Tayyibi or Bohra Ismailis), who experienced further
splintering, consider their Imam, al-Tayyib (of the mid-twelfth century), to
have gone into concealment, and thus they follow the authority of the head
of the teaching hierarchy, a position known as the *da'i mutlaq.*

There are many other small but significant Shi'i groups, such as the Zay-
dis, the Nusayris, the 'Alawis, the Shaykhis, and the Druze.

### Legal Developments

For the early Shi'ites, no empire existed to create a system of law for governing a society. There was, nonetheless, the need to create a body of rules
for conduct, drawing upon sources considered authoritative specifically for
Shi'is. The Qur'an, as sacred scripture, represented one such source. Another source, the *hadith* literature—which detailed the words and actions
of the Prophet and was a paradigm from which all Muslims could draw be-

havioral guidelines—laid primary importance upon the words and actions of the Imams. The canonical books of Traditions (*hadith*) for Shi'i Muslims were collected and written down at the end of the tenth and during the eleventh centuries by men such as Kulayni (d. 940), Ibn Babuya (d. 991), and al-Tusi, known as Shaykh al-Taifa (d. 1067). In the fourteenth century, these works were subjected to critical analysis and organization by 'Allama al-Hilli (d. 1325).

The town of Hilla on the Euphrates River became a center for Imami or Twelver Shi'i law. After the Mongol conquests in the mid-thirteenth century, Hilla superseded Qum and Baghdad as a major center of Shi'ite learning. A legal scholar from Hilla, Muhammad b. Idris al-'Ijli al-Hilli (d. 1202) had established the importance of the intellect (*'aql*) as a key source of legal judgment. Another scholar who had witnessed the Mongol invasion, Abu'l-Qasim Ja'far ibn al-Hasan al-Hilli (d. 1277), wrote a manual of Imami law titled *Laws in Islam.* However, credit for establishing the theoretical foundations of Imami law belongs to al-Hasan ibn Yusuf ibn 'Ali ibn Mutahhar al-Hilli ('Allama al-Hilli), who was a student of the celebrated astronomer, mathematician, philosopher, and theologian, Nasir al-Din Tusi (d. 1274). 'Allamah al-Hilli was the first to bear the title Ayatullah (literally, "sign of God"). Where the Sunni legal jurists had made the exercise of a jurist's intellectual reasoning allowable within the strictly definable limits of analogical reasoning, 'Allamah al-Hilli made intellectual reasoning a critical part of the jurist's reasoning by subsuming it under intellectual effort, or *ijtihad* (literally, "exertion"). This meant that a jurist was perfectly sound in his method in applying *ijtihad* in arriving at a legal ruling, thereby allowing reasoned argument as part of the process of legal judgment in a manner not so easily allowed to a Sunni jurist. *Ijtihad* was defined by him as "the discovery of decisions on the basis of general precepts in the Quran and Sunna and by weighing up contradictory arguments."[6] One who was authorized to use *ijtihad* or intellectual effort regarding legal matters had to be learned in the Qur'an and the *sunna* and the legal tradition. Ordinary people, then, who were not qualified to use *ijtihad,* should follow the legal ruling. 'Allamah al-Hilli further qualified the use of *ijtihad* as sometimes resulting in faulty decisions due to the human intellect; therefore, a *mujtahid* (one who exercises *ijtihad*) could always revise his opinion, or some other *mujtahid* might do so. Recognizing that a legal ruling could be erroneous and that it was subject to revision made the use of *ijtihad* critical in keeping the Imami legal system flexible and dynamic and far less subject to fossilization than is generally held. Thus, the four sources of law for Shi'ite jurisprudence are the Qur'an, the *hadith* literature, consensus (*ijma'*), and intellectual effort (*ijtihad*) that comprises the use of intelligence to arrive at a legal judgment.

With the rise of the Safavids under the leadership of Shah Isma'il (d. 1524)—who declared himself the sole legitimate representative of the Hidden Imam—a Shi'ite state was established in Iran. Isma'il established the office of the Sadr (literally, "head" or "chief") to oversee legal matters. Isma'il's Shi'ism is considered elementary at best, but his son, Tahmasp (d. 1576), invited the leading Shi'ite scholar of the day, Muhaqqiq al-Karaki (d. 1533), to propagate orthodox Shi'ism. Al-Karaki became known as the representative of the Hidden Imam, and the power of the clerics was further strengthened under the reign of Tahmasp's grandson, Shah 'Abbas I (d. 1629). Some scholars, such as Muhammad Amir Astarabadi (d. 1626), questioned the clerics' right to use *ijtihad*. Scholars who supported this contention against the use of *ijtihad* or intellectual reasoning came to be known as the Akhbari school, while those who included *ijtihad* were styled the Usuli school, both of which continued to coexist. Another scholar of note at this time was al-'Amili (d. 1622), who wrote a legal compendium still in use today.

## Intellectual Traditions

While the Hilla school dominated Imami or Twelver Shi'i legal discourse, the Isfahan school is known for its more philosophical and mystical understanding of Twelver Shi'i Islam. Two key proponents of these streams of thought in Shi'ism were Mir Damad (d. 1630) and Mulla Sadra (d. 1640). Mir Damad argued that revelation, human intelligence, and mystical visions were all equally valid means through which to arrive at the truth. Mulla Sadra and his celebrated pupils Lahiji, Qummi, and Kashani further contributed to the rich literature and philosophical and mystical ideas of this school. However, Isfahan philosophers and mystics were persecuted by the legalists, who accused them of being heretics and unduly influenced by Greek ideas. Muhammad Baqir Majlisi (d. 1700) mounted a campaign against philosophers and mystics in Iran and established a new orthodoxy that emphasized veneration of the Imams. He produced a 110-volume compilation of Shi'ite traditions (*hadith*) to assist legal scholars. The rising power of the clerics brought them into opposition with the power of the Shahs, and, in the eighteenth century, the Usuli school freed itself from the power of the state. It drew strength from its relationships with the landowners and merchants and thereby was in a position to oppose the central authority of the Shah and his tax collectors.

From 1722 to 1729 the Safavids succumbed to Sunni Afghan rule, and Iran was again restored to independence by Nadir Shah, who originally acted as an agent of the Safavids but then crowned himself Shah in 1736. Under his rule, the four main Sunni schools of law were reintroduced to Iran, and he sought to make Shi'a law the fifth school. Many Shi'ite clerics left at this time to settle in Iraqi centers such as Kazimayn, Karbala, and Najaf, thereby turning these into important centers of Shi'ite legal thought. After Nadir Shah's murder in 1747, the pro-Shi'ite Zand family came to rule. The Zands were vanquished by the Qajars in 1785 with the coronation of Agha Muhammad Khan.

Unlike the Safavids, the Qajars could not claim biological descent from the Imams, and the Shi'ite clergy therefore were able to strengthen their role as representatives of the Hidden Imam. Furthermore, their position from exile and their connections to the landowning and merchant classes enabled them to effectively mount opposition to the ruling power (eventually used to good effect by Ayatollah Khomeini in the twentieth century). Arguing that appeal to a dead legal authority is contrary to Shi'ite Islam, the Usuli school, which emphasized the use of intellectual reasoning (*ijtihad*), overcame the power of the traditional Akhbari school. During the nineteenth century, the *mujtahid* or legal scholars grew into a recognizable hierarchy, with one scholar named as the chief of the *mujtahids.* This person came to be recognized as the *marja' al-taqlid,* meaning one whose juridical opinions were to be followed.

As a representative of the Hidden Imam, the *marja' al-taqlid* could collect religious dues and income from religious endowments, thereby establishing his economic independence from the state. The *marja' al-taqlid* was responsible for leading the Friday prayer and delivering the sermon. He could impose corporal punishment and declare a *jihad* or holy war against unbelievers. For example, the Qajar ruler Fath 'Ali Shah was instigated by his crown prince to pressure the clergy to declare holy war against the Russians, a tactic that ultimately failed as it led to Iran's loss of the Transcaucasus in 1828. The senior *mujtahids* also claimed the right to excommunicate to defend orthodoxy. A person branded as a heretic could be persecuted. This strategy was used to good effect against the Akhbari legal scholars and then turned against the Sufis, against proponents of the Isfahan school, and then against the Babis and Bahais. Cooperation between the ruling power and the clergy was essential for peace; however, relations between the two were strained during the second part of the nineteenth century.

The installation of the Pahlavi dynasty in 1925 furthered the rift between the clergy and the state. Reza Shah, the first Pahlavi ruler, favored secular courts over religious courts; introduced civil law on the basis of French law; promoted Europeanized dress for men; forbade women from wearing the veil in 1936; and removed the notarial functions of the clergy for contracts, thereby depriving them of social status as well as an important source of income. In addition, only those with academic degrees could act as judges. Qum, meanwhile, was reestablished as a center for Shi'ite studies, and Ayatullah 'Abd al-Karim Yazdi Ha'eri was acknowledged as the *marja' al-taqlid.* One of his students was the young Khomeini. In 1948 several *mujtahids* joined forces to issue a ruling that forbade women from appearing in public without the veil. His successor, Ayatollah Tabataba'i Burujerdi, mounted opposition to the then-Shah, Muhammad Reza Pahlavi's tyrannical and foreign-influenced policies, including opposition to the land reforms proposed by the Shah, his pro-Israel policies, his advocacy of women's rights, and his extension of secular education intended to break the power of the clergy. These policies were perceived as foreign-instigated and part of the Shah's rule of tyranny that included civic violations by the Shah's secret police, the Savak. After Burujerdi's death in 1961, Khomeini briefly rose to prominence in calling for an end to the Shah's rule; he was exiled in 1964.

'Ali Shariati, a Sorbonne-trained sociologist, introduced the idea that the people of Iran could not be freed without a recognition of the importance of Shi'ite history and symbols. However, he criticized the clergy for their rote learning and reactionary ideas. The clergy, in turn, labeled him a foreign agent. Meanwhile, in exile in Najaf in Iraq, Khomeini wrote tracts denouncing the monarchy as anti-Islamic and was ultimately exiled from Iraq to France in January 1978. Clashes between the Shah's forces and the clergy took place in September 1978, leading to the Black Friday of September 8, 1978, during which mass demonstrations by the clergy and their supporters declared the monarchy un-Islamic. In February 1979 Khomeini returned to Iran amid public support and set in motion the Islamic theocracy in Iran. Khomeini's idea of the jurist as legitimate ruler was made real with the formation of the Islamic Republic of Iran, further ratified by an Islamic constitution that named Khomeini as the rightful ruler in the absence of the Hidden Imam and gave the clerics direct political control. Opposition by several clerics who did not see direct political control as part of their juridical mandate was quashed. Khomeini died in 1989. Today the role of the *marja‘* is held by ‘Ali Khamenei, and a council of guardians or experts continues to direct religious and political matters for Iranian Shi‘ites.

For Twelver Shi‘ites in other parts of the world, religious authority resides in the leader of their choice and must be established on a case-by-case basis.

## SUFI ISLAM

### Sources of Authority

Strictly speaking, the mystics of Islam could be either Sunni or Shi‘i in terms of their formal acceptance of ‘Ali as the legitimate spiritual successor of Muhammad. Sunni Sufis, for instance, by and large accepted ‘Ali's role as spiritual successor to Muhammad, but, unlike the Shi‘ites, did not accept that such spiritual guidance was bequeathed by ‘Ali to his physical descendants. Rather, for those who granted ‘Ali a position of primacy in spiritual matters, he was considered free to invest any one of his disciples with the mantle of spiritual mastery. Shi‘ite Sufis, on the other hand, gave credit to the twelve Imams beginning with ‘Ali as master guides along the spiritual path to gnosis or divine illumination. The Isma‘ilis shared many features with the Sufis, including their emphasis on the esoteric meaning of the Qur'an and the practice of ethical and spiritual exercises for the instruction of the soul, but they continued to see legitimate lines of spiritual authority in their Imams and those whom the Imams authorized as spiritual masters.

For all Sufis, whether Sunni or Shi‘i, the spiritual experiences of Muhammad became the focal point of what it meant to be a Muslim (Q. 41:53: "We shall show them our signs on the horizons and in themselves, until it is clear to them that [God] is the Truth"). The Qur'an and the *hadith* provided evidence of the mystical encounter between God and humans. The men and women who communicated with the divine being understood that no sense of self remains in the presence of the divine being. As the Qur'an says, "Everything upon [the earth] is ephemeral, but the face of your lord remains, full of majesty and glory" (Q. 55:26–27). Life in this world, then, had to be lived with a heightened consciousness that attachment to the power and glory and materiality of the world was foolhardy, since all ultimately perishes. Furthermore, life should be lived with the constant awareness that a person is held accountable for all thoughts and actions toward God, self, and others; hence, an ideal life was one invested in prayer, in disciplining the passions of the self to making morally upright choices, and in behaving ethically toward others.

As with all Muslims, Sufis also held that people needed to be taught how to open themselves to spiritual experience. While the Prophet's revelation (the Qur'an) was the guide par excellence, it had to be understood not just in literal terms but in its hidden meanings, known by those with spiritual insight. Thus, many Sufis trace such teachings back to the Prophet's son-in-law and spiritual successor, 'Ali, while others turn to his progeny, such as Ja'far al-Sadiq, for a spiritualized understanding of Islam. For instance, Ja'far's commentary on the Qur'an became important for Sufis; his usage of the terms *fana'* (perishing) and *baqa'* (enduring) was adopted by later Sufis to indicate the loss of a sense of self in the face of the divine, and its subsequent enduring as it returned to a consciousness of itself as a contingent being supported by divine power. The Qur'an specifies that God is beyond the grasp of human perception: "Vision does not encompass him; he encompasses vision" (Q. 6:103). Many of the *hadith qudsi* also record God as saying to the Prophet: "I fulfill my servant's expectation of Me, and I am with him when he remembers Me"; "My love belongs by right to those who love one another in Me, to those who sit together [in fellowship] in Me"; "My servant continues drawing nearer to Me through supererogatory acts until I love him; and when I love him, I become the ear with which he hears, the eye with which he sees, the hand with which he grasps, and the foot with which he walks."

In addition to the Qur'an and the *hadith*, Sufis drew inspiration from Muhammad as the prime example of a human who had attained closeness to God. The mark of distinction conferred upon Muhammad by God was made evident to Sufis in Qur'anic verses such as: "We only sent you as a mercy for creation" (Q. 21:107) and "Whoever obeys the messenger obeys God" (Q. 4:80). Especially important lessons from Muhammad's life were taken from his practice of seclusion and meditation as forms of practice that drew him closer to God and his ascent to the divine presence, a journey that all Sufis sought to emulate.

Men and women who experienced the divine being became authoritative guides along the spiritual journey. In the early days of Islam, such persons included Hasan al-Basri, Dhu al-Nun al-Misri, and Rabi'a al-Adawiyya. Much of the information about the early Sufis comes from the eleventh century, especially through the writings of al-Sulami (d. 1021). The derivation of the term Sufi comes from the Arabic word for wool (*suf*), as the Sufis were thought to wear garments made of rough wool as an indication of their rejection of a life of material pleasure. Other possible sources for the term Sufi include the Greek word for wise man, *sophos*, the Arabic word for bench, *suffa* (because the Prophet instructed Muslims in piety while seated on a bench), and the word for purity, *safa'*. Among the many definitions provided by Qushayri concerning Sufism are: "Sufism means that you own nothing and are owned by nothing"; "Sufism means entrusting the soul to God the most high for whatever he wishes"; "Sufism means kneeling at the door of the beloved, even if he turns you away"; and "The sign of the sincere Sufi is that he feels poor when he has wealth, is humble when he has power, and is hidden when he has fame. The sign of the false Sufi is that he acts rich towards the world when he is poor, acts powerful when he is humble, and is famous among his followers."[7] It has been suggested that the origins of Sufism go back to the tension felt by members of the early Muslim community who thought that the pomp and circumstance of the Umayyad court was contrary to the life of simplicity preached by Muhammad and who were mindful of the need to repent so as not to be consigned to hell on the Day of Judgment. Thus, Hasan al-Basri (d. 728), one of the earliest Sufis, writes:

> O son of Adam! You will die alone and enter the grave alone and be resur-
> rected alone, and it is with you alone that the reckoning will take place! O son
> of Adam! It is you who is intended! It is you who is addressed![8]

Sufis saw the greater *jihad* or holy war as one that had to be waged against the lower impulses of the self, and Sufis practiced an ascetic lifestyle as ex-emplified by Ibrahim ibn Adham (d. ca. 777), who put forward the idea of absolute trust in God. Since God is the provider of every need, the idea of absolute trust led to the practice of poverty, *faqr*, which meant to rely only on God for sustenance. The early Sufis rejected the material world since it was ephemeral and not worth lamenting over. However, at the beginning of the ninth century, a woman Sufi named Rabi'a al-Adawiyya declared that paramount over all was a human's love for God and worship of God for God's own sake, as this anecdote illustrates:

> She was seen one day in the streets of Basra, carrying a bucket in one hand
> and a torch in the other one. Asked the meaning of her action, she replied: "I
> want to pour water into Hell and set fire to Paradise so that these two veils
> disappear and nobody worships God out of fear of Hell or hope for Paradise,
> but only for the sake of His eternal beauty."[9]

The mystic Dhu al-Nun (d. 859 C.E.) was the first to view nature as a sign of God's presence:

> O God, I never hearken to the voices of the beasts or the rustle of the trees,
> the splashing of the waters or the song of the birds, the whistling of the wind

or the rumble of thunder but I sense in them a testimony to Thy Unity and a proof of Thy incomparability, that Thou art the All-Prevailing, the All-Knowing, the All-True.[10]

The idea of God's unity meant that there is nothing but God, not even self, even though humans experience selfhood as something distinct from God. Taken alongside *ma'rifah*, or experiential knowledge of God, it follows that the mystic in thrall of a divine experience cannot imagine him- or herself speaking, and this led to the tradition of ecstatic sayings in Sufism. The first to articulate such sayings was Abu Yazid Bistami (d. 875), who declared, much to the dismay of the legal scholars, "Glory be to Me!" While his utterance was excused as the outpouring of someone who was no longer in control of his selfhood, the celebrated mystic Mansur al-Hallaj (d. 922) was executed for making similar utterances, including the now famous, "I am the Truth." Two other mystics renowned for their ecstatic utterances are 'Ayn al-Qudat Hamadani, who was executed in 1131, and Ruzbihan Baqli (d. 1209). 'Ayn al-Qudat thought that seeing dualities between God and creation was itself a form of infidelity, for surely nothing other than God truly existed. Ruzbihan Baqli took the idea further to mean that every act of faith sustained duality, which was itself an infidelity; therefore, faith and infidelity were paired until the experience of final union with God, when all dualities vanished.[11]

As the Greek philosophical corpus was translated, absorbed, and adopted into Islamic intellectual discourse, mystical writers produced works of literature that examined philosophical and existential questions such as the nature of the soul, prophecy, creation of the cosmos, the role of the intellect, the secrets that could be known only by the heart, and the purpose and goals of human existence. Among the notable writers in this category are al-Farabi (d. 950); Ibn Sina (Avicenna, d. 1037); the Syrian Shihab al-Din Suhrawardi (killed on the orders of Saladin, 1191), who founded the Ishraqi or Illuminationist school and whose effect was felt in the Isfahan school of mystic thinkers such as Mir Damad (d. 1631) and Mulla Sadra (d. 1641); the tenth-century Brethren of Purity or Ikhwan al-Safa, a group of thinkers from Basra; Ibn Bajjah (Avempace, d. 1138); and Ibn Tufayl (d. 1185). The poetic literature generated by Sufis such as Omar Khayyam (d. 1123), Hafiz (d. 1390), and Rumi (d. 1273)—whose magnum opus, the *Mathnawi*, is often called the Persian Qur'an—and, more recently, the South Asian poet Iqbal (d. 1938) has come to be known worldwide as examples of the rich tradition of Muslim literature. Sufis also boast of a comic figure named Khwaja Nasiruddin, whose humorous stories convey subtle shifts in perception that embody mystical insights.

## Legal Developments

The legal regime followed by Sufis depended on whether they were Shi'ite or Sunni and on the local customs prevalent in their area. Sufis are not a separate sect in Islam but rather express an inward orientation to their understanding of Islam, so the transmission of Sufi ideas depended on the teachings of a master (known as *shaykh, qutb, murshid,* or *pir*), usually male, who instructed his disciples on an inward understanding of the Qur'an, on modes of expressing piety and engaging in prayer, and on the ethical principles that informed a Sufi's behavior toward others. Thus, beginning in the eleventh century and continuing to the present day, Sufis organized themselves into lodges where members live and study under the direction of a master. A master was usually initiated into spiritual mastery through a prior master, and such lineages often went back to Muhammad or 'Ali or to spiritualized prophetic entities such as Khidr (the "green" prophet), who conferred authority on the living master symbolically through the gift of a robe. Sometimes a master was given the spiritual mantle through the spirit of another teacher without ever having met him; this kind of initiation follows the model of Uways al-Qarani, a contemporary of the Prophet who had never met him but was spiritually instructed by him. It was customary for the disciples of a master to take an oath of allegiance to him and his teachings, and often a disciple took such oaths with several masters. It was important for a disciple to learn ethical behavior according to rules of moral conduct known as *adab.* So, for example, Abu Hafs al-Suhrawardi (d. 1234) described the master-disciple relationship in the following manner:

> When the sincere disciple enters under obedience of the master, keeping his company and learning his manners, a spiritual state flows from within the master to within the disciple, like one lamp lighting another. The speech of the master inspires the interior of the disciple, so that the master's words become the treasury of spiritual states. The state is transferred from the master to the disciple by keeping company and by hearing speech. This only applies to the disciple who restricts himself to the master, who sheds the desire of his soul, and who is annihilated in the master by giving up his own will.[12]

A Sufi order (*tariqa* or *ta'ifa*) was generally named after its founders and followed a distinctive understanding of what it meant to be a Muslim and how best to practice that understanding. So, for instance, the Mevleviyya order is named after Mevlana (or Mawlana) Rumi (d. 1273), whose practice of spinning in circles to emulate the rotation of the human soul around an axis representing the spiritual guide or the divine being has become well

known through the performances of the Mevlevi Whirling Dervishes of
Turkey. Orders often split into branches. Some orders resisted any political connections, preferring to support themselves through gifts or endowments (such as the Chishti order in South Asia), whereas others cultivated
political ties, such as the Ni'matu'llahi order in Iran, named after Shah
Ni'matu'llah Wali (d. 834).

## Intellectual Traditions

In their search for an experiential understanding of the divine being,
the early Sufis identified the heart as the location of mystical insight and
understanding. For instance, a Sufi from Baghdad named Sari as-Saqati (d.
867) declared:

> It is the custom of God to let the hearts of those who love Him have vision
> of Him always, in order that the delight thereof may enable them to endure
> every tribulation; and they say in their orisons: We deem all torments more
> desirable than to be veiled from Thee. When Thy beauty is revealed to our
> heart, we take no thought of affliction.[13]

The Sufi disciple was able, through spiritual exercises, to attain self-mastery
over a number of stations describing psychological and ethical qualities.
The number of such stations varied by author: Ruzbihan Baqli mentions
more than 1,000 stations, Qushayri (d. 1072) mentions close to 50, and
Ansari lists 100. Such stations might include repentance, fear of God, asceticism, fear, hope, sorrow, hunger, humility, trust in God, thankfulness,
patience, sincerity, truthfulness, magnanimity, recollection of God, chiv-
alry, generosity, poverty, vision, insight, yearning, thirst, tranquility, and
purity and the many stages of love such as intimacy, longing, and vision.
Stations were differentiated from states that were a grace from God and
overtook the seeker involuntarily: these sometimes overlap with the stations, and early classifications by al-Balkhi (d. 810) and al-Sarraj include
meditation, asceticism, fear, hope, longing, nearness to God, love, contemplation, and certainty.[14] The goal of the Sufi was to attain gnosis (ma'rifah)
through a submergence of the individual ego-self in the ocean of divinity,
often termed annihilation (fana'), before reemerging to everyday awareness
with an abiding consciousness (baqa') of the eternal.

The guide on the path toward illumination of the heart was the Sufi master. The Prophet was the paradigm of one who had attained the highest

spiritual mysteries and communed with the divine, and Sufis saw in him someone whose heart had understood what it meant to be the perfect servant (*'abd*) of God, one who bore the light (*nur*) of God's perfect creation. According to Sahl al-Tustari (d, 896):

> When God willed to create Muhammad, He made appear a light from His light. When it reached the veil of the Majesty, it bowed in prostration before God. God created from its prostration a mighty column like crystal glass of light that is outwardly and inwardly translucent.[15]

The philosopher-mystic, Shihabuddin Suhrawardi, Shaykh al-Ishraq, who was put to death by the legal scholars in 1191, understood existence itself as light:

> The Essence of the First Absolute Light, God, gives constant illumination, whereby it is manifested and it brings all things into existence, giving life to them by its rays. Everything in the world is derived from the Light of His essence and all beauty and perfection are the gift of His bounty, and to attain fully to this illumination is salvation.[16]

For Suhrawardi—who combined within himself knowledge of the Greek, Egyptian, and Persian traditions before him—a person's rank depends on the degree to which that person is veiled from or illuminated by the light. According to Suhrawardi, Gabriel is the guardian angel over all of humanity, and each person has a heavenly angel drawing the person closer to itself. This life is therefore significant, because the constant ethical striving of a person helps to remove the veils between the self and the divine source of illumination. Suhrawardi's impact was felt most in the Isfahan school and soon extended beyond the borders of Isfahan to form what is now called the Ishraqi tradition. This tradition combines philosophy, theology, and mysticism and flourishes in modern Iranian and Iraqi seminaries such as those in Qom, Mashhad, Tehran, and Najaf.

Another Sufi of note was Ibn 'Arabi (d. 1240), an Andalusian (Spanish) Sufi who has been called the greatest master or al-Shaykh al-Akbar. Educated by two women mystics, one of whom was Fatima of Cordoba, he understood the only reality to be that of divinity:

> When my Beloved appears,
> With what eye do I see Him?
> With his eye, not with mine,
> For none sees Him except Himself.[17]

Known for his theory of unity of being (*wahdat al-wujud*), Ibn ʿArabi believed that everything exists by being found or perceived by God, as expressed in his statement: "only their face that is turned to God is real, the rest is pure non-Being."[18] That is, human and divine are mirrors for each other: as a human looks into God, he or she understands his or her reality, and as the divine being looks at a human, the divine being sees which of its qualities has become manifest in that being. One must polish the rust off the mirror of one's soul through ethical and spiritual exercises to most clearly reflect the divine. Muhammad is the ideal mirror as his soul is the most perfectly polished, thereby earning him the title of the Perfect Man.

Another Sufi of note was Ibn al-Farid (d. 1135), an Egyptian poet whose odes are known for their exquisite beauty. He saw God as the puppet master and this world as a shadow-play behind which the divine hand lay. A tradition of love mysticism developed in the writings of mystics such as Ahmad Ghazali (d. 1126) (not to be confused with his brother, Abu Hamid al-Ghazali [d. 1111]), Jalaludin Rumi, and Fakhruddin ʿIraqi, for whom love is "a flame that burns everything save the Beloved...extinguishing everything that is other than God."[19] Fariddudin ʿAttar (d. 1220) wrote an influential work titled *The Conference of the Birds*, in which he explored the longing that creatures have for their spiritual home. In this tale, the bird is an analogy for the human soul (since it is capable of flight and soaring up toward the source of mystical illumination). Thirty birds undertake an arduous journey out of longing in search of the Simurgh, or king of the birds, only to realize at the end of the tale that they collectively are the *si murgh*, Persian for 30 birds, or Simurgh, the fabled king. Longing drives the search for spiritual illumination, and in union there is the joy of the soul having found its home.

Rumi, who had met ʿAttar and was blessed by him, was born in Balkh (present-day Afghanistan) and moved to Konya (in present-day Turkey) in his late teens. Konya was a center for intellectuals, poets, and artists fleeing from the Mongol invasions, and Rumi was initiated into mystical love by a figure about whom not much is known, Shams-i Tabriz, to whom Rumi devoted an entire volume of mystical verses. Rumi's magisterial work, the *Mathnawi*, contains more than 26,000 verses, and his total output exceeds 30,000 verses. The *Mathnawi* is often called the Persian Qur'an (this honor is also extended to the verses of another celebrated Persian mystic, Hafez). Drawing upon symbols taken from music and dance, Rumi opens the *Mathnawi* with the song of a reed-flute who longingly laments its being torn from its rush-bed and sings of the secrets of longing and union with its Beloved. One of Rumi's most renowned poems expresses the interrelatedness of all that exists and the upward journey of the soul through the different stages of its manifestation:

> I died as a mineral and became a plant,
> I died as plant and rose to animal.
> I died as animal and I was human.
> Why should I fear? When was I less by dying?
> Yet once more I shall die as human, to soar
> With angels blest; but even from angelhood
> I must pass on: all except God doth perish.
> When I have sacrificed my angel-soul,
> I shall become what no mind e'er conceived.
> O let me not exist! For Non-existence
> Proclaims in organ tones "To Him we shall return!"[20]

## ISLAMIC PHILOSOPHY

This chapter would not be complete without a brief mention of Muslim philosophers who, like the Sufis, expressed yet another orientation of what it meant to be Muslim. While the philosophers held either the Sunni or the Shi'i understanding of Islam, they thought, in addition, that the greatest gift to humankind lay in the intellect, or the capacity of humans to understand revelation in manners consistent with a rational investigation of the world, the cosmos, and the beings within it. They did not view faith as contrary to reason, but rather as an ally to reason, so that the goals of revelation and of rational or scientific investigation were the same—that is, to point to the greatness of divinity, the source of both revelation and the workings of the intellect.

The Muslim conquest of Egypt, Syria, and Iraq, where Hellenistic culture had flourished after the Emperor Justinian closed the philosophical academies in Athens, led to the translation of Greek philosophical and scientific texts. Alexandria in Egypt was the center for intellectual learning and the meeting place for Greek thought and Egyptian, Persian, Phoenician, Jewish, and Christian ideas. A significant school of thought that emerged from this encounter was Neo-Platonism, founded by the Egyptian thinker Plotinus (d. 270) and his Syrian disciple Porphyry of Tyre (d. 303). Plotinus's chief work, the *Enneads*, was organized by Porphyry into six books of nine chapters each, and portions of this work were translated into Arabic by Ibn Na'imah of Edessa (d. 835) under the title *The Theol-*

*ogy,* erroneously attributed to Aristotle. The centers of learning in Syria and Iraq included Antioch, Harran, Edessa, Qinnesrin, and Nisibis, where Greek texts were translated into Syriac as part of the intellectual culture and where Christian theological and philosophical work was produced. The Umayyad prince Khalid ibn Yazid (d. 704) is credited for patronizing the translation of medical, alchemical, and astrological works into Arabic, while the 'Abbasid caliph al-Mansur (d. 773) patronized the translation of philosophical works, chiefly those of Aristotle. The caliphs Harun al-Rashid (d. 809) and his son al-Ma'mun (d. 833) furthered the translation of texts, and the latter founded the House of Wisdom (*Bayt al-Hikmah*) in Baghdad in 830 to serve as a library and a center for translation. It was here that significant contributions were made to the translation movement by Hunayn ibn Ishaq (d. 873) and his disciples. Although the Greek corpus formed the bulk of what was translated into Arabic, Persian and Indian texts also were translated and studied.[21]

The translation movement sparked several centuries of scholarly reflection, analysis in the form of commentaries, and intellectual activity that sought to harmonize the "two truths" of revelation and reason, as well as intense productivity in the fields of science, philosophy, theology, medicine, astronomy, architecture, and music. Contrary to popular perception, the Muslims did not simply safeguard the translated texts until they were retranslated into Latin in Spain in the thirteenth and fourteenth centuries, but rather they used Greek, Indian, and Persian ideas to advance knowledge, whether it related to theories of optics or healing or the natural world. Indeed, without the advances made by Muslim thinkers, the European Renaissance might not have occurred when it did. (It is erroneous to call Muslim philosophy Arab philosophy, because most Muslim philosophers of note were not Arab, even though they wrote primarily in the lingua franca of the day, Arabic [Ibn Sina, for instance, also wrote in Persian].)

By and large, the philosophers espoused the view that all fields of knowledge provided windows into the workings of the divine being and, therefore, scientific investigation was not contrary to faith. Indeed, the first philosopher, the Arab al-Kindi (d. ca. 866) sought to buttress the Qur'an's claim of monotheism through mathematical proofs on the nature of eternity. He also attempted to show that time and motion are finite, so the world must have a definite beginning and end and therefore must have had a creator. Al-Razi (d. 925 or 935), a Persian who was the foremost medical authority of his day and a philosopher, made the point that revelation was in fact unnecessary for anyone who fully exercised his or her intellect, a view that earned him the displeasure of theologians and led to the burning

Man in front of Alexandria, Egypt, mosque. © Getty Images/21000054816.

of his vast philosophical output. His moral treatise, one of the few works to survive, argues that the healing of the soul lies in leading a virtuous life free of arrogance, envy, anger, lying, greed, gluttony, and the fear of death. Al-Farabi (d. 950), a Turk, styled the Second Master (after Aristotle, who was accorded the title of the First Master), is perhaps the most important Muslim philosopher to whom those who followed owed a profound debt. He paraphrased or wrote commentaries on all of Aristotle's logical works as well as on Porphyry's *Isagoge* and advanced the field of logic. The father of Muslim political philosophy, his work on the virtuous city explains his understanding of the workings of the universe that emanates from a perfect divine being and the operation of the virtuous city within that universe. Within the virtuous city is the soul, whose ultimate goal of happiness could not be attained without living in community with others and interacting with them in virtuous manners. Ibn Sina (Avicenna) (d. 1037), a Persian thinker who made significant contributions in the fields of medicine, science, philosophy, and mysticism, advanced a theory of prophecy in which the human intellect, based on al-Farabi's work, was capable through philosophical and scientific investigation of arriving at the same truths as the Prophet, who was a divinely appointed instructor for the human soul. Indeed, Ibn Sina's medical works continued to be used in European academies of learning until the nineteenth century. A group of tenth-century philosophers and scientists known as the Brethren of Purity (or Ikhwan al-Safa) are well known for their ecological fable, *The Case of the Animals vs. Man*, in which they argue for the capacity of all of nature to give thanks and praise to their Creator, while humans, who are blessed with free-will, misuse their moral privilege to ill-treat the earth and animals instead of acting in accordance with their divine appointment as stewards of the earth and all that is in it. Ibn Tufayl (d. 1185), a Spanish Muslim, wrote a fable titled *Hayy ibn Yaqzan*, in which Hayy, raised by animals on an island, comes to discover the secrets of the universe through reflection and meditation and by observing the world around him and the cosmos. When he finally meets a traveler from a civilized place who has been brought up in society and has learned about God and ethical behavior and the law through revelation, he realizes that he knows what the other has learned through revelation.

Islamic philosophy received a crippling blow through the efforts of the famous Persian theologian and mystic, Abu Hamid al-Ghazali (d. 1111). Trained as an Ash'arite theologian, he continued his studies in logic, theology, and philosophy with al-Juwayni in Nishapur. He was appointed head of the Nizamiyya school in Baghdad, a center for Sunni thought as well as anti-Isma'ili propaganda, much of which he authored. The school had been founded by Nizam al-Mulk, the powerful minister of the ruler Sultan Malik Shah. Both the minister and the ruler were assassinated by the Isma'ilis in 1092 and shortly thereafter, perhaps fearing for his own life, al-Ghazali left his position to wander for 10 years under cover as a Sufi. He resumed teaching in Nishapur five years before his death.

Al-Ghazali, a follower of the Shafi'i legal school, wrote works that examined theological, philosophical and mystical approaches to religion. He concluded that an intellectual approach to religion was not sufficient, whereas religious experience was capable of giving him peace and certainty. He criticized law, theology, and philosophy for attempting to make faith rational and for trying to organize human behavior according to their principles. Instead, he taught that anyone who believed in the principles of Islam was a believer and that certainty of faith could only be achieved from the exercises of the Sufis, leading the disciple to a religious experience of faith. Holding the view that only the learned should investigate religion because intellectual study would confound the masses, he made the connection that a good Muslim adhered to the *shari'a* and engaged in spiritual exercises to purify the soul and understand faith experientially. Perhaps his greatest achievement was to bring Sufism from the periphery to the center of orthodoxy; his greatest disservice was to destroy the credibility of philosophical thought in a work titled *The Incoherence of the Philosophers.*

The Spanish philosopher, physician, and jurist Ibn Rushd (Averroes, d. 1198), the foremost exponent of Aristotle after al-Farabi, attempted a rebuttal to al-Ghazali's attack on philosophy, titled *The Incoherence of the Incoherence,* with limited success. Indeed, Ibn Rushd's legacy lives on in the work of the Catholic theologian St. Thomas Aquinas (d. 1274), who accessed the Muslim philosopher's work through its Latin translation. Public opinion briefly turned against philosophical and scientific work, no doubt foreshadowing the deep anti-intellectualism that had found such an articulate champion in al-Ghazali a few decades earlier. Ibn Rushd was exiled in 1195, all his books burned, and, with the exception of medicine and astronomy, teaching in philosophy and the sciences was banned. He was called back from exile, but died soon after. Philosophical thought henceforth disappeared under the guise of what has been termed theosophical Sufism, such as the exponents of the Ishraqi school mentioned here. However, the emphasis placed on religious practice by al-Ghazali and many others remains an enduring legacy.

## NOTES

1. Wilferd Madelung, *The Succession to Muhammad: A Study of the Early Caliphate* (Cambridge, England: Cambridge University Press, 1997), 253.

2. Fazlur Rahman, *Islam* (New York: Holt, Rinehart and Winston, 1966), Chapter 6, fn.1.

3. Rahman, *Islam,* 101.

4. For this section, see John Esposito, *Islam: The Straight Path* (New York: Oxford University Press, 1992), Chapter 2.

5. See Marshall G. S. Hodgson, *The Venture of Islam: Conscience and History in a World Civilization,* Vol. 1: *The Classical Age of Islam* (Chicago: University of Chicago Press, 1974), Chapter 3.

6. For this section, see Heinz Halm, *Shiism* (Edinburgh: Edinburgh University Press, 1991); definition found on 69.

7. Carl Ernst, *Sufism* (Boston: Shambhala, 1997), 23–24.

8. Annemarie Schimmel, *Islam: An Introduction* (Albany: State University of New York Press, 1992), 102.

9. Ibid., 105.

10. Ibid., 106.

11. See Carl W. Ernst, *Words of Ecstasy in Sufism* (Albany: State University of New York Press, 1985).

12. Quoted in Ernst, *Sufism,* 124.

13. Annemarie Schimmel, *Mystical Dimensions of Islam* (Chapel Hill: University of North Carolina Press, 1975), 131.

14. Reynold A. Nicholson, *The Mystics of Islam* (London: Routledge and Kegan Paul, 1914, 1963), 29.

15. Annemarie Schimmel, *And Muhammad Is His Messenger: The Veneration of the Prophet in Islamic Piety* (Chapel Hill: University of North Carolina Press, 1985), 125.

16. Schimmel, *Mystical Dimensions,* 261.

17. Ibid., 266.

18. Ibid., 267.

19. Ibid., 294.

20. Ibid., 321–322. The word "Man" in the original has been changed to "human" in lines 3 and 5, and "him" in the last line has been capitalized to indicate divinity. The phrase in quotation marks is from the Qur'an.

21. For the translation movement, see Majid Fakhry, *A Short Introduction to Islamic Philosophy, Theology and Mysticism* (Oxford, England: Oneworld, 1997), especially the first chapter and appendix 1; also R. Walzer, *Greek into Arabic* (Cambridge, MA.: Harvard University Press, 1962).

# 4

# PRACTICE WORLDWIDE

As with every other major religious tradition, the 1.2 billion Muslims world-wide share many commonalities, even as they express what it means to be Muslim in culturally and regionally specific ways. Every Muslim reveres the Qur'an, contributes to charity, and fasts during the month of Ramadan. When possible, Muslims everywhere make the pilgrimage (*hajj*) to Mecca, and if this cannot be done due to economic, health, or political reasons, many Muslims, especially the mystically inclined, develop their individual spirituality to attain the Ka'aba of the heart.

## STRUCTURES OF RELIGIOUS AUTHORITY

All Muslims turn to the Qur'an for social and religious guidance; how-ever, the Qur'an's message is mediated through the structures of Islamic authority. The most immediate religious authority is the local preacher, or *imam* among the Sunnis and *mullah* among the Shi'ites. *Imams* and *mul-lahs* may receive their training at any one of many seminaries. The most prominent seminary for the Sunnis is al-Azhar in Egypt, and for the Shi'tes it is Qom in Iran. Different Muslim communities may have their own train-ing centers as well. Muslim social life is regulated through the legal system to the extent to which Islamic law is incorporated into state law. Until chal-lenged, customs are often understood as an expression of Islamic dictates. Many Saudi women now question the Islamic law that prohibits women from driving cars in Saudi Arabia. In many parts of West, Central, and South Asia, there is increasing criticism of honor killings, because a close examination of the Qur'an offers no justification for the practice of killing a woman to protect a man's honor. Contemporary Muslims in Europe, the Americas, and Australia have formed umbrella organizations to manage their religious, social, legal, educational, and political needs. In North America, for instance, the Muslim Public Affairs Council, the Council for American-Islamic Relations, and the Islamic Society of North America provide advocacy and advice. In other parts of the world, learned members of the community deliver legal rulings when authorized to do so by their training institutions and their respective governments. When not so authorized, they follow the rulings of recognized authorities. Many Sunnis submit to the jurists of Saudi Arabia and Egypt, although they defer even more to local authorities, such as those in Pakistan, Indonesia, Malaysia, or South Africa. Shi'ites abide by the authority of the chief of the *marja'-i taqlid* (models to be emulated) in Iran, but many will choose a particular *marja'* as their guide. So, for example, the Iraqi Shi'ite community in southern California follows the spiritual and religious leadership of Ayatollah Sistani in Iraq. Groups like the Druze and the Isma'ilis heed their own authorities in accordance with their social and religious duties.

## FORMS OF RELIGIOUS EXPRESSION

Muslims through the ages have developed diverse forms of religious expression in the arts; in devotional music; in the constructed environment of mosques, gardens, and cemeteries; in local traditions, such as visitations to shrines; and in the way life is honored. The Islamic arts are a celebration of the divine: geometrical and floral designs adorn screens and doorways, and tile work and intricate calligraphy grace Muslim architecture and public buildings. Muslim artists are noted for their illuminated manuscripts of the Qur'an, often embellishing the many different calligraphic styles with gold leaf and complex designs. Mosques and public buildings are often oriented in the direction of prayer toward Mecca, and domes symbolize the seven levels of ascent to paradise. Walls are covered in calligraphy with inscriptions from the Qur'an; interlocking geometric forms in tiled floors, walls, or screens denote the inexhaustible perfection of divinity; and controlled light entering a structure creates a serene atmosphere for prayer. The gardens that surround Islamic structures incorporate the sounds of flowing water, the calming presence of green foliage, and the play of natural light to evoke the gardens of paradise. The craftsmanship of Qur'anic manuscripts, demanding intense meditation and rendered in calligraphic styles that take years to master, pays homage to the divine word. Metal, glass, porcelain, and crystal arts incorporate similar inscriptions and geometric forms. Prayer rugs contain a place marker for the forehead and portrayals of pillars symbolizing the ascent to heaven. Carpets feature medallions, geometric designs, or the plants and creatures of divine creation.

Perhaps the best-known example of ceremonial fabric is the veil of the Ka'aba, with its inscriptions embroidered in gold. Ceremonial robes are also richly embroidered with inscriptions. Figural depictions of the Prophet and 'Ali are often represented (without facial features and surrounded by haloes indicating special dispensation from the divine being) in medieval Persian paintings. While the cantillation of the Qur'an in Qur'anic recitation is not strictly considered music, its resonant quality elevates the human voice as

Dome of a mosque. © Getty Images/21000054821.

an instrument of God's service and inspires listeners to a renewed commitment to faith and good works. Despite the common assumption that Islam frowns on music, Muslim theologians of the past condemned music only if it incited listeners to acts of passion and lust, and not if it edified. Many modern preachers, however, depending on their interpretation of Islam, consider music abhorrent and ungodly, despite the centuries-long tradition of Muslim musical virtuosity in which instruments like the oud, tar, sitar, flute, and the human voice have been used in mystical rituals and musical compositions of longing, praise, and supplication. The poetry of medieval Muslim mystics such as Rumi and Hafez is well known but represents only a small portion of the total body of Muslim devotional poems. Poetic and dramatic performances are part of the ceremony surrounding the rites of Muharram, during which Shi'ite Muslims commemorate the martyrdom of Husayn, son of 'Ali. Poetry honoring the Prophet is recited during the celebrations of his birth.

Shrine visitations are common in many Muslim countries, notably Egypt, India, Morocco, Iran, and others places where mosques built near the graves of noted personages are sites for festivals held in their honor, usually to commemorate a birthday, death, or anniversary. In Iran, for instance, the mausoleums of Rumi, Hafez, and Khomeini attract large numbers of pilgrims. While the "saint" in question is not always considered divine, it is hoped that the saint's elevated spiritual status will facilitate divine intervention on behalf of the supplicant. In Egypt, similar visitations to shrines occur during festivals, and Moroccan saints are honored throughout the year. The Moroccan government has instituted a Festival of Sacred Music that celebrates the devotional musical traditions of Moroccan and North African Muslims. The festival's success has led to the inclusion of other sacred musical traditions.

## RITES OF PASSAGE

The first words a Muslim newborn is likely to hear are the *shahada*, whispered into its ear by a proud parent, followed by the call to prayer. Then the opening verses of the Qur'an are recited. On the seventh day, the child is named, and sometimes the child's head is ceremonially shaved, a practice believed to date back to the days of the Prophet. After 40 days, the mother is deemed able to resume her ritual duties, from which she was exempted during pregnancy, birth, and recovery.

## Circumcision

Boys are circumcised soon after birth, in early childhood up to the age of eight, or at the onset of puberty. Although circumcision is not mentioned in the Qur'an, the practice has entered Muslim ritual and has pre-Islamic roots. The *hadith* literature contains references to Abraham's circumcision, suggesting its religious origin. How and when male circumcision is performed can vary from region to region and even from family to family, but it is usually accompanied by great ceremony. The child can be dressed as a bridegroom (in Southeast Asia, especially Java) or as a girl (in Egypt). On the day of circumcision, the child is sometimes placed on horseback in a procession, accompanied by musicians (as in Arabia). In parts of North Africa, communal ceremonies may be held every two years.

Female circumcision is recommended but not required by Islamic law. The earliest legal documents recommend a small removal of the skin in the highest part of the genitalia—a far cry from the extreme circumcision practiced in the Nile River region. The religious antecedents for female circumcision are found in a *hadith* in which Abraham orders Hagar to circumcise herself to appease Sarah's demand that he shed Hagar's blood—a product of the rivalry between mistress and slave. Female circumcision is now challenged by health workers and activists to curtail its more extreme forms, noting that there is no religious justification for the custom. Egypt has banned female circumcision, causing a backlash and an *increase* of the practice. Sudanese activists have initiated educational programs to dissociate female circumcision from Islamic requirements with a fair degree of success.

## Marriage

The Qur'an recommends abstinence until a male has the means to marry: "Marry the spouseless among you, and your slaves and handmaidens that are righteous; if they are poor, God will enrich them of His bounty.... And let those who find not the means to marry be abstinent till God enriches them of His bounty" (Q. 24:32, 33). In the *hadith* literature, Muhammad is reported as saying, "Marriage is half the religion." The mystics or Sufis were known to marry and have children even as they practiced corporal austerity. The Qur'an encourages marriage but considers it a legal contract and not a sacrament. Thus, many of the verses in the Qur'an pertaining to marriage are regulatory and have become the basis of Islamic family law.

Depending on where they live and the extent to which Islamic law has been incorporated, Muslims may or may not engage in polygamy; a wife may or may not have the right to initiate divorce; and child custody laws vary. In Muhammad's time, Qur'anic regulations were aimed at improving a woman's position in a marriage; however, reformers today identify the marital regime as deserving attention, all the more so because family laws are no longer as favorable to women and children as they once were. Thus, Muslim activists have spearheaded the revision of family legal codes in many Muslim nations including Tunisia, Morocco, Egypt, Indonesia, Pakistan, and Iran. Muslims in Europe, North America, and Australia follow the laws of their adopted lands, all of which ban polygamy.

Whether the families of the bride and the groom arrange the marriage of their respective children, or whether the bride and groom happen to meet and fall in love, families handle the details of the marriage. Preparations may include an exchange of gifts between the two families, ceremonies in which the marriage is arranged, bridal parties where the bride is decorated with henna and presented with a gaily packaged trousseau, and bachelor parties with similar rituals for the groom. The marriage ceremony involves the declaration and signing of the marriage contract, accompanied by a recitation of Qur'anic verses. After the wedding ceremony, local traditions may include a celebration with musicians, dancers, and food and traditional rites marking the union of the bride's and groom's families. In some regions, the bloody sheet from the wedding night is ritually displayed as proof of the bride's virginity, and in other regions the bride's virginity is considered a private matter. A key feature of Muslim marriages is the bridal gift from the groom's family. The gift is often gold jewelry or valuables and is the bride's to keep, even in the case of divorce (although this promise is not always honored). The marriage extends the wife's relatives to include in-laws with whom it is appropriate to maintain social relations, and without whom a woman may not entertain or otherwise interact socially with non-related males. Again, this aspect of Muslim social life is observed in relative degrees depending on region and culture.

### Death

A Muslim approaching death is positioned, if possible, to face Mecca. Prayers for the forgiveness of one's sins are recited around the deathbed and include chapter 36 from the Qur'an, a meditation on the reward and punishment of deeds good and evil. After death, the body is washed ritually three times with soap and water, and scent is added to the final washing. The cleansing begins with the parts of the body that are normally washed for prayer. Once cleaned, the body is wrapped unembalmed in a white shroud. A special prayer is recited over the body before burial, preferably not in a coffin, and often the corpse is placed on its right side facing Mecca. Between the time of the death and the burial ceremony, family members and friends gather to pray at the home of the deceased or in a mosque. Prayers are recited for 40 days, after which special prayers are recited every month until the end of the first year and, from that point forward, every year on the anniversary of the death.

## CONTEMPORARY MUSLIM ISSUES

Religion can be a powerful tool for social change. Religious teachings and ideas have inspired throughout history and achieved a place of particular social prominence in the twentieth century, as exemplified in Dr. Martin Luther King, Jr.'s struggle to bring about civil rights for African Americans. People of faith do not lead compartmentalized lives. They see the challenges of human existence through a lens of religious values, placing the needs of society in conversation with what they believe are God's intentions. More recently, deep religious convictions have been at the root of activism like Dorothy Day's Catholic Worker Movement and the Latin American churches of the poor, both of which condemn the social injustice of poverty and call on people of faith to effect a change. If God is merciful, loving, and just, they argue, is it not our responsibility to care for all humanity, and not just for ourselves? So to understand religious behavior, we must understand the conditions in which people live, as they look to their religious traditions for comfort, guidance, and support. Contemporary religion is no longer the exclusive domain of houses of worship or something mystical expressed in rituals; it plays an important role in all fields of human endeavor, from law, economics, and science to politics, sexuality, ethics, and how we deal with people of different faiths from other countries with dissimilar cultural traditions.

After the horrific events of September 11, 2001, it has become more important than ever to understand how religion affects social behavior and how social conditions evoke responses pursuant to religious sentiments. With respect to Muslims, the two most urgent questions concern political Islam and the treatment of women. Both these issues must be placed in a historical, social, and political context. Every world religion today has a political dimension and has witnessed the struggle for gender rights. The nineteenth- and twentieth-century movements for the political, legal, and economic rights of women go hand in hand with the efforts of Christian and Jewish women to reinterpret sacred texts in a way that is different from traditional male interpretations that devalued them.

## Political Islam

European colonization in the eighteenth, nineteenth, and the first half of the twentieth centuries left an indelible print on all countries with Muslim majority populations. The only Muslim countries that did not experience direct colonization were Saudi Arabia, Turkey, and Iran; however, these countries felt the impact of European policies. Colonization reversed the autonomy Muslims had enjoyed for centuries and created a crisis that was economic as much as it was cultural and religious. There is little doubt that the economies of all colonizing nations—England, France, Spain, Portugal, The Netherlands, Germany, and Russia—richly benefited from the resources of the colonized countries. Although the impact of colonization on Muslim countries awaits a thorough assessment, it is clear that local economies, administrative structures, and social arrangements were adversely affected. An imposed Europeanized education created a compliant bureaucracy that served the interests of the European elite. As a trade-related infrastructure was built—roads, railways, harbors, and communications systems—missionaries followed, introducing modernized health care and education but also converting the locals to Christianity as part of their commitment to "civilize" the natives by bringing them into the saving grace of Christ.

Socially and religiously, the more devastating impact of colonization was the way in which Europeans formed a view of the colonized that justified colonization to the people at home. Edward Said, author of a landmark study titled *Orientalism* (1979), argued that Europe defined itself as the apex of Western civilization by creating an image of the Other, or the Oriental, who was despotic, unable to think for himself, exotic, child-like, given to pleasure and eroticism, and very much in need of enlightened European civilization, culture, and religion. The Other was barbaric and needed to be tamed, civilized, and saved. European colonizers were thus able to rationalize the need to colonize "barbaric" peoples, although the primary motive was the tremendous wealth that colonization generated. European scholars also suggested that colonized Muslims were spiritually

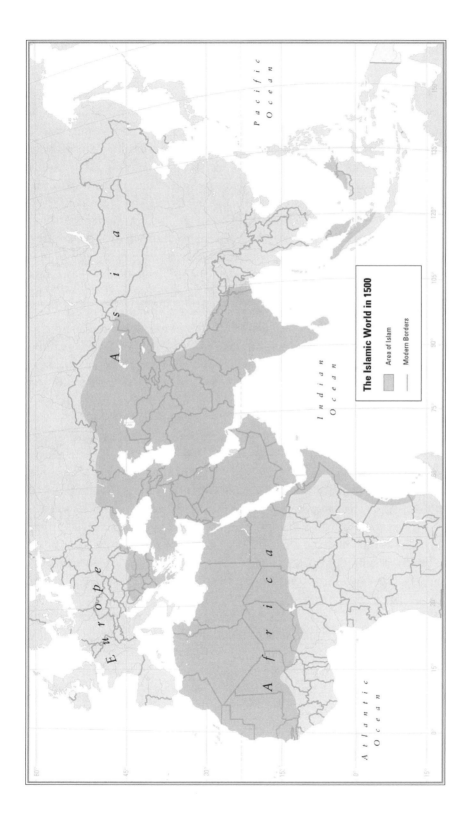

The Islamic World in 1500

Area of Islam
Modern Borders

backward and all that it took to prove this backwardness was to point out
how women were treated in Islamic societies. These claims were advanced
even though the suffragette movement in Europe was barely underway
and European women fared little better than their Muslim counterparts.
Entertaining such views allowed the Europeans to continue reaping huge
economic benefits from a brutal colonial system. By claiming moral ascen-
dancy, Christian missionaries were sent to save the souls of the brutalized.

The link between politics and Islam can be understood in the context of
colonization; it has been argued that Islamic political movements formed
in opposition to colonization. These are the *revivalist* movements of the
eighteenth and nineteenth centuries, the *reformist* movements of the nineteenth and early twentieth centuries, and the *fundamentalist* movements
in the twentieth and twenty-first centuries. Examples of revivalism are the
Wahhabi movement in Saudi Arabia, initiated by Muhammad ibn Abd al-
Wahhab (d. 1792 C.E.), who explained Muslim political weakness as stem-
ming from a deviation from the straight path of Allah, and for which the
only solution was to return to the beliefs and practices of the original seventh-century Muslim community. Other examples of revivalism are the
movement sparked by Uthman Dan Fodio (d. 1817) in Nigeria, by Muhammad ibn ʿAli Sanusi (d. 1859) in Libya, and the Mahdi (d. 1885) in the Sudan,
all of which combined militancy with a reaffirmation of Islamic practice.
In India, Sayyid Ahmed Barelewi (d. 1831) called on Muslims to purify
themselves of all practices at odds with strict monotheism and to conduct
a *jihad,* or holy war, against non-Muslim rulers: first the Sikhs and then the
British. The key features of the movement are, first, that revivalists sought,
in reaction to diminished Muslim political power, to revitalize Islam from
within by returning to the origins of Islam. All practices that would lead
to the fragmentation of the Muslim community were to be purged. Second, revivalists held that religion was integral to state and society and that
Islamic government should prevail, regulated by Islamic law. Third, the
struggle to reestablish Islam's rightful place in society required moral self-
discipline and, if necessary, armed struggle.[1]

Around the turn of the twentieth century, revivalism gave way to reformist movements that attempted to address internal social and political
weaknesses, as well as the external threat of colonization. Many Muslims
wondered whether they had lost favor with God to find themselves governed by non-Muslims acting on non-Muslim laws and whether Christianity was in fact the superior religion. Some Muslims argued that traditional
practices no longer applied to the modern world and that state and religion

should occupy separate spheres. Other Muslims blamed the loss of Muslim political power on the deviation from traditional Islamic practices, and they rejected Western culture and Christianity. Still others, who became known as the reformists, sought to influence rather than reject outright the challenges of colonization and Western Christian power. Men like Jamal al-Din Afghani (d. 1897), Muhammad 'Abduh (d. 1905), Rashid Rida (d. 1935), Sayyid Ahmed Khan (d. 1898), and Muhammad Iqbal (d. 1938) believed that the loss of Muslim power and prestige was associated with an unhealthy attachment to the past and an inability to change, and they called for reform through renewed interpretation of the Qur'an and the adaptation of Western ideas amenable to Islam.

Afghani traveled widely to Afghanistan, Egypt, Turkey, Iran, India, Russia, France, and England with the message that reason, science, and technology that were once the hallmarks of Islamic civilization must be re-appropriated within Islamic discourse to strengthen Muslim society and to meet the challenge of the West. Islam, he believed, had been weakened by a fatalistic belief in justice in the world after death; at the same time, he thought that the Western separation of religion from all other arenas of life was unwarranted. Rather, he argued for Islam to be a comprehensive way of life that must inform how Muslims conduct their legal, political, and social as well as ritual lives, and that Muslims must struggle to bring about justice on earth in this life as well as in the next life. In this manner, he sought to mediate between Muslims who sought to restrict religion to a private realm (known as secular Muslims, not because they lacked in faith, but because they sought to separate state from religion) and traditionalist Muslims who saw the application of reason to religious matters as contrary to tradition. Afghani held that Islam was capable of responding to contemporary challenges, and he challenged traditional thinkers for refusing to allow scientific endeavor among Muslims, arguing that rationality was important and must be brought back through *ijtihad,* or interpretation of the Qur'an and of sacred law, the *shari'a,* in contrast to the blind obedience propagated by the jurists. Afghani's movement is known as the *salafiyya* movement.

Afghani's disciples, Muhammad 'Abduh and Rashid Rida, continued his modernist vision. 'Abduh wrote *The Theology of Unity* (1897), in which he argued that reason and revelation were complementary and that there was no contradiction between revelation and science. He, too, argued for interpretation and against blind obedience on the basis that religion was comprised of unchanging fundamental principles and their applications, which could change over time. Thus, while the rules governing worship (prayer, fasting, pilgrimage) were unchangeable, the rules governing social affairs should be reinterpreted to meet changing historical and social circumstances. He campaigned for women's rights to education and argued against polygamy.

Rashid Rida took these ideas a step further and argued that the implementation of Islamic law required an Islamic government, and he grew increasingly more conservative over time. He was greatly influenced by the Wahhabi movement in Saudi Arabia, a more puritanical form of Islam. He had no interest in engaging with the Western world, which to him simply had to be rejected. He considered Islam self-sufficient, in contrast to both Afghani and 'Abduh, who thought that it was important to maintain a dialogue with the West and not to reject it outright. Rashid Rida greatly influenced the thought of the founder of the Muslim Brotherhood in Egypt, Hassan al-Banna (1906–1949) (discussed in the later section on fundamentalism).

Sayyid Ahmed Khan (1817–98) and Muhammad Iqbal (1875–1938) of the Indian subcontinent are among the reformist Muslim thinkers whose legacies survive today, largely under progressive Muslim movements. Sayyid Ahmed Khan faced a situation in India under colonial British rule, in which most Muslim *'ulama'* (the religiously learned) had rejected the British and wanted nothing to do with them. Khan argued that the British political power had to be accepted and that Islam needed to be revitalized from within by allowing interpretation and moving away from blind obedience. In his view, Islam was eminently capable of being relevant to contemporary social and political conditions. Further, he argued that there was nothing incompatible between Islam and scientific activity; he saw no contradiction between the word of God (revelation) and the work of God (nature). He, along with the third Aga Khan, Sir Sultan Muhammad Shah (1887–1957), created the Anglo-Muhammadan Oriental College, now Aligarh University, to promote Western-style education and translate Western scientific work. He also called for a reinterpretation of the Qur'an, a reevaluation of the veracity of the *hadith* literature, and a reexamination of Islamic law or *shari'a.*

Muhammad Iqbal, his younger contemporary, lived at a time when the educated elite were well conversant with Western education and Muslims and Hindus were gearing up for struggles of independence from British rule. The key challenge facing Muslims was whether, as a minority, they would receive equal treatment under a Hindu majority government should India be granted independence from Britain. Drawing equally from his Is-

lamic learning and from his training in Western philosophy, Iqbal understood the role of the humans as carrying out God's will in every area of their
lives. He did not compartmentalize the spiritual and the worldly, but rather
saw them as two sides of one coin. A lawyer by training, Iqbal stressed the
importance of Islamic law for fair and just governance; however, he did not
advocate the adoption of Islamic law as it had been developed ten centuries earlier. Rather, he thought, like other reform-minded thinkers before
him, that *ijtihad* or interpretation had to be employed to make the law
relevant to contemporary social circumstances. He did not view the *shari'a*
as fixed and immutable; rather, he thought the principles of Islam had to
be applied according to the needs of the time. He did not support nationalist efforts, because he thought that nationalism would split the Muslim
community into various nations—unlike his older contemporary Sayyid
Ahmed Khan, who believed that pan-Islamism, or a united Muslim world,
was unrealizable under current political conditions. However, by 1930, as
Iqbal witnessed the independence movement in India and greater calls for
a Hindu nationalism, he realized reluctantly that it would be impossible
for Indian Muslims to live in harmony with a government comprised of
Indian Hindus. He came to believe that a separate state—not necessarily a
separate country—for Muslims was necessary for Indian Muslims to retain
their identity. As a result, he is often considered the ideological founder of
Pakistan even as Muhammad Ali Jinnah is considered the political founder
of Pakistan. The latter, a secularist Muslim who believed in separating religion from politics nonetheless gradually moved toward the realization that
a separate Indian state for Muslims would not provide sufficient guarantees
for Muslim identity and representation under a largely Hindu-controlled
Indian National Congress.

Reformist thought (often referred to as *salafiyya*) influenced parts
of the Muslim world from Morocco to Indonesia. In all cases, *salafiyya*
movements formed a response to internal stultification largely due to the
*'ulama*'s insistence on *taqlid* or blind obedience and external political
threats posed by ongoing colonization. All the reformist thinkers called
for renewing interpretation or *ijtihad* of sacred and other authoritative
sources and for applying the fundamental and unchanging principles of
Islam in rational and creative ways that would make Islam relevant to contemporary Muslim societies. Many called for reforms governing the status
of women, and education that would be scientific and humanistic while
also including Islamic education. Many also turned their energies to social welfare programs to address the living conditions of Muslims. They

also advocated an Islamic government that would administer a reformed Islamic law. However, in practice, none or very few of these recommendations were carried out, and no large-scale program to reform Islamic law was instituted. Education remained bifurcated in that students either went to Western style educational institutions or continued to receive traditionalist Islamic education supplemented with mediocre Western education. The reformers' intent was miscast as an attempt to accommodate the West rather than an attempt to revitalize the meaning of Islam and how it related to contemporary life. Instead, many reformist movements were overshadowed by the rise of fundamentalist movements that continue to hold sway today through their ability to influence political powerbrokers, even though reform-minded Muslims likely make up the unheard, and politically impotent, majority.

Often called neo-revivalist movements, fundamentalist movements owe their origin to two or three thinkers: Hasan al-Banna (1906–49) and his chief ideologue, Sayyid Qutb (executed 1966) in Egypt, Mawlana Abu'l 'Ala Mawdudi (1903–73) in India and Pakistan, and Ayatollah Ruhollah Khomeini (d. 1989) in Iran. These men blamed the ills of Muslim societies internally on the lack of religiosity among Muslims and named Western secularism, Marxism, and capitalism as the chief external causes. The context of fundamentalist thought in Islam must be clearly identified as a reaction to Western colonization and the subsequent political turmoil experienced by almost every post-colonial state in the world. It is no wonder that the commonalities among fundamentalist thinkers include the notion that Islam is a self-sufficient system, capable of generating a political realm within which Muslims self-govern through the instrument of the *shari'a*; that Islam has no need of Western secularization or materialism; indeed, the West and all it stands for must be rejected in favor of a life in which the principles and traditions of Islam, as they understood them, would reign supreme. These thinkers "called for a return to the Quran, the Sunna of the Prophet, and the practice of the early community to establish an Islamic system of government."[2] Although they espoused the necessity of interpretation and the rejection of blind imitation, they saw no need to reform traditional family law, believing that such calls for reform were Western inspired. Indeed, unlike the reformists who saw value in adopting Western methods of education and analysis to revitalize Islam from within, these thinkers believed that there was nothing Islam needed from outside as all the tools required for living an Islamically oriented life in all realms of human activity—whether law, politics, economics, or gender issues—could be found from within the Islamic tradition. Such ideologies form an inward-looking reaction to the political, cultural, economic, and military power of the West and can be seen as a form of resistance to global Western influence. Nonetheless, they mark the entrance of Islamic political parties to the public scene due to their understanding of Islam as a form of government, styled theo-democracy by Mawdudi and enacted as a form of theocracy by Khomeini in Iran—for Muslims, by Muslims, according to Muslim law, and in accordance with Islam. Further, because of the emphasis on social justice at the core of fundamentalist ideologies, welfare and social service agencies are important activities of the institutions created by these movements. These movements—termed Islamist—also emphasize strict adherence to ritual and the acquisition of the necessary technological skills for social development, thereby integrating all aspects of a person's life within a religious framework.

The organizations spawned by these thinkers, the Muslim Brotherhood in Egypt and the Jamaat-i Islami in Pakistan, often were in confrontation with the state in both countries due to the state's unwillingness to cede control to Islamic political parties. The Muslim Brotherhood was banned in Egypt, and its founder, Hasan al-Banna, was assassinated in 1949; Sayyid Qutb, its chief ideologue, was imprisoned and then executed in 1969. The Jamaat-i Islami, although often criticized and its members sometimes imprisoned, was able to enter the political process in sufficiently strong numbers so as to work within the system. The military coup by General Zia ul-Haq in 1977 delivered to the Jamaat a military ruler who took significant measures aimed at Islamizing the government and the judiciary, resulting in rolling back civil and legal rights for women and for non-Muslim minorities as well as Muslim groups that were considered aberrant, such as the Ahmadiyya Muslims.

Thus, since the 1960s, all areas of the world in which majority Muslim populations reside have witnessed growth in the external representation of Muslim identity through dress, ritual observance, and public institutions—especially law, political rhetoric, and social service agencies. The Six Day War of 1967 between Israel and several Arab nations (Egypt, Syria, and Jordan) and the defeat of these nations by Israel and the consequent loss of the Golan Heights, the West Bank, and East Jerusalem led to disillusionment with pan-Arab and pan-Islamic movements and again brought to the forefront the question of Muslim weakness, not just within Arab nations, but wherever Muslims resided worldwide. Again, the responses to this question were to identify Muslim laxity in religious practice as an indication of God's punishment as an internal factor and identify Western support of Israel and their combined disregard and antipathy for Muslims as an external factor. These notions again led to the idea that Islam was a self-sufficient system and did not need foreign ideas or institutions for social organization and governance, and the Western idea of secularism, or the separation of religion and state, once again was questioned. Many Muslims thought that Islam as a way of life provided a viable alternative to the Western secularist model insofar as Muslim societies were concerned.

Still, the governments of countries with Muslim majority populations, if they were not kingdoms, attempted to retain at least the façade of Western-style democratic government. Many such governments (for example, Libya, Egypt, Iran, Sudan, Pakistan, and Malaysia) have used Islam as an ideology to gain legitimacy for their policies. However, their failures to provide much-needed social services and maintain robust economies that provide employment, education, health, and decent living standards for their populations and their authoritarian and militaristic modes of governance led to further calls for establishing authentic Muslim states that would restore the former greatness of Islamic civilization to Muslim societies. In addition, Islamist organizations have called for resisting the foreign influence of Western foreign policies and the Western encroachment of local economies through globalization.

The removal of the Shah of Iran during the Iranian revolution of 1978–1979 was the logical outcome of such resistance among Iranians. In this instance, the fact that the Iranian revolution was a Shi'ite revolution did not matter; Sunnis and Shi'ites all over the world saw this as a model and as an opportunity to agitate against their own governments in the hopes that Islam as a religion and as a state would address the ills they believed were prevalent in their societies. They felt that the struggle against injustice, corruption, and lack of religiosity in their own societies must be turned into a holy war (*jihad*), as must the attempt to stave off Western-style secularization of society. Although not all Muslim political groups espouse the use of violence in such a *jihad,* many do in the service of attaining their ends, and these are referred to as radical Islamic groups. For them, rejecting Western cultural and political models does not mean that Western technology should be rejected, for although Western cultural and political penetration is perceived as a threat to Islamically understood means of organizing and governing society, technology is seen as something that belongs to all of humankind.

Most politicized Muslims engaging in social *jihad* or war against injustice aimed at strengthening Muslim societies from within and resisting Western-imposed political or economic models and globalization that they think are counterproductive for their societies do so through Muslim organizations that actively work in the fields of social services, education, politics, and law, without the endorsement of violence. Extremist or radical groups do, however, endorse the use of violence and turn this at will against anyone or anything they deem stands in the way of creating an Islamic society governed by *shari'a* law. Not all Muslim political parties endorse the use of violence, even though all turn to Islam as a way of life that should include political matters, and all are wary, if not outright rejecting, of Western influence. The key difference between Muslim political organizations that endorse violence and those that do not is that the latter work toward strengthening Muslim societies from within through the delivery of services intended to improve people's living conditions and address the many challenges Muslims face. In the case of organizations that espouse violence, the reasons for such violence can be understood in the context of perceived inequities and systemic inequities that exist between the West and the parts of the world in which many Muslims live. For instance, observers of Palestinian violence toward Israelis have noted that the Palestinian population has become so impoverished—not only economically, but also in terms of education, health, and hope—that radical youth believe they have nothing to lose (including their own lives) by resisting what they consider the past and ongoing U.S.-aided Israeli occupation of their lands and resources with acts of self- and other-inflicted violence.

That said, radical or extremist Muslim political organizations terrorize their own populations as much as they do the rest of the world; a case in point is the Taliban in Afghanistan. However, the complexities surrounding the rise of the Taliban make it clear that the group came into existence largely through Western efforts (and support) to create an indigenous fighting force, the Mujahideen, which was encouraged to perceive removing the Russians from Afghan soil as a holy war, or *jihad*. The Taliban stepped into the vacuum that was created after the removal of the Russians. No rebuilding efforts were undertaken in Afghanistan, despite promises to do so; thus creating the material and economic conditions that enabled radical and extremist Islamic political groups to bring home their point: the ills of society can be addressed through recourse to Islam as a way of life. For all their excesses, the Taliban succeeded in demilitarizing the population of Afghanistan and in almost eradicating the cultivation of opium-producing poppies. At the same time, their governance points to the same problems with the so-called radical Islamic solution: the Taliban moved to standard-

ize all Muslim ritual practice; the *sharï'a* as implemented by the Taliban was
not only outdated and outmoded, as argued by the reform-minded Muslim
thinkers discussed, but was also considered immutable, thereby subjecting
the Muslim population to a reign of terror with respect to the delivery of
justice. Furthermore, women were cloistered; not allowed to work outside
the home; refused education; and forced, rather than allowed to choose, to
wear the veil. Finally, the Taliban were unable to keep the West out; toward
the end of their time in power, discussions were already underway with
Western nations regarding the building of a pipeline to carry oil through
Afghanistan.

The Taliban are an extreme case of what happens when radical extremists find their way into political power; another case is that of Iran after
the Iranian revolution. Although the two can hardly bear comparison since
the Iranian mullah leadership is far more sophisticated and more highly
educated, it can be fairly said two decades after the revolution that, while
it is possible to implement Islamic law and principles as a form of social
organization and management, such a move entails understanding that
Islam is neither a fixed ideology nor a fixed body of law that can simply be
implemented at will anywhere in the world. Rather, as the Iranian case has
shown, Khomeini's initial attempt to remove women from the public economy proved counterproductive and, as women have argued, un-Islamic;
similarly, in the economic realm, refusal to work with Western (and, for
that matter, non-Western and non-Muslim) nations in a global economy
is simply not realistic. In other words, the reformists' attempts to suggest
that a dynamic Islam, through the application of human intelligence, was
capable of meeting the challenges of contemporary times remains as true
today as it was several decades ago before the fundamentalist movements
shifted the understanding of what it means to be a Muslim toward blaming
internal Muslim lack of piety and external Western encroachment as the
key factors to be "corrected."

The challenges facing Muslims today are (1) how to have viable economies in a world economy in which the industrialized nations of the world
profit through globalization, as the poor get poorer; (2) how to ensure the
delivery of health, education, and justice within Muslim majority population countries rife with authoritarian or militaristic governments, poorly
constructed economies, and lax educational, health, legal, and social service systems; (3) how to deal with the degradation of the global environment; (4) how to prevent Islam or any other ideology from being used in
the service of power-mongering; and, finally, (5) how to address growing

world militarism on the one hand, and lingering internal patriarchal and external racist attitudes, on the other. Imposing "solutions" on a country without taking into account its history, culture, and social arrangements will fail, and any efforts made internationally to ameliorate conditions in a country need to be undertaken as a process of dialogue, and solutions must be tailored to the context for which they are intended. What works in Rome simply does not necessarily work in Jakarta, although Italians and Indonesians might, through dialogue, find a way to make it work.

## Women and Islam

This discussion of political Islam has made it clear that what the Qur'an says about women is not sufficient to determine the place of women in Muslim societies. Rather, the fact that religion and religious attitudes permeate all areas of human activity means that social attitudes, treatment under the law, cultural practices, and access to health, education and social services all have a religiously informed dimension for Muslim women.

Islam, as with all major world faiths, provides in its sacred scripture the possibility for women to attain their full potential as members of the human race and as moral and spiritual agents. Indeed, the Qur'an advances the view that women are created equal to men, and, although their biological capacities differ, women are as responsible as men are for their moral actions and will be judged according to their works and degree of faith, after which they will be sent to either heaven or hell. The notion that women were created out of men (for instance, from the rib of Adam) is missing from the Qur'an, as is the notion that women were created to be of service to men. Thus, according to Islam, women were created neither from men nor for the purposes of men; rather, the two sexes were created from a single soul so that they might find comfort in each other. As a seventh-century document, the Qur'an is remarkable in giving women rights to property, inheritance, and alimony and the right to give testimony in a legal court, rights that Western women did not have until many centuries later. However, at the same time, those rights are conveyed within the social structures of the day. For instance, women may inherit, but only half of what their brothers might, and men are allowed polygamy whereas women are expected to remain monogamous. Nowhere does the Qur'an mention that women must cover their heads, although they are asked to cover their bosoms and their private parts, and modesty of dress and behavior is enjoined on both men and women.

Regardless of what the Qur'an grants to women and says about them, as with all sacred scriptures, the role of interpretation was critical in translating Qur'anic injunctions and statements on women and their rights and responsibilities into socially applicable edicts such as found in the law or *shari'a*. As with other religious traditions, men carried out much of the interpretation of sacred texts. Until the large-scale questioning of patriarchal assumptions and attitudes that came to the forefront with women's activism in the nineteenth and twentieth centuries, the men who interpreted sacred texts and set up social institutions such as the law and access to the workplace and property were imbued with the patriarchal assumption that the role of women in society was to support men in their endeavors and that women were not capable of doing anything other than their fulfilling their biological destiny of bearing and raising children and caring for families and living a life of service to family, community, and religious institutions. There are actually two movements occurring side by side: there are male-generated texts that define what women can and cannot do, and there is the reality of what women in fact do, in spite of what male-written and -interpreted texts say they can or cannot do.

In contemporary times, Muslim women's status varies by location, class, and situation. It is difficult to make broad generalizations pertaining to all Muslim women. However, some factors can be considered with respect to the status of Muslim women.

## The State

The state is a key determinant of women's place in the social structure of the country and their access to fair treatment under the law. Since the state has, as its major interest, the economic viability of the country within an international economic system, it is important for the state to harness the work and production capacities of women, who usually make up half of the population. In this regard, various states with majority Muslim populations have made public education available to women to ensure their entry into the workplace despite religiously informed social attitudes that prefer women to stay at home and care for the children. Reform-minded Muslims identified women's lack of education as one of the key factors holding Muslim societies back from development, if for no reason other than that an educated mother raises the level of awareness in her children. The age of marriage increases and fertility rates decline with higher levels of education. Literacy rates for women have improved substantially in the Middle

East and North Africa, ranging from over 80 percent in Bahrain, Jordan, Kuwait, Lebanon, Qatar, and the United Arab Emirates to lows of between 22 and 44 percent in Egypt, Iraq, Morocco, Sudan, Yemen, and Afghanistan.[3]

The state is also responsible for family law. As such, it has to contend with those agitating for family law reform and with Muslim political parties and fundamentalist organizations that consider the family to be the building block of an Islamic society and therefore wish to safeguard traditional gender roles. Whereas colonization replaced Islamic law with Western laws adapted to suit the colonized region, family law was not similarly replaced by colonial administrators, but rather assigned to religious governing bodies for interpretation. Thus, any modification of family law is perceived by fundamentalist Muslims as tampering with the core of Islam, akin to tampering with laws regulating ritual behavior such as washing before prayer and almsgiving. Yet, for women's rights activists, family law reform is key to improving the status of women, because *shari'a* law, depending on how it is applied, can allow for polygamy, the unilateral right of divorce reserved for men, child custody for the father after the children have reached a certain age depending on their gender, the inability of a woman to work or travel without her husband's permission, and so forth.

The struggle between family law reformers and conservative extremists has continued throughout the twentieth century and will likely persist until states can pass and implement reforms in the interests of the nation. Thus, for instance, in Iran, women were compelled by the imperial ruler, the Shah, to remove the veil in 1936, a move that was not considered to have been made in the interests of women even by women. However, on a more positive note, in 1966, women were accepted into the judiciary and police and armed forces, and in 1967 under the Family Protection Law, women were granted the right for mutual consent in divorce. Women also entered the political arena and held 22 seats in the 270-member parliament. With the Iranian revolution of 1978 and the establishment of Islamic law, this number fell to 2 under Khomeini. Meanwhile, the Family Protection Law of 1967 was suspended in February 1979, and, for a while, women were not allowed to practice in the medical and legal professions.[4] Similarly, in Egypt, Syria, Jordan, Pakistan, and India, reformists succeeded in reinterpreting Islamic law to the greater benefit of women; these gains were in part rolled back in places such as Pakistan under General Zia ul-Haq, who embarked on a program of Islamization masterminded by Mawlana Abu'l 'Ala Mawdudi and the Jamaat-i Islami. The Hudood Ordinances were introduced in 1979, marking a major reversal in women's rights; among other objections, the lines between adultery and rape were blurred, making the rape victim subject to punishment for adultery. Tunisia reformed its family law in 1956, after the end of French colonial rule, and continued with further reforms in the 1980s and 1990s. Justifying these reforms as new interpretations and as Islamic, the new code abolished polygamy, removed the right of men to divorce their wives unilaterally, made provisions for child custody and alimony consequent upon divorce, and increased the age of marriage as a measure against child marriages. In Egypt, family law reform passed in 1979 was recalled after some conservative opposition, and Egyptian women lost the right to remain in the family residence after divorce.

## Fundamentalism, or Islamism

Fundamentalism, often referred to in the media as Islamism, has made strides among women. The contemporary revival of Islam in all areas of life has had both positive and negative consequences for women. On the negative side, Islamic revivalism has focused a great deal of its energy on the dress, comportment, and role of Muslim women as bearing the moral burden as well as the representational responsibility of a Muslim identity as distinct from that of the once-colonizing West. Just as colonial discourses blamed Islam for the backwardness of Muslim societies—exemplified through the treatment of women in Muslim societies (veiling, seclusion, absence from the public sphere) through which colonization and Christianization was justified as bringing civilization to the natives—post-colonial Islamic discourses use the same framework of making Muslim women the symbol of Islamic identity and using that symbol to express difference from Western civilization and culture. As a result, Muslim fundamentalists or Islamists portray any attempts to change women's status in Muslim societies as Western-inspired plots to further weaken Islamic society, accusing secularist-minded Muslim activists of being tools of Western governments and Western feminism.

At the same time, fundamentalist thinkers such as Mawdudi sought to outline women's role in Islam in traditional ways, restricted to mothering and child-care and care of the family, working only when circumstances warranted, and continuing to view women as requiring men to oversee their financial and marital matters and, in some cases, their mobility. Other fundamentalist or Islamist thinkers such as Sayyid Qutb saw the role of women

Muslim girls praying. © Getty Image/21000054824.

as essential to social development and argued that women should be the managers of their own affairs and be educated as well as socially and morally responsible. A key supporter of Hasan al-Banna's Muslim Brotherhood (to which Sayyid Qutb belonged, in Egypt), Zaynab al-Ghazali (b. 1918), who founded the Muslim Women's Organization at the age of 18 in 1936 (the organization was dissolved in 1965 at her imprisonment) as a parallel organization to the Muslim Brotherhood, articulated the need to struggle on the behalf of women from an Islamic, not a Western feminist-inspired, perspective. For her, the notion of liberation for Muslim women was outrageous; in her view, Islam provided women with everything they needed, if only women knew of their rights and responsibilities under Islam. Her organization taught women about Islam, provided social services such as welfare and employment counseling for women, assistance for poor families, and an orphanage. She concurred with the revivalist and fundamentalist view that Muslim societies were backward because they did not practice Islam well and that an ideal Muslim polity should be governed by returning to the Qur'an and the practice of the Prophet—and, by extension, Islamic law. In her words, the role of women is as follows:

Women [are]...a fundamental part of the Islamic call....They are the ones who build the kind of men that we need to fill the ranks of the Islamic call. So women must be well educated, cultured, knowing of the precepts of the Koran and the Sunna, informed about world politics, why we are backward, why we don't have technology. The Muslim woman must study all these things, and then raise her son in the conviction that he must possess the scientific tools of the age, and at the same time he must understand Islam, politics, geography, and current events. He must rebuild the Islamic nation. We Muslims only carry arms in order to spread peace. We want to purify the world of unbelief, atheism, oppression, and persecution.... Islam does not forbid women to actively participate in public life. It does not prevent her from working, entering into politics, and expressing her opinion, or from being anything, as long as that does not interfere with her first duty as a mother, the one who first trains her children in the Islamic call. So her first, holy, and most important mission is to be a mother and wife. She cannot ignore this priority. If she then finds she has free time, she may participate in public activities. Islam does not forbid her.[5]

Al-Ghazali did not follow her own proscriptions. She married twice and both times stipulated in her marriage contract that she held the right to divorce her husband should he get in the way of her mission. Indeed, she divorced her first husband on those grounds. Thus, her own first priority was the mission to be an Islamic activist and to work for the establishment of an Islamic state, not, as she recommends for all other women, the "first, holy, and most important mission" of wife and mother.

Nonetheless, al-Ghazali presages how Islamist women have found fundamentalism a positive force in their lives and in their struggles for change. Certainly, there were and are Muslim women activists, many of whom are secularist in orientation and feminist in inspiration; however, the growth of women's Islamist organizations has far overrun secular and feminist organizations in popularity and number. While the use of the veil as a political tool by women—whether in resistance movements against colonization such as during the Algerian war of independence or during the Iranian revolution where the Shah was perceived as a dictator who had sold off Iranian economic and political interests to the West—increasingly, under Islamist ideology, women began to use the veil as a sign of their proud identification with Islam as an alternative ideology to Western secularization. The emphasis by women's Islamist organizations on education in the quest for women's rights and responsibilities under Islam has enabled such Muslim women to enter the public and the political sphere to campaign for rights that they argue are given to them under Islam. More secular-minded Muslim women's organizations have had to learn to cooperate with these larger Islamist women's organizations. In Morocco, for instance, a campaign to remove polygamy was met with overwhelming resistance from Islamist women who argued that removing polygamy would leave many women with no other means through which to support themselves in the absence of readily available jobs for women. Another positive effect of Islamist women's organizations is that women are coming together to provide much-needed social services and are negotiating for women to gain access to education, the workplace, fairer legal treatment, and public policy—as can be seen in organizational advances being made in places as distant as Iran and Indonesia.

Many secular Muslim women, however, are wary of Islamist organizations that claim that a Muslim state and Islamic solution is the only way Muslim societies can flourish and prosper and that reject all that is Western with the exception of technology. However, perhaps this is a phase through which Muslim societies must pass to address the many social and political issues they face.

### Woman-friendly Interpretations

As Muslim women acquire the tools for studying sacred texts and the law, challenges to time-honored male and patriarchally informed interpretations are being made. Among the most recent can be counted Amina Wadud's *Quran and Woman* (1992) and Asma Barlas's *"Believing Women" in Islam: Unreading Patriarchal Interpretations* (2002), both of which make the case that traditional interpretations suggesting that the Qur'an supports polygamy, wife-beating, seclusion, male guardianship, and inequitable treatment under Islamic law can no longer be sustained. Rather, they argue, if the Qur'an is read from a contemporary consciousness and with full awareness of the patriarchal assumptions of prior male readers from the eighth century onward, then it is clear that the Qur'an is much more an advocate of human equality between the sexes and of human accountability to God in moral terms than it is of men's rights over women. Women's groups in Indonesia and women's magazines in Iran are also finding that the Qur'an does not curtail women's rights to self-development in the manner understood to date. It remains to be seen whether such efforts will eventually translate into social change.

### Hot-Button Issues

Wearing of the veil is sometimes automatically seen as a symbol of oppression for Muslim women, but their relationship to it varies depending on the woman's cultural and social location. The forcible removal of the veil by Reza Shah in Iran in 1936 distressed many women who felt naked without it. For many women it is a time-honored cultural tradition and a sign of their piety. Furthermore, many Muslim women think that the West's fixation on the veil prevents addressing the real concerns of Muslim women: access to a decent standard of living, health care, education, the workplace, legal equity and fairness, clean water, safe neighborhoods, and peace.

Apart from the veil, two issues plague Western perceptions of Muslim women: female genital surgery and honor killings, both of which have been justified in the name of Islam. Honor killings have been claimed in the Middle East, North Africa, and South Asia as the male right to discipline women who dishonor their families through being accused of adultery or perceived intimacy with men not among the familial relatives. The problem has been further compounded by social attitudes toward female sexuality, male privilege and honor, and judicial failure to take the perpetrators to task. Indeed, an Amnesty International report on honor killings in Pakistan found that prevailing social attitudes result in the killings often going unreported or, when they are reported, neither the police nor the judicial system responding in ways that would hold the killers to task. Furthermore, in Pakistan and in other places where honor killings occur, the law allows for the perpetrator to go free or receive a reduced sentence if it can be shown that the man was subjected to undue provocation (and sometimes the hint of an illicit relationship is sufficient grounds for undue provocation). There is often an economic motive underlying the honor killing, as a new wife will bring with her further bride wealth.

Activists have sought to address the issue of honor killings in different ways. Asma Jehangir, a human rights lawyer and head of the human rights organization in Pakistan, has argued that the state must do more to protect its female citizens, and that the practice has nothing to do with Islam. Riffat Hassan, a Pakistani American, Muslim academic, and activist, has argued that prevailing social attitudes toward women in Muslim societies must be addressed by examining the theological reasons for women's low estimation and status in society. She has shown that the biblical notion of woman as created from the rib of the man for the purpose of the man entered Muslim discourse on the Qur'an and thereby contributed to making women secondary citizens in Muslim societies. She has met with General Pervez Musharraf and discussed the importance of disengaging such practices from Islam, especially with respect to protecting women in the legal sphere. Honor killings have since been criminalized in Pakistan, and activists in other regions with Muslim majority populations are attempting to bring about similar results.[6]

Female genital surgery occurs primarily in the region along the Nile River in Africa, although some cases have been reported in Indonesia and elsewhere. Muslims do not practice female genital surgery anywhere else in the world (although immigrants, whether Muslim or not, from regions where it is practiced illicitly continue the practice in the countries to which they migrate, including North America and Europe), and it is not mentioned in the Qur'an (neither is male circumcision). Although the practice predates Islam and was a local cultural practice already in effect when Muslims reached Africa, it appears to have been absorbed into Islam and is practiced in those regions by tribal groups, as well as by Coptic and Jewish communities in Egypt. The Islamic rationale for circumcision being a Muslim practice was apparently provided by the *hadith* literature, which stated that Abraham asked Hagar to pierce herself in three places to draw blood and appease Sarah's (his wife's) anger against Hagar for giving Abraham a son and for being haughty about it. The practice is referred to as purification (*taharah*); apart from its Islamic rationale, it is a traditional practice that is thought to contain a woman's sexuality and prevent her promiscuity. Female genital surgery varies in scope; at its worst, it entails removing all external female genitalia and sewing closed the vaginal opening, which is ritually opened at the time of marriage. Apart from the psychological problems it causes, the painful procedure also poses severe health risks for women and can lead to complications during childbirth. Researchers have noted that denouncing the practice only leads to resistance, because women who participate in the practice believe that it is a traditional custom that must be retained to improve opportunities for marriage, for aesthetic reasons, and to be considered a good woman. Instead, researchers suggest that activists work within the cultural and social context of the practice so as not to eradicate it but to minimize its scope and impact, perhaps through a symbolic "nicking" of the genitals rather than removal of parts. Muslim organizations in Egypt and the Sudan have begun campaigns to show that Islam neither requires the practice nor supports it. In Egypt, initial attempts to eradicate the practice were met with opposition from conservative elements until the Shaykh of al-Azhar, the premier training facility for Muslim clergy, issued a statement saying that Islam did not require such a practice.

## WESTERN PERCEPTION OF ISLAMIC PRACTICES

Since 9/11, Muslims all over the world have struggled with the Western perception of Islam as a violent and misogynist faith; indeed, for many, the war on Afghanistan was not seen as an attempt to remove the Taliban for refusing to hand Osama bin Laden over to the United States, but as a war to remove the Taliban for their ill treatment of women. In the United States, Muslims have come under greater scrutiny with regard to their movements and their political activities and affiliations, and their charitable organizations have been shut down or closely examined because of the fear that they may be involved in terrorist activities. At the same time, many faith organizations and educational institutions have attempted to learn more about the Muslims in their midst and to understand Islam in an attempt to build bridges of understanding. In Europe, fears of Muslim fundamentalism and terrorism have resulted in the banning of veils for women in France and in parts of Germany. For some European Muslims, this is seen as part of the ongoing racism against Muslims; for other Muslims, this move is applauded as upholding Western secularist separation of church and state. However, banning the veil does not address the issue of fundamentalism or terrorism, for as long as Muslims continue to feel threatened or impoverished, there will continue to be those who preach the return to Islam as a solution for social ills. Palestinian, Chechen, Filippino, and Kashmiri Muslims struggling for nationhood continue to be labeled Muslim terrorists in their own countries, and violence in those regions will can be expected to continue as long as the political issues are not addressed. The genocide in the Sudan is an example of intra-Muslim warfare as well as Muslim-Christian warfare that has at its root the struggle for control of valuable resources.

Many Muslims in different parts of the world believe that they need to retake the public sphere from fundamentalist voices that have been heard most loudly there. As Muslims debate the uses to which their faith has been put, and as local and international organizations work to address the living conditions of peoples around the world, many hope that the foundational values of Islam—such as good works, charity, compassion, justice, and good will toward all of humankind—will prevail.

## NOTES

1. See also John Esposito, *Islam: The Straight Path* (New York: Oxford University Press, 1998), Chapter 4, for a fuller discussion of Islamic political movements.

2. Ibid., 152.

3. Valentine M. Moghadam, *Modernizing Women: Gender and Social Change in the Middle East,* Second Edition (Boulder, CO: Lynne Rienner, 2003), 140.

4. Bruce B. Lawrence, *Shattering the Myth: Islam Beyond Violence* (Princeton, NJ: Princeton University Press, 1998), 113–114.

5. Quoted in Leila Ahmed, *Women and Gender in Islam* (New Haven, CT: Yale University Press, 1992), 199, citing the translation of Valerie J. Hoffman, "An Islamic Activist: Zeinab al-Ghazali," in *Women and the Family in the Middle East,* ed. Elizabeth Warnock Fernea (Austin: University of Texas Press, 1985), 236–237.

6. Although Islam is used to justify the practice in Muslim areas, a similar practice in India is justified through Hinduism, suggesting that honor killings belong in the larger realm of violence against women globally, justified locally through whatever ideology is available.

# 5

# RITUALS AND HOLIDAYS

Muslim law books generally begin with ritual practices, and it is here that the notion of five or six pillars of Islam as minimal ritual obligations for all Muslims is found. Traditionally, the five main pillars are the witnessing (*shahada*), prayer (*salat*), payment of obligatory alms or charity (*zakat*), fasting (*sawm*), and pilgrimage (*hajj*). *Jihad,* or struggle in the path of God, is often considered a sixth pillar; however, it will not be considered in this chapter because each Muslim interprets *jihad* in a manner most consistent with his or her understanding of Islam. For some, this term has political overtones; for others, it translates into social justice activism; for yet others it means the struggle to uphold moral parameters of doing good to self and others and to desist from any harmful acts or thoughts.

Muslims engage in many forms of ritual activity to express their faith that go far beyond the pillars. For instance, Muslims may take care to wash their hands scrupulously before every meal in emulation of the Prophet's custom of doing so; others may engage in night-long repetitions of one of God's names (an activity known as *dhikr*); others may perform or attend sessions of devotional poetry set to music and executed with a high degree of musical virtuosity and vocal mastery (*qawwali*); others may visit shrines of saints and make entreaties directed at God through them; and others may deliver food or supplies anonymously to those in need at regular intervals. This chapter explores the pillars as well as a few other ritual observances common to many Muslims, including commemorative days such as the birthday of the Prophet, the ascension of the Prophet, and the two 'Id celebrations.

## WITNESSING

The act of witnessing (*shahada*) by uttering the statement, "There is no god but God, and Muhammad is (God's) messenger"—to which Shi'ites will often add "and 'Ali is the Master of the believers"—has no clearly defined limits on when and how it must be uttered. As a cardinal belief, it must be uttered over newborn children to attest to their membership in the Muslim community; it is spoken publicly by those who convert; and it is heard and uttered daily by Muslims during the call to prayer. Muslims will recite it during prayer and at times of strain or death and commemorate it in inscriptions in tile, pottery, and coins. As an article of faith, theologians, mystics, philosophers, artists, and poets meditate upon the *shahada.*

## PRAYER

Many forms of personal and communal prayer (*salat*) are observed by Muslims for the purposes of giving praise to God; thanksgiving; making supplications; expressing lamentation; and asking for intercession, help, and guidance. Such prayers are known variously as *du'a, munajat, girya-u-zari, tasbih,* and *dhikr* and are considered meritorious and purifying. The formal, legally obligatory prayers observed by Muslims at regular times during the day are called *salat,* and they comprise bodily postures and recitations from the Qur'an, oriented toward the Ka'aba, a cubed structure in Mecca, Saudi Arabia.[1] Prayer is performed five times a day by Sunni Muslims at specified times: early morning (*al-fajr*), noon (*al-duhr*), mid-afternoon (*al-'asr*), sunset (*al-maghrib*), and evening (*al-'isha*). Shi'ite Muslims pray three times a day and combine the noon and mid-afternoon prayers, and the sunset and evening prayers. Muslims are not required to be in congregation for daily prayers, although they are encouraged to congregate at the mosque to do so. The Friday noon (*al-jum'a*) congregational prayer is required, accompanied by a sermon (*khutba*). Other obligatory prayers are those performed at funerals and at eclipses of the sun and moon. The prayer performed during the two 'Id celebrations are recommended but not required.

In preparation for the prayer, a believer must perform ablutions called *wudu,* through which minor impurities may be removed. Impurities are of two kinds: major and minor. A person enters a state of major impurity through seminal emissions or other bodily emissions such as menstruation and postpartum bleeding. In such cases, ritual purity is restored by bathing, and it is recommended that every Muslim bathe before attending the Friday congregational prayer. Minor impurities are brought about by sleeping; bodily functions such as urinating, defecating, or passing wind; touching the genitals; or sexual contact short of engaging in sex. These may be removed by performing ablutions, which entail, according to Qur'anic prescription (Q. 5:6) washing the face and hands up to the elbows and wiping the head and the feet to the ankles, all of which must be done with water, with the right side being washed first, following the Prophet's custom. If water is unavailable, such as when traveling, then sand or dust may be used instead. Many mosque compounds have areas where the faithful may perform ablutions. Short prayers (*du'a*) are often recited as each bodily part is washed; for example, while the feet are being washed, one might say, "God, Make my feet firm on the Path, on the Day when the feet easily slip away from the Path!"[2] Along with purification, the believer must take care to be appropriately dressed and to approach the prayer with proper intention (*niyya*). The believer's intention to pray is articulated and the number of cycles of prostration the believer intends to perform are specified. The believer—having been purified and dressed appropriately—then faces Mecca in a mental and emotional frame of mind that is appropriate to the performance of prayer.

At the approach of the time for prayer, the call to prayer (*adhan*) is sounded, usually by the *mu'adhdhin* (one who calls to prayer). Travelers to Muslim countries often awaken to the recitation of the call to prayer as it is broadcast through loudspeakers. Often several calls to prayer may be seconds apart emanating from different mosques in the city. The call to prayer, recited in Arabic, consists of the following statements:

> God is the Most Great (four times)
> I testify that there is no god but God (twice)
> I testify that Muhammad is the Messenger of God (twice)
> Hasten to prayer! (twice)
> Hasten to salvation! (twice)
> Prayer is better than sleep (only before the dawn prayer; not recited by Shi'ites)
> Hasten to the best of actions (said twice by Shi'ites only)
> God is the Most Great (twice)
> There is no god but God (Sunnis once, Shi'ites twice)

Those who wish proceed to the mosque (in Arabic, *masjid*, "place of prostration") and line up in rows facing Mecca, usually with men in the

Tile panel from a mihrab, Iran, early 14th century. Molded stone-past; painted underglaze with color and overglaze with luster. Courtesy of the Freer Gallery of Art and Arthur M. Sackler Gallery, Smithsonian Institution, Washington, D.C.: Gift of Charles Lang Freer, F1909.319.

front and women and children either behind them or in a separate room or balcony. In many contemporary mosques in North America, men and women stand in rows side by side, separated by a curtain or a space. In a mosque, the direction of Mecca is traditionally marked by a recess in the wall, and here the leader (*imam*) of the prayer stands, the rows of the congregation behind him. Each person silently whispers his or her intention (*niyya*) to pray, and the *salat* proper begins.

The basic unit of the *salat* consists of a cycle, called *rak'a,* and each *salat* has a specified number of cycles. The morning *salat* requires two cycles; the noon, afternoon, and evening *salats* each require four cycles; and the evening *salat* requires three cycles. These numbers of *rak'a* are obligatory, and worshipers may increase them if they wish.

## ALMSGIVING

The payment of alms (*zakat*) is a legal obligation on all Muslims, introduced by Muhammad in Medina, based upon various Qur'anic passages that identify the giving of alms as a virtue (Qur'an 23:4), a sign of righteousness (Qur'an 76:8), and as sharing the benevolence bestowed on humans by God (Qur'an 35:29). The term is used almost synonymously with *sadaqa*, which means giving charity and was known to pre-Islamic Arabs through the Jewish practice of the same name. The key difference between almsgiving and charity is that, in later Islamic law, almsgiving is made a legal obligation whereas charity remains voluntary. In the Qur'an, the terms are used interchangeably. For example, in verse 9:60, the recipients of charity are named as the poor, the needy, those who care for them, and travelers. That verse, along with Qur'an 2:215, which names parents, relatives, orphans, travelers, slaves, and the poor and needy as among those meriting almsgiving, became the basis for later laws governing the disbursement of funds collected through obligatory donations.

Almsgiving expresses the human relationship to God in the form of giving thanks for all the bounties that God has made available and is considered an extension of worship. In addition, almsgiving establishes a relationship with one's community, redistributing wealth in ways that materialize the values of care and compassion for others. The notion of purity is embedded in almsgiving: by giving alms, a Muslim purifies what remains and renders it lawful wealth in the sense that it is hoped that the remainder will cause one no harm but rather will benefit oneself and others. Wealth that has not been thus purified is considered unclean.

At the Prophet's death, many Bedouin tribes refused to continue paying *zakat*, and Abu Bakr, the first caliph, institutionalized its payment as a form of religious tax. The legal regimes that developed thereafter maintained almsgiving as a religious obligation on all adult Muslims (most legal schools consider 16 years to be the age at which adulthood is attained). Crops, fruit, livestock, gold and silver, and merchandise were taxed, and payment formulas were developed. For instance, the tax on crops was ten percent to be paid at harvest, whereas the tax on gold and silver was two and a half percent, payable at the end of each year. Under the caliph system, *zakat* was due to an appointed tax collector and then was disbursed by the government; in contemporary times, *zakat* may be paid, depending on the Muslim's country of residence, to a government-authorized tax collector, a mosque organization, a charitable organization, or directly to the categories of recipients mentioned in the Qur'an. Most legal schools also made it obligatory for all who could afford it a special category of *zakat* payable at the end of the fasting period in Ramadan, *zakat at-fitr*, entailing the provision of one day's food for a needy person. Both obligatory giving and voluntary giving are considered extremely meritorious and a source of purification, which is the basis of spiritual development. By and large, almsgiving today is a matter of individual conscience. Almsgiving in its many forms is considered part and parcel of the Muslim ethic of social justice, echoed throughout the Qur'an, as in 2:261–3: "Those who spend their wealth in Allah's way are like a grain that grows seven ears, in every ear a hundred grains.... Those who spend their wealth for the cause of Allah and afterward make not reproach and injury to follow what they have spent, their reward is with their Lord. No fear shall come upon them, nor shall they grieve.... A kind word with forgiveness is better than almsgiving followed by injury."

## FASTING

Fasting (*sawm*) occurs during the month of Ramadan. The Arabic term for fasting, *sawm*, meaning "to be at rest," is connected also to silence, according to the Qur'anic reference found in Qur'an 19:26, in which Mary is told to say: "I have made a vow of *sawm* to the Merciful, wherefore I speak to no one this day".[3] Qur'an 2:183–185 prescribes fasting for Muslims, just as it was prescribed "for those before you" (that is, the Jews and the Christians) during the month of Ramadan, "in which the Qur'an was sent down, a clear guidance for humankind." Exceptions are made for the ill and for travelers, for Allah "desires not hardship for you." Qur'an 2:187 specifies that eating, drinking, and sexual relations are permitted until "the white thread becomes distinct to you from the black thread of the dawn," at which time the fast must be observed until nightfall. During the period of fasting, God exhorts fasters to "be at your devotions in the mosques." Technically, the fasting period ought to begin as soon as the new moon has been sighted heralding the month of Ramadan; often this occurs on the last days (29th or 30th) of the previous month, Sha'ban.

Muslim legal scholars defined fasting as abstinence from those things that break the fast. They also devised qualification criteria for fasting: a person had to be a Muslim in full possession of his or her senses; it was obligatory for a child older than 10 years of age to fast; a fasting woman must not be menstruating or just have given birth; and the person fasting must be physically fit. People who intend to fast must declare their intention to do so in their prayers. The fast was considered invalid if food or drink were ingested during the fast or if the person engaged in sexual activity. Legal scholars also determined that the fast would be invalidated in cases of deliberate vomiting, inhaling tobacco smoke, deliberate sexual emission, menstruation, intoxication, and being of an unsound mind. Missed days of fasting because of travel or illness may be made up at a later time.

Ending the fast (*iftar*) should be a conscious, deliberate act. The fast ends as soon as the sun sets, and Muslim tradition holds that the Prophet typically ended his fast with two dates and water before the evening prayers were recited, after which a full meal was eaten. Muslims will often celebrate the end of the fast with gatherings of family and friends, during which poetry and other entertainments are enjoyed.

Obligatory fasting includes fasting during the month of Ramadan and may be undertaken for other reasons, such as during a period of drought or if one has taken a vow that entails fasting. Voluntary fasting is recommended on the day of 'Ashura' (see the discussion of Muharram later in this chapter) and, if possible, on the day preceding as well as the day following it; on the day of 'Arafa (discussed in the section on pilgrimage); for six days from the second to seventh of the Muslim calendar month Shawwal; for ten days in the Muslim calendar month of Dhu al-Hijja; and on the day of Mi'raj. Additional days historically recommended include every Monday and Thursday; the first, middle, and last day of each Muslim calendar month; and the days of the "white" nights of each lunar month (12th, 13th, 14th, and 15th) and the days of the "black" nights (28th, 29th, 30th, and sometimes the 1st). The *hadith* literature further reports that the Prophet recommended the practice of fasting every other day. A well-known *hadith* reported by the legal scholar and theologian Ahmad b. Hanbal declared, "The scent of the breath of a fasting man is more pleasant than the scent of musk" to God. Fasting is forbidden during the two 'Id celebrations, 'Id al-Adha and 'Id al-Fitr.

Al-Ghazali (d. 1111 C.E.), the noted medieval theologian, jurist, and mystic, considered fasting to be an antidote to the workings of Satan, who led humans astray through their enjoyment of eating and drinking. For al-Ghazali, fasting enabled humans to discipline their passions, and he considers fasting not just on the physical level of abstaining from food, drink, and sexual activity, but also on the moral and mental level of abstaining from all sinful desires and actions. Fasting at any time, whether obligatory or voluntary, is considered a time for atonement of past transgressions and the renewing of a commitment to be more mindful of one's ethical behavior toward God, oneself, and others. Many view fasting as a time in which to reflect with gratitude on the bounties provided by God and a time during which awareness of the need for compassion for those who go hungry or suffer is strengthened for the whole year.

## PILGRIMAGE

The pilgrimage (*hajj*) to Mecca is considered to be a duty incumbent on all adult Muslims who are able-bodied and financially able to undertake the journey at least once in their lifetimes. Another person can be appointed to make the pilgrimage on one's behalf, especially if the Muslim is elderly or infirm.[4] The pilgrimage is traditionally performed during the month of pilgrimage—Dhu al-Hijja—from the eighth to the twelfth days, although a Muslim may make the *hajj* at any time of the year (another popular pilgrimage time is during the Muslim calendar month Rajab). The pilgrimage consists of the many rites that make up the lesser pilgrimage (*'umra*); a visit to the plain of 'Arafat to observe standing; stone-throwing at the plain of Muzdalifa; a ritual sacrifice in observance of the Festival of Sacrifice ('Id al-Adha); and the concluding rite of haircutting (*taqsir*) that signals the end of the *hajj*. Once the pilgrimage is over, Muslims may continue with a visit to Medina to sites such as the Prophet's tomb before returning to Mecca and leaving for home. The pilgrimage season lasts the three months of Shawwal, Ramadan, and Dhu al-Hijja. Many pilgrims arrive during the month of Shawwal, observe the fasts of Ramadan while in Mecca, and remain for the pilgrimage in Dhu al-Hijja, celebrating 'Id al-Adha before returning home. A pilgrim is henceforth accorded the title *Hajji*, meaning "one who has performed the pilgrimage."

There are pre-Islamic antecedents to the ceremonies performed during the pilgrimage, but the rites performed at the Ka'aba in Mecca were introduced by Muhammad seven years after the Muslim emigration from Mecca, which occurred in 622 C.E. Muhammad was unable to undertake the pilgrimage to Mecca until the year he died, in 632 C.E. The annual performance of the pilgrimage dates from this time. Because Islam follows a lunar calendar, the period of the pilgrimage cycles through different seasons, falling 10 to 11 days earlier than the previous year and completing the entire cycle of seasons every three decades or so.

In preparation for the annual pilgrimage, the Ka'aba is draped in a gold-embroidered black brocade covering known as the *kiswa,* prepared in Egypt each year. The *shahada* or testament to faith is woven in gold embroidery into this covering, along with fine calligraphy of Qur'anic verses in a band about two-thirds of the way down the cloth. The garment is taken down each year in the Muslim calendar month Dhu al-Qada, and pieces are sold off as keepsakes, and a new garment is placed on the Ka'aba at the end of the pilgrimage rites.

In pre-modern times, pilgrims traveled to Mecca by land in caravans or by sea; the journey was long and difficult, punctuated by stops on the way for supplies and to rest. Car, air, and rail travel options have made getting to Mecca for the annual *hajj* much easier, resulting in between 2 and 3 million pilgrims attending each year, in contrast to the figure of approximately 200,000 pilgrims noted at the turn of the twentieth century. Pilgrims are responsible for settling all debts as well as their affairs before embarking on the pilgrimage and to have drawn up a will in case they die before returning from the pilgrimage. A person who dies while on pilgrimage is considered to be an extremely fortunate martyr and is guaranteed entrance into paradise. Advances in health care have significantly reduced the number of pilgrims who die each year on the strenuous journey.

Before arriving in Mecca, the pilgrim puts on garments called *ihram,* signifying entering a state of holiness and readiness for the pilgrimage. For men, the *ihram* is a white, seamless, two-piece garment that erases all traces of class and status, thereby rendering the pilgrims equal before God. Women may also wear an *ihram*-type garment, but most dress according to their regional customs, displaying the diversity of cultures espoused by Muslims.

Pilgrims enter Mecca through a number of checkpoints, beyond which non-Muslims may not progress. If they have not already done so, pilgrims must don the *ihram* at this point. Each pilgrim renews his or her intention (*niyya*) to perform the pilgrimage and its rites; henceforth, until the end of the pilgrimage, the pilgrim is forbidden to have sexual intercourse, clip nails, hunt, wear perfume or jewelry, cut hair, and argue. As they approach Mecca, and throughout the *hajj,* pilgrims recite the *talbiyya:*

> Here I am, O our God, here I am! (*labbayk allahumma labbayk!*)
> You who are without any associate, here I am!
> To You are praise, blessing and power.

Pilgrims proceed into Mecca through the Gate of Peace (*bab al-salam*) to recitations of verses from the Qur'an and continue onward to walk around the Ka'aba in a counterclockwise direction seven times, in a rite known as the *tawaf.* This rite is performed three times: once upon entering Mecca, once after the ritual haircutting after the sacrifice, and once before leaving Mecca. Pilgrims extend their arms toward the Black Stone embedded five feet above the ground in the eastern corner of the Ka'aba if they are not close enough to touch it; the Black Stone is considered a sign of God's covenant with Abraham and Ishmael.

After the *tawaf,* pilgrims perform two cycles of prostration prayer at the Place of Abraham (*maqam Ibrahim*), believed to be the place where Abraham worshipped while building the Ka'aba. The pilgrims then perform the rite of *sa'y,* running or walking seven times between the two hills Safa and Marwa, in emulation of Hagar's panic-stricken search for water for Isma'il (Ishmael), her son by Abraham. Legend has it that Isma'il's heel struck water where he had been left, and the wellspring is named Zamzam, from which pilgrims take a vial of water. The total distance covered amounts to a little less than 10,000 feet. At this point, pilgrims symbolically mark the end of the *'umra* rites. Now begin the rites related to the pilgrimage proper, beginning with a sermon on seventh day of Dhu al-Hijja at the Grand Mosque of Mecca reminding pilgrims of their duties during the pilgrimage.

On 8th of Dhu al-Hijja, pilgrims move eastward toward Mina, where they stop for the night, or to 'Arafat. The 9th of Dhu al-Hijja is spent standing in the valley or plain of 'Arafat; pilgrims are expected to stand for at least an hour between noon and sunset. The act of standing (*wuquf*) is the central and obligatory rite of the pilgrimage, for during it pilgrims contemplate, each in his or her aloneness with God, the test to which Abraham was put when asked by God to sacrifice his son. 'Arafat also derives its significance as having been the place where the Qur'an "descended" or was revealed to the Prophet, and it was here that the Prophet stopped to deliver a sermon to those who had accompanied him on his final and only pilgrimage to the Ka'aba in Mecca, during the year of his death. For those on pilgrimage, this is a time for solitary prayer, repentance, renewal of commitment, and the giving of praise and thanks to God. At sunset, the pilgrims move to the plain of Muzdalifa, and communal prayers combining the evening and night prayers are recited, after which 49 pebbles are collected for stone-throwing rites.

The next day, after the morning prayers, pilgrims leave Muzdalifa for Mina, where at a site called *jamrat al-'akaba* seven pebbles are flung at the devil for having attempted to dissuade Isma'il from cooperating with his father's decision to comply with God's command to sacrifice him. On this day, if the pilgrim wishes, a goat or a sheep may be ritually slaughtered. In contemporary times, the Saudi government has much of the meat packaged for later use and distribution. The 'Id al-Adha is celebrated; pilgrims may now proceed with the ritual shaving of the head or *taqsir* (sometimes a token piece of hair is cut off) and return to Mecca for another *tawaf* around the newly adorned Ka'aba. The pilgrims will spend the next three days in Mina, congregating and visiting in a festive spirit, with the obligation of casting seven stones at each of the three pillars within Mina, ending finally with stoning the pillar of 'Aqaba. Pilgrims usually leave Mina on the 12th or 13th, stopping one last time at Mecca to perform a final *tawaf* around the Ka'aba before going home or visiting sites connected to the early days of Islam such as the Prophet's tomb and mosque in Medina.

Through the centuries, Muslims have reflected extensively on the spiritual significance of the pilgrimage. According to the *hadith*, performing the pilgrimage results in the forgiveness of all sins. Here Muslims become cognizant of the vastness and international nature of the worldwide Muslim community (*ummah*), a community of fellowship and surrender to God. Muslims reenact their connection to Ibrahim (Abraham), mentioned in the Qur'an as the first to have surrendered to God's will—that is, the first

Tent city for the *Hajj* pilgrims on the Plain of Arafat. Courtesy of the Saudi Information Office, Washington, D.C.

*muslim*. They reflect on the difficult ethical choices made by Abraham regarding whether to obey God, by Isma'il (Ishmael) regarding whether to succumb to the devil's entreaty that Isma'il not comply with his father's wishes, and by Hagar regarding whether to trust in God's compassion and benevolence as she hungered in the desert fearful for herself and her son, and they see a sign of God's bounty and grace as Isma'il's heel strikes the ground to reveal the flowing waters of the well known as Zamzam.

The many linkages to Abraham and his family are brought to mind as Muslims remember that Abraham is thought to have built the Ka'aba (according to legend, the place where Adam and Eve fell to earth) with Isma'il; close to the Ka'aba there is a dome in which is preserved a tablet bearing the imprint of Abraham's feet. There is also a trough that is remembered as the place where Abraham and Isma'il mixed the mortar for the Ka'aba. At the northwest corner of the Ka'aba is a circular wall where Isma'il and his mother Hagar are said to be buried.

As they stand at the plain of 'Arafat, Muslims reflect on the Qur'an as a source of guidance revealed as a sign of God's compassion and mercy for humankind. And because 'Arafat is significant at both the beginning and end of the Prophet's career, Muslims also reflect upon the difficult mission of the Prophet as he introduced monotheism in a polytheistic environment and suffered hardship while preaching the revelation. It is not surprising to find that meditations on the pilgrimage and what it signifies for the development of the soul continue long after the pilgrim has returned. In a famous poem, the Central Asian poet and philosopher Nasir Khusraw (d. 1074) chides a returning pilgrim for not having thrown out his shameful actions when he cast the stones at Satan, for not having sacrificed his ego when he sacrificed the lamb, and for not having surrendered his soul to God while standing at the plains of 'Arafat.[5]

## BIRTH OF THE PROPHET

The Prophet's birthday celebrations are held on the Muslim calendar date of the 12th of Rabi' ul-Awwal (which is believed by some to be also the date of his death). The birthday of the Prophet is generally referred to as his *maulid,* and the alternative term, *milad,* is also used. The Egyptian historian Maqrizi (d. 1442) described a *milad* celebration from Fatimid records dating from the tenth to twelfth centuries, on which occasion scholars delivered lectures and sermons, sweets were distributed, and alms were given to the poor. The Mamluks, a dynasty that ruled Egypt during the fourteenth and fifteenth centuries, continued such traditions. A thirteenth-century eyewitness account described *milad* celebrations entailing elaborate food preparation for guests, prayer meetings and sermons, mystical dance performances, candlelit processions, and shadow plays. In Turkey, mosques are festooned with candles or lights. Many *maulid* celebrations include the recitation of poetry in honor of the Prophet, often expressing the deep love felt by the poet for the blessing received by humankind in the person of the Prophet. Tapes of such recitations may be found in bazaars or marketplaces throughout Muslim countries. In some regions, such as South Asia, the 12 days leading up to the birthday of the Prophet were commemorated through the sounding of drums, special prayers for the Prophet, exhibitions of paintings, lectures, dance, acrobatics, and the performance of heart-stirring poems (*na'ats*) in praise of the Prophet. Such popular manifestations of love for the Prophet were often denounced by theologians who deemed only recitations of the Qur'an and sermons to be appropriate modes of celebration of the Prophet's birth. In contemporary times, it is not unusual to find cities with large Muslim populations festooned with flags and other decorations. There also might be special features on radio and television and in print media and gatherings where poetry, music, sermons, and lectures are enjoyed. During these gatherings, attention is often drawn to the miraculous events surrounding the Prophet's birth.

Such miracle stories relate that the angels and spirits (*jinn*) congratulated themselves on the Prophet's birth, that gardens blossomed, and the sky came close to the earth as his birth took place. Muhammad's associations with light metaphors are expressed—for example, his mother's womb is thought to emanate a light at his birth, and poets have drawn upon the Qur'anic epithet for Muhammad, "a shining lamp," to tell of how the whole world was illuminated at his birth. Some stories relate how a light shone from his father's forehead on the night that Muhammad was conceived. The *hadith* literature records that Asiya, the wife of the Pharaoh, who raised Moses, and Mary, the mother of Jesus, attended Muhammad's mother, Amina, during her labor. Not only is Muhammad considered to have been born free of all physical impurities, but apparently he was also born circumcised, a detail that is the basis of popular Muslim justifications for male circumcision, which is not mentioned in the Qur'an. The Turkish poet Suleyman Chelebi (d. 1419 C.E.) celebrated such details in verse, and versions of his poem are still recited during *milad* celebrations in Turkey, in which Muhammad is described as "he so pure/Will suffuse the world with light."[6]

## NIGHT OF POWER

*Laylat al-Qadr* or the Night of Power, which falls on the 27th night of the Muslim lunar calendar month of Ramadan, is described in Sura 97 of the Qur'an as a night that is better than a thousand months, during which the angels descend with blessings. During the night, the Qur'an was first revealed to Muhammad. Muslim communities around the world often commemorate this occasion by staying up all night for prayer and sermons and recitations of the names of God and hymns of praise. The Night of Power culminates the days of fasting undertaken during the month of Ramadan and is considered to be the night when human and divine are at their closest proximity.

## NIGHT JOURNEY AND ASCENSION

Qur'an 17:1 alludes to an event that graphically portrays for Muslims Muhammad's ability to traverse the distance between the physical world and the spiritual world, from the plane of humanity to the realm of divinity: "Praise Him, who traveled in one night with His servant from the Masjid al-Haram to the Masjid al-Aqsa, whose surroundings We blessed, in order to show him Our signs." According to Muslim tradition, the one to be praised is the angel Gabriel, the servant is Muhammad, the Masjid al-Haram is the Ka'aba in Mecca, and the Masjid al-Aqsa is a reference to Jerusalem, whether in its earthly or in its heavenly form. The term *mi'raj*, understood as Muhammad's ascension to God's presence, means a ladder, and there are several Qur'anic references to a ladder connecting heaven and earth.

The *hadith* literature furnishes great detail on the ascension. It is reported that angels came upon Muhammad while he was sleeping, opened his heart, and washed away all doubt, idolatry, and error with water drawn from the well of Zamzam and filled him instead with wisdom and belief. Thus purified, Muhammad was then taken on his nocturnal journey (*isra'*) from Mecca to Jerusalem and then on the ascent to the heavens. Other *hadith* narrate that the purification of the heart took place during Muhammad's childhood, separating it from the account of the ascension.

The earliest biography of Muhammad related that the angel Gabriel came to Muhammad while he was asleep and led him to a white animal,

half mule, half donkey, with wings on its sides, named Buraq (popular ar-
tisan depictions of Buraq give the flying animal a woman's head and face).
Gabriel and the Prophet rode on Buraq to Jerusalem, seeing all the marvels
of heaven and earth on the way. In Jerusalem, they found Abraham, Moses,
and Jesus among a company of the prophets. There the Prophet led them
in prayer and then was offered water, wine, and milk, of which he chose
the milk. Upon drinking it, he was told by Gabriel that in so choosing, he
would be rightly guided, as would his people. Thereafter, it is reported that
Muhammad was brought a ladder "finer than any I have seen. It was that to
which the dying man looks when death approaches." Here begins the ascent
to the lowest heaven, under the command of the angel Isma'il, who oversaw
12,000 angels, each with 12,000 angels under its command (Qur'an 74:34:
"And none knows the armies of God but God").

One of these angels, Malik, the keeper of Hell, showed Muhammad the
flames of hell. Muhammad then continued his ascent to the second heaven,
where he met Jesus and John; to the third, where he met Jacob; to the fourth,
where he met Idris (Enoch); to the fifth, where he met Aaron; to the sixth,
where he met Moses; to the seventh, where he met Abraham; and, finally, to
paradise, where he saw a beautiful red-lipped woman before proceeding to
the immortal mansion. There he sees "the lote-tree of the furthest bound-
ary," the divine throne, and a house called the *bayt al-ma'mur* (considered
the celestial counterpart to the Ka'aba), and he enters the divine presence,
where he is given the prayers ordained for his community. The narrative
goes on to relate that it was there that the duty of 50 prayers was placed
upon Muslims, but when Muhammad began his descent, Moses sent him
back repeatedly until the number of prayers had been reduced to five.[7] It is
said that when Muhammad returned to his bed after the journey, a tumbler
of water that had spilled when he arose from his bed had not yet completed
running out, suggesting that the entire journey and its momentous experiences took place in the blink of an eye—that is, in a time not of this time.[8]

Muslims commemorate the occasion of Muhammad's ascent through
various ritual observances. Usually celebrated on the Muslim calendar date
of the 27th of Rajab, ritual observances, which vary from region to region
and from community to community, may entail fasting, recitations of the
Qur'an, readings from texts detailing the journey, lectures on its importance and meanings, poetry performances, and silent or communal prayer.
The *mi'raj* legend inspired poets, artists, and thinkers through the ages,
resulting in a significant amount of literature and art depicting, elaborating
upon, and exploring the significance of the *mi'raj*. Theologians, for instance,

argued about whether Muhammad's night journey was undertaken in spirit or entailed the body, since a *hadith* reports 'A'isha as commenting that Muhammad's body was not missed during the night on which he experienced the ascent. Evidence of Muhammad's high stature among all the prophets was found in the Qur'anic verse stating that, during the divine encounter, Muhammad's eye did not rove (Q. 53:17), suggesting that no one else was able to behold the divine presence without flinching. The question has also been raised as to why Muhammad did not remain in the divine presence, but rather chose to return to earth to communicate the divine message, thereby staking a claim to his mission to improve the lot of creation.

The word *'abduhu* (God's servant) applied to Muhammad in the Qur'anic account of the ascension has suggested to Muslims that, despite his access to the divine, Muhammad remained a created being, and, thus, the story of the ascension reinforces the possibility for humans to ascend to the divine presence, with Muhammad being a model for this possibility. Muhammad's negotiations on behalf of his community with the divine being concerning the number of prayers to be observed establishes Muhammad's role as intercessor between the divine and the human, a role that the Wahhabi form of Islam denies to centuries of Muslim understanding. Muslim poets and artists through the ages and in different locales have elaborated upon the ascension legend, and in popular folk art, the image of Buraq, with the head of a woman decked out in bridal finery is often found on walls or even painted on trucks in Pakistan. Works such as the fifteenth-century manuscript titled the Book of the Ascension (*Mi'rajnama*) from Herat (in present-day Afghanistan) depict Muhammad in a green robe. The circular dance of the Mevlevi tradition in Sufism has been described by its founder, the celebrated mystic poet Rumi, as "a ladder that leads higher than the seventh sphere," because the whirling dervish's aim is to attain proximity to the divine being. Indeed, a Sufi's mystical ascent is often paralleled with Muhammad's experience of *mi'raj*. Scholars have suggested that the ascension legend was circulated in the Mediterranean region during the Middle Ages and may have contributed to Renaissance poet Dante's descriptions of heaven and hell.[9]

## 'ID AL-ADHA

'Id al-Adha—also called 'Id al-Kurban, 'Id al-Nahr ("sacrificial feast"), 'Id al-Kabir ("major feast"), Bakri 'Id in South Asia, and Kurban-Bairam in Central Asia—marks the ending of the pilgrimage to Mecca and commemorates the Abrahamic sacrifice commanded by God. Abraham's difficult decision to comply with God's wishes and to sacrifice his son as a token of his loyalty, devotion, and obedience to God is remembered during this 'Id or celebration, during which an animal is slaughtered. At least two-thirds of the animal is to be shared with the community, in remembrance of the goat or lamb that replaced Abraham's son on the sacrificial altar. The day occurs on the Muslim calendar date of 10th of Dhu al-Hijja. One does not have to be a pilgrim to observe this commemorative celebration, and it is observed wherever Muslims live. Pilgrims participating in the pilgrimage to Mecca make their sacrifice in the valley of Mina. The festival lasts two or three days, and, for this 'Id as well as the one following, special 'Id prayers are recited in lieu of one of the regular prayers at the commencement of the 'Id. For both festivals, the 'Id al-Adha and the 'Id al-Fitr, Muslims put on their best clothes, visit friends and family, exchange or give gifts, and celebrate in myriad ways.

## 'ID AL-FITR

'Id al-Fitr, the festival marking the ending of the period of fasting during the month of Ramadan, is also called the minor festival, 'Id al-Saghir, even though it is celebrated with intense joy at having suffered through fasting for the entire month of Ramadan with equanimity. It is celebrated on the Muslim calendar date of the first of Shawwal and lasts two to three days. Muslims are enjoined to have paid their alms or religious dues by the time the festival begins, and the 'Id begins with special prayers, as with 'Id al-Adha.

## NEW YEAR

The festival of *Navruz* (literally, "new day") is observed primarily by Shi'ite Muslims influenced by Iranian culture. Coinciding with the vernal equinox, when day and night are of equal length, the date of *Navruz*, March 21, has been celebrated from ancient times to the present in Persian civilization. The Achaemenid (559–330 B.C.E.) and Sassanian (226–652 C.E.) kings celebrated the festival with public feasts and the giving of gifts, while the populace lit fires and sprinkled water on each other. Among the customs observed by the Sassanids, the number seven figured prominently; for instance, seven kinds of seeds were sown in small containers; and seven kinds of grain, along with seven kinds of twigs and seven silver coins, were submitted to the king. This ancient memory is still preserved in modern-day Iran in the *haft-sin,* where seven items beginning with the letter *sin,* or s, are gathered together in the household (apples, vinegar, garlic, sumac, sorbapple, silver coins, and fresh grass).

Originally, *Navruz* was thought to have been a pastoral festival marking the seasonal transition from winter to spring. Under the Zoroastrians, the festival, observed on the first day of Farvardin, the first month of the Iranian solar year, came to denote the withdrawal of ancestor spirits and the ending of the old year. It was thought that these ancestor spirits came to visit their households during the period of this festival and, accordingly, homes were cleaned and food and drink readied for them. *Navruz* was held to be a time of sacred commemoration for Zoroastrians, who believed that fire was created on that day, along with its celestial guardian. Prayers were also offered to the deity Mehr, who was said to appear on *Navruz* to welcome the new season.

The festival was secularized under the Sassanids and in some parts came to be associated with the summer solstice, a time of harvesting and rejoicing, used by later non-Persian and non-Shi'ite Muslims as the time when revenues were collected. Under the Seljuq (Turk) Sultan Malikshah (1072–1092), scientists such as the celebrated poet 'Umar (Omar) Khayyam (d. 1123) worked to fix the date of *Navruz* on the first day of Farvardin, that is, the 21st of March. This date remains constant on the Iranian solar calendar by adding one day before the New Year festival once every four years. Under the Muslims, who vanquished the last of Sassanid rulers in 651, *Navruz* became invested with Islamic and specifically Shi'ite symbolic importance. The Shi'ite Imam Ja'far al-Sadiq (d. 765) established its importance to Shi'ites with his statement: "And there is no Navruz but that we have ordained that some divine felicity takes place therein because it is one of our days and the days of our Shi'a." According to him, this day is associated with primordial time as the Day of the Primordial Covenant recorded in Qur'an 7:172, when God asked humanity collectively: "Am I not your Lord?" to which humanity replied in affirmation. It is the day on which the sun first rose at the dawn of creation and, in prophetic time, the day on which Noah's ark came to rest on Mt. Judi, an event referred to in Qur'an 11:44.

The *Bihar al-Anwar,* an encyclopedic collection of Shi'ite *hadith* prepared in the seventeenth century by Muhammad Baqir Majlisi (d. 1699), further reported on the authority of Imam Ja'far al-Sadiq that *Navruz* was the day on which the Prophet designated his cousin and son-in-law, 'Ali ibn Abi Talib, as his successor and *amir al-mu'minin* (Commander of the Faithful). It is also the day on which the Prophet and 'Ali destroyed the idols in the Ka'aba, just as Abraham had destroyed idols on that same day many generations ago. Finally, *Navruz* is recorded as the day on which the messiah will appear at the end of time and destroy the archenemy of justice, al-Dajjal, at Kufa.

In commemorating the first day of spring and the religiously significant events associated with it, *Navruz* is important in both the natural seasonal order and the religious order, both of which are necessary to sustain humans. In including that which is necessary for human physical well-being (spring makes the harvest possible in the summer and fall) and that which is necessary for spiritual growth and self-realization (revelation is a benefit to humankind, and the guidance of the Imams, according to the Shi'ites, is essential in understanding the meaning of revelation so as to attain a state of inner enlightenment), *Navruz* marks the significance of new beginnings in both the physical and the spiritual worlds. The Persian philosopher and poet Nasir Khusraw (d. ca. 1074) made a point of examining the natural order as evidence of a Creator who invested the world with all that was necessary for humankind to flourish, including revelation and those who are empowered by God to interpret that revelation.

In Nasir Khusraw's exploration of the inner significance of manifest things, spring reveals the true state of a tree in winter. During the winter, a tree whose roots have dried up and which is no longer able to bear foliage or fruit appears to be the same as a tree whose roots are healthy and which will bear healthy foliage and delicious fruit during the summer. In the spring, the true state of the tree is revealed, for the tree whose roots have dried out will gradually reach a state whereby its branches break; it is unable to rejoice in the springtime sun. Similarly, the soul of a human in this world is like a tree in winter; if it is alive, like the healthy tree, it has an "eye" watching for the advent of spring or renewal.[10]

In keeping with the theme of renewal—in the natural as well as in the spiritual order—preparations for *Navruz* typically include the planting of grains in small containers. The resulting grass (*sabzi*) is a symbolic decoration gracing tables laden with offerings. Decorated eggs, along with fresh fruit and sweet baked goods are elements of observing *Navruz,* along with new clothing for family members. Visiting friends and relatives and special prayers are parts of the New Year celebration. In Iranian Muslim homes, the *Navruz* table will likely include grass (*sabzi*), *haft-sin,* a mirror, a copy of the scripture observed by the household, a bowl of water in which leaves and flowers are set afloat, and sweets. The New Year "season" lasts about 12 days, and on the thirteenth day, the *sabzi* is cast into running water, which, it is hoped, will remove the tribulations of the previous year.

In Shi'ite communities where *Navruz* is incorporated into liturgical observance, each community has its own ways of marking the occasion and its significance. Among some communities including the Isma'ilis, for instance—packets of grain are handed out to symbolize the prosperity with which it is hoped the family will be blessed in the new year heralded by *Navruz*.[11]

## MUHARRAM RITES: 'ASHURA AND THE TRAGEDY AT KARBALA

Muharram is the first month of the Muslim lunar calendar (also the first month of the Jewish calendar). This month is significant for various reasons. Early Muslims considered Muharram to be one of the four sacred months (the name means "that which is sacred") during which no blood could be shed. The first of the month is the New Year, not to be confused with the Persian New Year (*Navruz*) described, but rather, the first day of the New Year according to the Muslim lunar calendar. The 10th of Muharram is significant to Sunnis and Shi'ites for entirely different reasons, although as a mark of respect to Jewish tradition due to its connection to Abraham and as a mark of respect to the family of the Prophet, both communities remain mindful of the multiple reasons for which the day is commemorated.

For many pious Muslims regardless of whether they are Sunni or Shi'i, the 10th of Muharram is called 'Ashura' and is spent fasting according to the Prophet's decision to adopt as a practice for Muslims the Jewish Day of Atonement observed on 10th of Tishri (the Jewish month). In Muhammad's time, the Jewish practice of fasting from sunset to sunset was observed; however, the practice was made voluntary rather than obligatory when Muhammad's relations with the Jews deteriorated. Since that time, fasting on the day itself rather than from the sunset of the previous day to the sunset of the following day is highly recommended rather than obligatory. Also on this day the Ka'aba's doors are opened to visitors.

For Shi'ite Muslims, this day has additional significance as the day on which the Prophet's grandson Husayn was martyred in 680 C.E. on the battlefield by Yazid, the son of Mu'awiya, founder of the Umayyad dynasty, as he attempted to restore his claims to the caliphate. Imam Husayn, the son of the Prophet's daughter Fatima and his cousin 'Ali, is held in great reverence by Shi'ites as the holder of the Imamate. This is a day of intense mourning for Shi'ites, and pilgrimages are made to Karbala in Iraq, the town closest to the battlefield, and especially to Mashhad Husayn, the place at which the decapitated bodily remains of the Imam were buried.

The mourning rites for Husayn are observed during the first 10 days of Muharram. During this time, the sufferings of Imam Husayn are recited, culminating in the story of his martyrdom. Acts of mourning or *matam* are performed, usually by men's guilds, at religious assemblies held at shrines called Husayniyya in Iran or *ashurkhanas* or *imambara* in India and Pakistan. The battle standards of Husayn and his fellow martyrs and replicas of Husayn's tomb are brought out from storage, and passion plays known as *ta'ziya* depicting the fateful events at Karbala are performed over several days, moving the faithful to tears and cries of lamentation. Mourning ceremonies may take the form of street processions, during which performers will ritually engage in acts of *matam,* most often expressed through a stylized beating of the chest or through repetitive motions during which chains, sometimes fastened to razor blades or small knives, are struck on the performer's back, drawing blood. Acts of mourning are performed to rhythmic chants. The flags are often in the shape of a hand, with the names of the five holy persons (Muhammad, 'Ali, Fatima, Hasan, and Husayn) from the family of the Prophet or the *ahl al-bayt* ("people of the house") written on the them. Some flags also depict 'Ali's sword, Dhu al-fiqar.

The following is an eyewitness account of a religious gathering in Hyderabad, India:

> The *majlis* [religious gathering] typically begins with a *marsiyeh,* the reciting of funeral laments by a chorus of some half-dozen men. A sermon is then given by a *zakir* or preacher. The structure of the sermon is fixed according to tradition: invocation of God's blessings and praise of the Prophet's family; *faza'il,* description of the merits of the martyrs of Karbala, with reflections on how their virtues may guide our conduct today; *masa'ib,* evocation of the sufferings endured by the martyrs and the rapacious cruelty of their persecutors. The sermon may last from twenty minutes to somewhat over an hour; and the assembled congregation takes a very active role therein. As the *zakir* embarks upon the *masa'ib* and his voice quivers with ever more emotion in recalling the sorrows of the martyrs, those listening express their grief: quietly at first, in low groans and sighs, then more and more loudly, till by the conclusion of the *masa'ib* virtually all are crying, slapping their thighs or heads, or concealing their faces with handkerchiefs as they sob. At this point the sermon will end. An emotional decrescendo is provided as all stand and ritual prayers are recited quietly in Arabic in honor of the twelve Imams; while standing, the participants bow, first in the direction of Najaf

and Karbala, then to Meshhed, and finally to Samarra (these are shrines and burial sites associated with the Imams).[12]

Although preachers will vary their sermons as they see fit, traditionally, sermons delivered on the first to third of Muharram will focus on the arrival of Husayn to Karbala and his refusal to acquiesce to Yazid, the commander of the Umayyad army. The fourth day is devoted to Hurr, a commander in the Umayyad army who repents his opposition to the family of the Prophet and joins Husayn. The fifth day celebrates the lives of Husayn's nephews, his sister Zaynab's sons Aun and Muhammad, who were also martyred at Karbala. The sixth day commemorates Husayn's infant son 'Ali Asghar and his 18-year-old son 'Ali Akbar, who was killed in battle. On the seventh day, the wedding of Husayn's daughter Fatima Kubra to his brother Hasan's son Qasim is detailed in its poignancy, for Qasim dies soon thereafter on the battlefield. The eighth day remembers the bravery of the water-carrier, 'Abbas, in his frantic search for water for the warriors and the holy family. On the ninth and tenth days, Husayn's grisly martyrdom on Yazid's orders at the hands of his commander Shimr is recalled amid much lamentation.[13] Processions then spill into the streets, often led by horses signifying 'Abbas's search for water, followed by a float on which are hoisted the battle standards of Husayn and his fellow martyrs and a replica of Husayn's tomb, followed by chanters and young men performing *matam*.[14]

## SUFI RITUALS

According to the *shari'a* (the legal codes developed by Muslim legal scholars in the centuries following Muhammad's death), it is incumbent on Muslims to observe the five pillars of faith. However, different communities of interpretation within Islam observe other rites and rituals, often in addition to the pillars (for instance, the Muharram rites described). Sufi communities have also developed practices key to their worldview and their goal of attaining internal or experiential knowledge of closeness to God. A famous *hadith*, the Hadith of Gabriel, recounts an encounter with the Prophet in which Gabriel asks the Prophet to define what have come to be understood as the three stages of religiosity. The first, surrender (*islam*), constitutes the pillars. The second, faith (*iman*), comprises what might be called a creed: "Faith means you have faith in God, His angels, His books, His messengers, and the Last Day, and that you have faith in the measuring out, both its good and its evil." The third, virtue or excellence in conduct (*ihsan*), is defined as "Doing what is beautiful means that you should worship God as if you see Him, for even if you do not see Him, He sees you."[15]

Sufis understand the path to virtue as consisting of various devotional acts that will polish the mirror of the soul so that it reflects the divine being, impelling the one in service to God to act in a manner that reflects a continual consciousness of accountability to and awareness of the divine being. This spiritual path involves being initiated into a community of fellow seekers under the tutelage of a spiritual teacher who is already the recipient of divine grace and has an experiential understanding of what it means to be a servant of God. Once initiated, a member of a Sufi order is expected to attend regular meetings for communal recitation of supplicatory prayers (called *wird*); for the continual repetition of the divine name specified by the master of the order (a practice known as *dhikr*); to listen to the master's teachings, often interpretations of Qur'anic verses or instruction in rules of conduct; and to participate in *sama'*, a concert at which sacred devotional poetry may be recited or sung, sometimes with music and dance or whirling. In addition, Sufis engage communally or individually in various types of silent contemplation or meditation.

*Wird*, often translated as litany, is intended to focus the Sufi on God. Formulas taken from the Qur'an, such as "God is the Most Great" (*allahu akbar*) or "All praise is due to God" (*subhan allah*) are recited aloud in congregation, as many as 33, 100, or 1,000 times.

*Dhikr*, meaning remembrance, involves the continual repetition of a name or quality of God, following the Qur'anic statement, "the *dhikr* of Allah is the greatest thing" (Q. 29:45), and injunctions found elsewhere in the Qur'an such as "Remember Me, and I will remember you" (Q. 2:152) and "God guides to Him...those who believe and whose hearts are at rest in God's remembrance because surely, in God's remembrance are hearts at rest" (Q. 13:27–28). *Dhikr* reinforces not only the awareness of one's Creator, but also the Creator's connection, compassion, and beneficence to all living things. The supplicant is enjoined to engage in *dhikr* in a spirit of humility and often to recite the so-called 99 names of God such as, "O the Living, Immutable One!" (*ya hayy, ya qayyum*) and "O the Compassionate, Merciful One!" (*ya rahman, ya rahim*). Such phrases are often recited with the help of a string of 99 prayer beads (*tasbih*), each bead for a different name. Or, an entire *tasbih* may be devoted to the repetition of one name. Phrases such as "There is no god but God" (*la ilaha illa allah*) or simply

Sufi women performing Dhikr in Volubilis, Morocco. Courtesy of Karen Torjesen.

"God" (*Allah*, often *Allah Hu*, God Is) are also recited, as are other divine names suggested by the master. *Dhikr* may be performed loudly or silently, in congregation or in solitude.

*Sama‘* consists of singing hymns taken from devotional Sufi poetry, many of which are in praise of God for the blessings given to creation or supplications. The name Allah may also be invoked during *sama‘*. Here is a description of the Shadhili Sufi form of invocation of the name Allah:

> At the start of this rhythmic invocation, all the participants stand side by side and join hands, forming one or more either concentric circles or rows facing one another. In the center stands the shaykh or one of his assistants. This arrangement, which is also found among the whirling dervishes, evokes the symbolism of the circle of angels or the rows of angels that surround the Divine Throne. The session begins with a slow rhythm. The dancers pronounce the Divine name in unison, bowing the trunk of the body rapidly and fully at the moment of exhaling the second syllable, *lah*. When they inhale, they stand erect again. The rhythm increases in tempo little by little, and the movements of the body always accompany the two phases of the breath. The name *Allah* is soon no longer clear and only the last letter *ha'* remains,

which all the chests exhale in an immense burst of air. Each of these exhalations symbolizes the last breath of man, the moment when the individual soul is reintegrated into the cosmic breath, that is to say, into the Divine Spirit, which was blown into man at the time of creation and through which man always remains in communication with the Absolute. Keeping with the movements of the chest, the body is alternately lowered and raised as if at each instant it were being pulled toward the sky and then sent back toward the earth. All the eyes are closed; the faces express a kind of painful rapture. One need not fear pointing out that, if breathing of this *dhikr* evokes that of a rapture of a more sensual order, it is not an accident. There are precise correspondences between the higher order and that here below. That is why, for example, earthly love is able to serve as the point of departure for the realization of Divine Love."[16]

The whirling dance that characterizes the *sama‘* of the Mevleviyya order comprises many symbolic elements, including the items of dress that are worn to perform the ritual. For instance, the tall hat, usually made of felt, symbolizes the vertical dimension free from desire and passion even as it evokes the tombstone and reminds the wearer of the inevitable end of life in death and the perennial quest for a transcending Truth. The black robe worn to the ceremony is removed at the beginning of the dance, symbolizing leaving the individual self behind. The white robe that remains signifies the white shroud in which the body will be wrapped at the time of burial, harkening at the same time the joy of meeting the divine. The reed flute that provides musical accompaniment is reminiscent of Rumi's opening lament in his *Mathnawi*, where he likens the human soul to a reed torn from its bed of rushes, separated from its true home and singing in sorrow. The dancers arrange themselves in concentric circles around a dervish who serves as the axis or pole, in emulation of the orbits of the celestial bodies. The dance begins with hands crossed over the chest in an attitude of humility, after which they are spread wide, with the right hand open to the sky and the left hand pointing to the ground, suggesting a movement originating with grace from above to compassion for those below the celestial realm. In rotating, robe gracefully billowing outward, the dancer affirms the presence of the divine in all directions: "Wherever you turn, there is the Face of God" (Q. 2:115).[17]

Another popular ritual practice is the visitation to shrines (*ziyarat*) dedicated to those considered to have been perfect servants of God, or who are honored by tradition as holy people, or who are considered Imams or spiritual masters. While never losing their connection to humanity, such

persons are considered to have attained a spiritual station that leads sup-
plicants to entreat them for help with their difficulties, sorrows, and tribulations. The saints, as they are often called, are celebrated on the days of
their birth or investiture, lamented on the days of their death, and visited
at their shrines. In the next chapter on major figures in Muslim civilization
and culture, some of these saints are discussed.

## NOTES

1. The *salat* is the most commonly observed form of obligatory ritual
prayer among Muslims, but communities such as the Ismailis observe the
Qur'anic injunction of obligatory prayer through a cycle of prostrations and
recitations of Qur'anic verses interspersed with praise giving and prayers of
supplication. See Tazim R. Kassam, "The Daily Prayer (Du'a) of Shi'a Isma'ili
Muslims" in Colleen McDannell, ed., *Religions of the United States in Practice*,
Vol. 2 (Princeton, NJ: Princeton University Press, 2001), 32–43.

2. Quoted in Frederick Matthewson Denny, *An Introduction to Islam* (New
York: Macmillan, 1994), 117. See Denny for a detailed description of the words
and bodily movements of the prayer.

3. C.C. Berg, "Sawm" in H.A.R. Gibb and J.H. Kramers, ed., *Shorter
Encyclopedia of Islam* (Leiden: E.J. Brill, 1974), 504.

4. Many of the details on *hajj* are taken from B. Lewis, A.J. Wensinck,
and J. Jomier, "Hadjdj" in the *Encyclopedia of Islam*, CD-ROM, Edition v.1.1.
(Leiden: E.J. Brill, 2001).

5. Annemarie Schimmel, *Make a Shield from Wisdom* (New York: Kegan
Paul International, 1993), 95–96, with minor changes.

6. Quoted in Annemarie Schimmel, *And Muhammad Is His Messenger*
(Chapel Hill: University of North Carolina Press, 1985), 153–154.

7. Ibn Hisham, Abd al-Malik, *The Life of Muhammad*, trans. A. Guillaume
(London: Oxford University Press, 1955), 181–187.

8. Schimmel, *And Muhammad Is His Messenger*, 161.

9. Ibid. See Chapter 9.

10. Nasir-I Khusraw, *Six Chapters* (Leiden: E.J. Brill, 1949), 85.

11. "Nawruz" in Mircea Eliade et al., eds., *The Encyclopedia of Religion*, Vol.
10; "Nawruz" in John L. Esposito, ed., *The Oxford Encyclopedia of the Modern
Islamic World*; Marshall G.S. Hodgson, *The Venture of Islam*, Vol. 2; Moojan
Momen, *An Introduction to Shi'i Islam* (New Haven, CT: Yale University
Press, 1985); W. Ivanow, trans., *Six Chapters or Shish Fasl by Nasir-i Khusraw*
(Bombay: Ismaili Society, 1949).

12. David Pinault, *The Shiites: Ritual and Popular Piety in a Muslim Community* (New York: St. Martin's Press, 1992), 115–116.

13. Ibid., 117–118.

14. For accounts of the Muharram rites, see Vernon James Schubel, *Religious Performance in Contemporary Islam: Shiʻi Devotional Rituals in South Asia* (Columbia: University of South Carolina Press, 1993); Pinault, *The Shiites,* and Momen, *An Introduction to Shiʻi Islam.*

15. This *hadith* is found in Muslim, under *Iman,* 1, and Bukhari, under *Iman,* 37, quoted in Sachiko Murata and William C. Chittick, *The Vision of Islam* (New York: Paragon House, 1994), xiv.

16. Jean Louis Michon, "The Spiritual Practices of Sufism" in Seyyed Hossein Nasr, ed., *Islamic Spirituality: Foundations* (New York: Crossroad, 1997), 282.

17. Ibid., 283–84.

# 6

# MAJOR FIGURES

In Islam, the material and spiritual life are viewed as an integrated whole. As a result, notable Muslims since the inception of Islam include not only individuals who have made contributions to theology, mysticism, and religious literature, but also those who attained high levels of excellence in the sciences, architecture, and the arts. Inspired by the well-known prophetic saying—"seek knowledge even in China"—Muslims have sought to understand and work on the achievements of non-Muslim civilizations to make significant contributions within a variety of fields. In what follows, only a few of the many key figures have been included.

Few women are included among the people cited here because the effort to recover Muslim women's writings and contributions to history has only begun in recent decades. Muslim women who have played a central role in Islamic history include: Khadija (d. 619), wife of the Prophet; 'A'ishah b. Abi Bakr (d. 678), wife of the Prophet; Fatima b. Muhammad, daughter of the Prophet (d. 633); Rabi'a al-'Adawiya (d. 801), Sufi mystic noted for her ardent devotion to God; Zaynab and Nafisa (d. 824), descendants of the Prophet, whose Egyptian shrines are considered worthy of visitation to this day; Arwa, Queen of Yemen (d. 1138); Shajarat al-Durr (d. 1257), ruler of Egypt; Raziyya Sultana (d. 1240), briefly ruler in parts of India; Jamal Khatun (d. 1639), considered a saint in the Qadiriyya Sufi order; Jahanara (d. 1689), royal granddaughter and mystic; Jahanara's niece, Zaybunnisa (d. 1689), an accomplished mathematician and poet. Among the many illustrious, prolific, and, in some cases, incendiary and revivalist twentieth-century and contemporary women writers, activists, and thinkers, all of whom critique the position of women in Islamic societies, one may draw attention to Hoda Sha'rawi (d. 1947), Ismat Chugghtai (d. 1992), Zaynab al-Ghazali, Bint al-Shati, Halide Edib, Parvin Ettesami, Nawal El Saadawi, Fatima Mernissi, Assiya Djebar, Sahar Khalifeh, Anis Sabirin, Zainah Anwar, Rose Ismail, Riffat Hasan, and Laila Ahmed.

## Hasan al-Basri (642–728)

Al-Hasan b. Abi'l-Hasan al-Basri was born in Medina in 642 and settled in Basra, where he earned a reputation for his piety, mystical tendencies, depth of learning, and eloquence. He died there in 728. Present at a time of immense political and theological turbulence, Hasan al-Basri lived through the assassination of the third caliph, 'Uthman, and the beginnings of the Alid movement that supported 'Ali's claims to the caliphate. Eminently re-spected as a theologian, mystic, and *hadith* scholar, he adhered to the doc-trine of free will as opposed to predestination. This doctrine had political implications, because if God predetermined human events, then Muslims would be obligated to accept the rule of an unjust caliph or ruler. Another major debate at this time concerned the religious status of the grave sinner: should such a person be considered a Muslim? The Kharijites (those who split off) held that the grave sinner should not be considered a Muslim, while the Murji'ites (those who delayed judgment) wavered on the issue. Al-Basri was an ascetic who proposed that a true religious life should in-clude reflection and self-examination with an attitude of surrender to God's will. He held material goods and the pleasures of this life in contempt, be-cause they stood in the way of reaching harmony between individual free will and God's will.[1]

## Wasil b. 'Ata' (699–748) and the Mu'tazila School

Wasil b. 'Ata' (d. 748 C.E.) was the founder of what came to be known as the Mu'tazila school —a group of theologians whose position was be-tween that of the Kharijites and Murji'ites. While Hasan al-Basri held to the doctrine of free will, and therefore suggested that grave sinners were fully aware of what they were doing and, therefore, were to be held accountable, Wasil b. 'Ata' proposed that such sinners should be placed in an intermedi-ate position between faith and infidelity, with God as the final judge.

The cornerstone of the Mu'tazilite theological position, officially sanc-tioned under Caliph al-Ma'mun (786–833), was that God's ways are rational and that good and evil are concepts that can be understood independently of scripture. So God forbids something because it is bad, not that something becomes bad because God forbids it. God does not command anything that is contrary to reason, nor disregard the welfare of creatures, as doing so would compromise God's wisdom or justice. In other words, the Mu'tazilites held that God worked within the bounds of justice, mercy, and wisdom. The Mu'tazilites also upheld the notion that human beings had the capacity to act freely—in contrast to some theologians who held that God alone, who was omnipotent, had the power to act freely and that not only did God determine what a person was going to do, but also that no human action could take place without God's permission. The Mu'tazilites were troubled by this position because it implied that God was responsible for the evil in this world; in attributing free will to humans, they protected God from such responsibility.

The key doctrines associated with the Mu'tazila school are: (1) God's Absolute Unity, or the profession of monotheism against any kind of dualism; (2) God's Justice; (3) God's Promise and Threat (heaven and hell), entailing discussions of what constitutes belief and what constitutes sin; (4) The Intermediate Position, whereby a grave sinner was still considered part of the Muslim community because it was up to God to judge; and (5) Enjoining the Right and Prohibiting the Wrong, which examines the question of to what extent Muslims are responsible for ensuring that other Muslims live rightly.

The Mu'tazilites flourished politically until the commencement in 847 of the reign of the caliph Mutawakkil, who mounted an attack against them on behalf of the *hadith* scholars such as Ahmed b. Hanbal. After that point, Sunni orthodox thought was found in the Ash'arite school of thought, founded by al-Ash'ari, who was trained as a Mu'tazilite theologian before creating a middle path between the *hadith* scholars and the rationalist theologians.

## Al-Kindi (ca. 800–866)

Abu Yusuf Ya'qub b. Ishaq al-Kindi, considered the first Arab philosopher, was born in Kufa, Iraq, educated in Basra, and lived for the remainder of his life in Baghdad. There he served under the patronage of three 'Abbasid caliphs—al-Ma'mun, al-Mu'tasim, and al-Wathiq—before arousing the ire of their successor, al-Mutawakkil, who was not well disposed toward philosophy. Al-Kindi's philosophic and scientific output, of which little remains, was prodigious and is quoted by later authors. The bibliographer

Ibn Nadim attributes 242 works to him that dealt with logic, metaphysics, arithmetic, spherics, music, astronomy, geometry, medicine, astrology, theology, psychology, politics, meteorology, topography, prognostics, and alchemy.[2] Al-Kindi belongs to the Islamic Aristotelian tradition, so reading his work requires a close familiarity with Aristotelian thought.

As a scientist, philosopher, and theologian, al-Kindi sought to understand revelation in ways that would be consistent with rational understandings of reality (as did the Mu'tazilites, considered the first rationalist theologians) while at the same time defending revealed knowledge as something beyond the grasp of the human mind. As a result, he disagreed with the Aristotelian and Neoplatonic thinkers on issues such as the creation of the world, prophecy, bodily resurrection after death, and miracles. However, he built a strong case for the importance of studying the works of ancient philosophers such as Aristotle and Plato and for honoring knowledge whatever its source, because "nothing should be dearer to the seeker after truth than truth itself."[3] Nor should philosophy, in his view, be rejected by those who are religious, for knowledge of material things comes through the senses, and knowledge of immaterial things comes through rational cognition and proofs, such as the proofs for the qualities of the divine being. For al-Kindi, material things were created, whereas immaterial things were divine. Accordingly, the study of material things is called physics, and the study of immaterial things is called metaphysics. He identified the study of mathematics as essential preparation for engaging in metaphysical thinking, and his attempts to understand the qualities of the divine being, such as its being eternal or unitary, drew upon mathematical understandings of his day.

The realms of knowledge to be investigated by a Muslim included the religious and the secular because both are dimensions of total reality. At the same time, al-Kindi held the view that, while philosophy and scientific investigation were essential to the human striving for truth, knowledge about the divine being cannot be made known except by God, who imparts knowledge of divine realities through prophecy. Thus, the role of philosophy was not to supplant the role of revelation but rather to support it. For al-Kindi, the study of metaphysics—that is, that which is beyond physics or material things—entailed the study of the divine being.

## Abu Yazid (Bayazid) al-Bistami (804–875)

Abu Yazid al-Bistami, an ecstatic mystic, was born in Bastam, Northern Iran, and followed the mystical path, subjecting himself to severe austerities to diminish his human needs and instead meet God face to face, as it were. He died in 875, having earned the reputation of being given over to ecstatic utterances while in thrall with the divine. For example, he is recorded as having said: "Glory be to Me, how great is My Majesty," speaking as though he were God from within a state of consciousness in which all consciousness of self had been lost and only consciousness of the divine being remained. In a report of a conversation with God, he said: "Once [God] lifted me up and placed me before Him and said to me: O, Abu Yazid, my creation desires to see thee. And I said: Adorn me with Thy unity and clothe me in Thine I-ness and raise me up unto Thy oneness, so that when Thy creatures see me they may say: We have seen Thee [i.e., God] and Thou art that. Yet I [Abu Yazid] will not be there."[4] Scholars have suggested that some of his ideas of divinity may have originated in India because his teacher was an Indian convert to Islam.

## Al-Junayd (ca. 830–910)

Abu'l-Qasim al-Junayd of Baghdad is an important early Sufi best known for his sober mysticism and his development of the notions of passing away (*fana'*) and abiding (*baqa'*) in God's presence. Drawing a clear distinction between the Creator and creation, he held that all created things ultimately pass away, leaving behind only "the Face of God" (Q. 55:27). The covenant established between God and humans before the creation of humans (Q. 7:172) was central to al-Junayd's thought, indicating, as the Qur'anic verse notes, that humanity replies in affirmation when God asked, "Am I not your Lord?" Once humans experience the reality of being that is, in essence, an idea in God's mind prior to actual creation, then they can become dead to the transience of this embodied existence and awakened to eternal life within God. Unlike ecstatic mystics such as Bayazid al-Bistami, al-Junayd maintained that Sufis should remain within the bounds of *shari'a* and maintain spiritual sobriety at all times.

## Al-Hallaj (ca. 858–922)

Al-Husain b. Mansur al-Hallaj, an ecstatic mystic, was taught, among others, by al-Junayd, who was his spiritual director for two decades. Al-Hallaj is said to have stood in the hall of the mosque at Mecca during his first pilgrimage for an entire year, apparently not even lying down to sleep. He spent his time preaching, traveling as far as Gujarat in India. In an intoxicated state of mystical awareness, he declared, "I am the Truth! [i.e., God]," and it is ostensibly for making such utterances that he was sentenced to death by crucifixion in 922, a sentence that was carried out with intense cruelty on the orders of the officiating vizier. When asked to defend his utterances, al-Hallaj responded with the explanation that when the mystic is in a state of union with the divine being, it is God who speaks and acts through the mystic.

## Al-Razi (ca. 864–932)

Abu Bakr Muhammad b. Zakariya al-Razi (Latin: Rhazes) was born in Rayy in the province of Khurasan, Iran. He was considered the foremost medical authority of his day and was also well known as an independent-minded Muslim philosopher, for which reason most of his books were burnt. His extensive medical compendium, *Kitab al-hawi fi al-tibb,* a 23-volume work that shows evidence of his knowledge of Greek, Near-Eastern, Indian, Arabic, and possibly Chinese medical knowledge, was translated into Latin in 1279 and was in use in European medical circles until the nineteenth century. Another, smaller text, *On Smallpox and Measles,* also was widely used, and al-Razi was the first scientist to draw a connection between the two diseases. He wrote on Plato, Plutarch, and Socrates and also on many philosophical and scientific topics. He was also familiar with Indian thought.

His approach to medicine was holistic, attaching importance to the well-being not only of the mind and body, but also the soul. One of his texts that survives is an ethical treatise, the *Spiritual Physick,* in which he followed Plato's tripartite division of the soul into the vegetative, the animal, and the rational. Al-Razi advocated the middle path of moderation in all things as leading to spiritual health and well-being. In a manner reminiscent of Plato, Pythagoras, and the Gnostics, al-Razi viewed the soul as originally a formless, living, eternal, and perfect entity that was seduced by matter and its pleasures and became caught in embodiment. As a result, God endowed the soul with reason to awaken it from its bodily slumber by reminding it of its original perfection and participation in the world of divine realities, thereby enabling the soul to attain its salvation. Al-Razi departed from mainstream Islamic thought in putting forward a theory of five uncreated eternal principles (rather than just one, God, who alone is uncreated): matter, space, time, the Soul, and the Creator. As opposed to al-Kindi, who held that God created *ex nihilo* (out of nothing), al-Razi held that the Creator did not create out of nothing, but that creation was the act of combining these eternal entities to form what we understand as creation. Al-Razi earned the wrath of other Muslim thinkers by stating that humans need rationality, not prophecy, to understand reality. He thought that prophecy was unnecessary to attain eternal truths, and God did not need prophets to reveal divine knowledge to humans, nor did humans need prophets as mediators between human knowledge and divine knowledge.

## Al-Ash'ari (873–935) and the Ash'arite School

Theologian Abu'l-Hasan al-Ash'ari was born in Basra and studied with al-Juba'i, the head of the Mu'tazilite school of thinkers, before breaking away from them at the age of 40. Legend describes a conversation between the two men that illustrates al-Ash'ari's departure from the Mu'tazilite belief in human responsibility for actions. According to this conversation, al-Ash'ari asked his teacher what would be the fate in the afterlife of three brothers—one who died in a state of grace, one in a state of sin, and one in a state of innocence, that is, before he reached maturity. Al-Juba'i's response was that the first went to heaven on the strength of his good works, the sinner went to hell as a result of his sinful deeds, and the third would be in an intermediate state. If the third brother were to protest that he would have performed good deeds and lived a righteous life if he had been given a long life, then the response would have been that God knew that he would not, and therefore, a life in hell was spared the third brother by placing him in an indeterminate state. At this point, the second brother protested why had God not curtailed his life as well and save him from hellfire. The anecdote reports that al-Juba'i had no answer to this.

For al-Ash'ari, such thinking placed humans on the level of divinity by making them the architects of their own fate, whereas such a responsibility and privilege belonged only to God. If humans have no free will in which to conduct their actions, and all their actions are preordained and foreseen by God, then does not such a view contradict the notion of God's justice? Al-Ash'ari held that, to the contrary, injustice can never be applied to God. Rather, he came up with the theory of *al-kasb*, or acquisition, according to which a person's actions are created by God but acquired by the human or imputed to him or her. That is, God creates the action, but the person "acquires" it, thereby keeping intact God's power to create and not allowing the human to share in that power. The following quotation illustrates al-Ash'ari's position:

We believe that God has created everything, by simply bidding it: Be, as He says [in Koran 16, 42]: "Verily, when we will a thing, our only utterance is 'Be' and it is"; and there is nothing good or evil on earth, except what God has preordained. We hold that everything is through God's will and that no one can do a thing before he actually does it, or do it without God's assistance, or escape God's knowledge. We hold that there is no Creator but God, as He said [in Koran 37, 94]: "He has created you and what you make"... and we hold that God helps the faithful to obey Him, favors them, is gracious to them, reforms and guides them; whereas he has led the unfaithful astray, did not guide or favor them with signs, as the impious heretics claim.... We believe that good and evil are the outcome of God's decree and preordination: good or evil, sweet or bitter, and we know that what has missed us could not have hit us, or what has hit us could not have missed us, and that creatures are unable to profit or injure themselves, without God.[5]

While such a statement reflects the piety of a person who believed that people were utterly powerless before God, al-Asha'ari's education, training, and subtle mind used the language of philosophical and theological sophistication to underscore an anti-rationalism directed against the philosophers, scientists, and rationalist theologians. He went on to found a theological school that characterizes mainstream Sunni Islam and that subsumes all rational knowledge to its interpretation of revelation. For al-Ash'ari, God's omnipotence and sovereignty of the world are paramount, and it is the duty of every faithful Muslim to obey God's decrees. To impute free will to humans was the same as making a human co-creator with God, and yet to absolve humans of all responsibility for their actions was to impute evil to God, neither of which were acceptable positions. Al-Ash'ari addressed this dilemma by developing the doctrine of *kasb*, or the acquisition of the merit or demerit of the deed done. According to this doctrine, a person's voluntary actions were created by God, but their merit or demerit was acquired by the human; the distinction being that God created the act out of eternal power, but the human acquired the created act in temporal time. Al-Ash'ari thought that this verbal distinction kept God's omnipotence intact while at the same time making humans responsible for acts committed. The distinction between his position and that of Ibn Hanbal, the traditionalist founder of the Hanbali school of law, was that Ibn Hanbal's credo, "ask not how" prevented the asking of questions regarding scriptural ambiguities, while al-Ash'ari held that asking questions was fine but one had to keep in mind that the human mind could not know the mysteries of what scripture taught, and scripture held primacy in investigating truth.

Al-Ash'ari went on to become the key formulator of Sunni theological doctrine, consolidating the methods of the Mu'tazilites with the concerns of the traditionalists who opposed Mu'tazilite viewpoints. He founded a school of theology that included the celebrated theologian, al-Ghazali, and continues to the present day, for instance, at al-Azhar, the famous training ground for Sunni theologians located in Cairo, Egypt. Al-Ash'ari's theology was further developed by al-Baqillani (d. 1013), who systematically developed Ash'arite doctrine; al-Baghdadi (d. ca. 1040); al-Juwayni (d. 1086); and al-Ghazali (d. 1111) and found among its most recent exponents Muhammad 'Abduh (d. 1905), the grand Shaykh of al-Azhar.

### Al-Farabi (ca. 870–950)

Muhammad b. Muhamad b. Tarkhan al-Farabi (Latin: Abunaser) came from Farab in Central Asia; grew up in Damascus, where he worked as a gardener and read philosophy; studied logic in Baghdad; and, after traveling to Egypt, settled in Aleppo, Syria. He soon earned fame as the leading authority on Plato and Aristotle and surpassed the reigning master of the day in logic, Matta, a Nestorian Christian scholar. He wrote works on physics, metaphysics, politics, and logic and is known as "The Second Master" (the first being Aristotle). Indeed, an anecdote relates that Ibn Sina did not understand Aristotle's *Metaphysics,* despite having read it 40 times, until he read al-Farabi's commentary on it.

Al-Farabi's emphasis on ethics (practical philosophy) and knowledge (theoretical philosophy) going hand in hand for the attainment of happiness (the title of one of his works) became a key feature of subsequent Islamic thought. He categorized all the sciences of his day under the following eight topics, each of which has further divisions: linguistic, logical, mathematical, physical, metaphysical, political, juridical, and theological. All of these, as with Aristotle's classification of the sciences, form an organic unity. Moreover, they are all viewed within an overriding framework of the Unity of God's creation. Al-Farabi is remembered chiefly for his contributions to metaphysics and to politics, for he saw one as relating to the other. Thus, his *Virtuous City* presents the idea that the gift of reason enables humans to strive for their own perfection vis-à-vis God through reflecting on the divine being and developing an ethical way of being in the world. Doing so enables the principles through which communities of humans can live together in harmony in cities or states. Thus, human relations with God, self, and others form an organic unity governed by the application of rationality.

## Ibn Sina (ca. 980–1037)

Abu 'Ali al-Husain ibn Sina (Latin: Avicenna), the foremost philosopher and medical authority of his day, was born in Afshana near Bukhara in Central Asia and educated in Bukhara. His father was an Isma'ili Shi'ite (one of the branches of Islam), an affiliation that Ibn Sina did not claim for himself, although his interest in philosophical and mystical subjects may have been nurtured from a very young age because of this. A precocious child, he had mastered the Qur'an by the age of 10, going on to the study of logic, physics, metaphysics, and medicine; by the age of 16, he was a practicing physician. His studies in metaphysics were aided greatly by his reading of al-Farabi's commentaries on Aristotle. He wrote prodigiously on all manner of subjects. His key philosophical text is the *Kitab al-Shifa'* (Book of Healing), an encyclopedic work that he later condensed into the *Kitab al-Najat* (Book of Salvation). He wrote these works in Arabic, but also wrote a philosophical work in Persian titled *Danesh-Nameh* (Book of Knowledge), thereby contributing to the development of philosophical vocabulary in Arabic and Persian.

Ibn Sina continued much of al-Farabi's thought, especially on the nature of the divine being, the intellect, and prophecy. He identified the divine being as the Necessary Existent or Being, upon whom all other existence is contingent: "For everything derives from it, but does not share with it [in anything], and it is the source of all things, without being any one of the things posterior to it."[6] The human reasoning faculty or intellect has many stages of development and depends for its knowledge of reality on mediating sources such as the sense organs or the inner senses (the imagination, for example, or the instinctual ability to see danger). Nonetheless, Ibn Sina held that there are a few persons in this world whose rational faculties were developed to the extent that they did not need such mediators to understand reality; these were the prophets, who were in possession of something that Ibn Sina called holy reason. It is through the prophets that knowledge of divine things was revealed to humankind.

Ibn Sina also wrote mystical treatises in the form of allegories, exploring the idea that the soul is imprisoned, like a bird, in the cage of matter and mortality and must struggle to become free. Once freed, the bird-soul must journey to find a place of safety from which it can never be imprisoned again. The allegory also explored the idea of love as something noble and capable of freeing humans from the lust of material enjoyment into the goodness of virtuous existence. He conveys the struggle of a journeyer who travels away from the bondage of corporeality and the ephemeral (or fleeting) pleasures attained through the five external senses into a life of spiritual awakening and the eternal pleasures experienced through proximity to the source of all being, God.

The contributions made by Ibn Sina to medical knowledge were immense. His encyclopedic work on medicine, *al-Qanun* (The Canon), was divided into five books that covered all aspects of medicine then known to the Greeks and within the Islamic purview, with sections on medical instruments and pharmaceutical substances. Together with al-Razi's *al-Hawi*, the two works became the standard textbooks in European medical training facilities for several centuries after they were translated. In some of his writings, Ibn Sina explored the connection between emotional and bodily health, assessing the impact of the environment and music on overall health.[7] For all his brilliance, Ibn Sina led a life of tribulations under various patrons, oscillating between excessive work and pleasure, leading to his untimely death at the age of 58 in Hamadan, Iran (where he is buried).

## Ikhwan al-Safa' (Tenth Century)

Otherwise known as the Brethren of Purity, the Ikhwan were a group of Muslim philosophers and scientists who flourished in Basra in the tenth century and whose work rapidly spread through Muslim lands and into Spain in the eleventh century. They are most well known for their encyclopedic work, the *Rasa'il* or Epistles, comprising 52 chapters on wide-ranging topics concerning the nature of both the physical and spiritual worlds, including mathematics, astronomy, logic, geography, music, ethics, nature, botany, life and death, pleasure and pain, mystical love, resurrection, moral and spiritual purification, angels and demons, politics, prophecy, and creation. Informed by Pythagorean and Neoplatonic ideas, their work evinced the unity of knowledge thought to underlie all branches of investigative sciences ranging from the physical to the metaphysical. For the Brethren, the study of mathematics—which included the study of arithmetic, geometry, astronomy, geography, music, logic, arts, and crafts—was essential for moral and intellectual development and preparatory for knowledge of the soul, which itself was a preparation for the highest knowledge, knowledge of God. Powerful as the human mind is, it could not grasp the realities of divine concepts such as God's majesty and must defer to the prophets and revelation for such knowledge. However, the Ikhwan held firmly to the notion that philosophical/scientific investigation and divine revelation were not at odds with one another, for the goal and purpose of philosophy and revelation was the same—that is, emulation of divinity according to human capacity.[8] One of their epistles, "The Case of the Animals Versus Man," is an ecological fable in which animals take humans to court for ill treatment.

## Miskawayh (ca. 932–1030)

Remembered more for his ethical treatises than for his philosophical expositions or historical works, Abu 'Ali Ahmad b. Muhammad b. Ya'qub Miskawayh was born in Rayy, Iran, and died approximately a hundred years later, in 1030. He studied the works of the great Muslim historian al-Tabari. His *Tahdhib al-Akhlaq* (Cultivation of Morals) influenced later luminaries such as al-Ghazali and Nasir al-Din Tusi, as well as the modern Egyptian scholar Muhammad 'Abduh. Miskawayh identified four cardinal virtues— wisdom, temperance, courage, and justice—as the middle path between the two extremes representing the vices that an unrestrained appetitive or passionate faculty would generate.[9] He thought that the soul, following Plato's division, had three faculties: the rational or angelic faculty located in the brain, which mediates between the appetitive or bestial faculty located in the liver, and the passionate or leonine faculty located in the heart. Thus, for instance, the greed of the appetitive faculty could be tempered by the rational soul such that it is balanced into using just what is sufficient for one's needs; the anger generated by the passionate faculty could be tempered into forbearance and compassion.

Miskawayh distinguished between happiness on earth and spiritual happiness. Although the latter far outweighs the former because it is eternal and self-sufficient, earthly happiness is to be sought in a life of action, in moderation in all things, in the friendship of others, and in the various forms of love, including the love of God, nurtured by a contemplative life. He thought that the two most debilitating afflictions of the soul were sorrow and the fear of death. The fear of death must be overcome by the realization that death is nothing other than the process by which the soul attains a higher level of purity and bliss, for, being eternal, the soul cannot disintegrate, but only transforms from one form to another. Sorrow must be overcome by an understanding that all possessions in life are ephemeral, as is earthly existence itself.[10]

## Ibn Hazm (ca. 994–1064)

Abu Muhammad 'Ali b. Ahmed b. Sa'id ibn Hazm was born in Cordova, Spain, and became famous as a poet and theologian. He left Cordova for political reasons, was imprisoned briefly for supporting the Spanish Umayyad caliphate after its loss of power, and returned to Cordova after a five-year absence. He briefly held a high position in court but was then imprisoned again for his theological views before being back in favor at court briefly before he was once again reviled for attacking the works of legal scholars such as al-Ash'ari, after which Ibn Hazm's books were burned. His famous work, *The Ring of the Dove*, established him as a mystic poet, and the great Sufi Ibn al-'Arabi is thought to have drawn inspiration from his mystical writings.

However, Ibn Hazm's major preoccupation was with theology and the study of language. Although he began as a follower of the Shafi'ite school of law, he soon adopted the Zahirite (or Literalist) school of thought according to which any laws not based on revelation or the *hadith* ought to be rejected. He attacked the Mu'tazilite and Ash'arite theories of God's attributes, although he turned to spiritual interpretation when faced with the anthropomorphic verses describing God in the Qur'an—for instance, verses referring to God's face or hand. In his view, only knowledge based on sense perception and what was immediately intellectually perceptible was valid, unless it was laid down in scripture. He argued that knowledge of God comes only from revealed scripture and all forms of theological discussion about God's attributes are futile and irrelevant, for a human can never understand the mysteries of God's ways.

## Al-Ghazali (1058–1111)

Theologian Abu Hamid Muhammad b. Muhammad al-Tusi al-Shafi'i al-Ghazali was born in Tus, Iran, and educated there and in Nishapur under al-Juwayni, an Ash'arite theologian. He served for a while at the Seljuk court under the vizier Nizam al-Mulk until he was appointed the head of the Nizamiya school of religious sciences in Baghdad, where he wrote theological and polemical works in defense of Sunni orthodoxy. He began his study of philosophy in 1090 and a serious study and practice of Sufism in 1093 after which, disillusioned with teaching, he left to travel for 10 years. He resumed teaching in Nishapur and died there in 1111. In his autobiography, *Deliverance from Error,* he discussed his ardent search for a certain knowledge that was not open to doubt, and his profound studies in law, theology, philosophy, and mysticism led him to conclude that neither the knowledge derived from sensory experience nor the knowledge received from the use of reason was free from error.

After a period of intense doubt, he thought he was saved by the grace of God, through "a light which God infused into his heart." Henceforth, he declared that the theologians, philosophers, and Shiʿite esoteric groups such as the Ismaʿilis were all prone to error. Although he acknowledged the usefulness of theology (provided its study was restricted to those who were capable of doing so and not the general masses), he saw no merit in the works of esoterically minded groups or the philosophers. He argued against the view of the esoteric groups such as the Batiniyya or Ismaʿilis that certain levels of knowledge could be obtained only through instruction from an infallible teacher, the Imam, since the Prophet already functioned as an infallible teacher in bringing revelation from God. Contrary to the philosophers, he argued that reason alone could not have knowledge of the immortality of the soul or the pleasures or pains experienced by the soul after death, for such knowledge only comes through revelation and experience. Thus, the Sufis, who were also esoterically inclined, enabled a human to practice the faith in such a manner that it opened the heart to ecstatic experience, which alone was to be trusted as knowledge free from error. In addition, a good Muslim was obliged to observe the *shariʿa* and to emulate ethical principles in all their undertakings. Al-Ghazali's devastating attack on the philosophers in his work *The Incoherence of the Philosophers* rendered the study of philosophy suspect among pious circles, causing philosophical investigation thereafter to be largely merged with mysticism.

Although al-Ghazali ostensibly discredited the study of philosophy and the views of esoterically inclined communities of interpretation such as the Ismaʿilis, in his own mystical work, he relied heavily on both, albeit implicitly and without open acknowledgment. For instance, in his well-known mystical treatises, the *Mishkat al-Anwar* (Niche of Lights) and *al-Risalah al-Laduniyah* (Treatise on Mystical Knowledge), he relied upon a Neoplatonic hierarchy of being as the underpinning of his mystical universe.[11] Thus, for him the visible world was—as held by Plato and Plotinus—a shadow or replica of the invisible or spiritual or intelligible world, and an entity's position in the hierarchy of being was determined by its proximity to the source of all entities, God or the Supreme Light. Thus, in tacit agreement with the Ismaʿilis, al-Ghazali thought that scriptural texts needed to be understood metaphorically to access their significance with respect to spiritual realities. For instance, the notion of God's face mentioned in the Qurʾan was not to be taken at face value as per the argument of literalists such as Ibn Hanbal, the traditionalist founder of a legal school, or those who refused to ask why or how God might have a face because divinity was not human; rather, God's face must be understood metaphorically to indicate that nothing in the world was eternal, everything was subject to perishing, and that God alone was everlasting—that is, the only entity to have had an enduring "face" or presence.

## Ibn Bajjah (ca. 1095–1138)

Abu Bakr Muhammad b. Sayigh, known as Ibn Bajjah, was born in Saragossa, Spain, lived in Seville and Granada, and was poisoned in Fez (Morocco) in 1138. Considered the first major Spanish Arab philosopher, he was both a philosopher and a scientist who drew attention to Aristotle's works. He is remembered for his exploration of the state of the person he called the stranger or the solitary being, who is the philosopher living in a corrupt rather than in a virtuous city. Such people, whose aim is to foster spiritual growth and attain philosophic wisdom, must become solitary beings if they are impeded along the path to intellectual perfection. Once they have prepared themselves to the extent humanly possible, then final perfection may be given to them through divine grace.

## Ibn Tufayl (ca. 1100–1185)

Abu Bakr b. Tufayl was born near Granada, Spain, educated in Seville and Granada where he studied medicine and philosophy, served as the caliph's physician, and died in 1185. He wrote works on medicine, astronomy, and philosophy. Of the latter, only one survives to this day, the celebrated tale, *Hayy b. Yaqzan,* which was translated into several European languages and thought to have influenced Daniel Defoe's novel *Robinson Crusoe* in its form, if not content. The story traces the life of a child, Hayy, brought up by a gazelle on an uninhabited island. As the child grows, he questions the purpose of his existence and begins to observe and emulate nature. Hayy finally arrives at an experiential and intellectual understanding of reality and his place within it, through what he understands as divine grace. Soon after, he meets a traveler named Absal from a neighboring island, whose people are guided by revelation, and it becomes clear from conversations that the truths Hayy has arrived at through observation, introspection, and emulation are similar to the truths brought by revelation and the practices introduced through prayer and other ritual observances. However, when Hayy travels back with Absal to Absal's island, he realizes that not all people have the capacity to understand higher truths of religion in philosophic or intellectual terms. He returns to his island to resume his solitary life.

Ibn Tufayl addressed the issue of the harmony between philosophy or the efforts of human rational thought and revelation. He incorporated the mystical path of practice to give equal weight to knowledge (theoretical philosophy) and ethics (practical philosophy) in the attainment of truth and emphasized the importance of divine grace. In religious terms, this would be understood as following scripture and participating in ritual observance to prepare the soul for illumination through divine grace.

## Al-Suhrawardi (ca. 1154–1191)

Considered the founder of the Illuminationist school of thought, Shihab al-Din Yahya al-Suhrawardi from Aleppo, Syria, was named al-Maqtul (the Slain) or al-Shahid (the Martyr) as a result of being put to death by the Ayyubid caliph Saladin at the behest of theologians who disfavored his philosophical and mystical views.[12] His major work is titled *Hikmat al-Ishraq* (The Science of Illumination). He rejected Aristotelian thought in favor of a higher wisdom, which he termed illumination, with antecedents in the writings of Hermes (identified as Idris or Enoch), Asclepius, Pythagoras, Zoroaster, Plato, Plotinus, and Aristotle. Al-Suhrawardi sought to show that what Aristotle meant in his work was far different from what later Aristotelians made of it. He also argued against Ibn Sina's proof of the existence of the Necessary Being. Ibn Sina had suggested that being is something added to essence, which precedes it. Rather, for al-Suhrawardi, although people could logically distinguish between essence and existence, existence was always found with essence, and hence the proof of the existence of the Necessary Being must be found in realizing that all things had a cause, and the ultimate cause of all being was the Necessary Being, which itself required no cause, because causes could not continue in an infinite series.

In another of his works, al-Suhrawardi reported that Aristotle came to him in a dream and indicated to him that self-knowledge was the basis of all higher knowledge. Thus, theoretical knowledge must be balanced by experiential knowledge. One who was master of both could rightly be considered the vicegerent of God on earth without whom the world cannot subsist, and his instruction to others was indispensable in pointing the way to self-illumination. For al-Suhrawardi, the key element in the world was light, which was all-pervasive, and all things in this world formed a hierarchy depending on the extent to which light permeated them. Humans admit both light and darkness. Light illuminated both itself and other things; at the top of the hierarchy of lights was the Light of Lights, upon which all other lights depended, and hence it must necessarily have existed as the terminus point of all the lights that emanated from it. The Light of Lights was characterized by unity, and the lights more highly placed in the hierarchy exerted an overwhelming or irresistible power over those below them, with those below being attracted to those above through love. The holy spirit, or Gabriel, conferred light on the human embryo, and this constituted the human's soul. Thus, a human was equally capable of domination and of love, and, through experiential exercises and theoretical knowledge, the soul could catch glimpses of the splendors of the eternal world and be released to it upon death. Al-Suhrawardi described some aspects of the soul's journey into illumination through a series of delightful tales written in Persian, translated under the title, *The Mystical and Visionary Treatises.*[13]

## Ibn Rushd (1126–1198)

Abu'l-Walid Muhammad b. Ahmed b. Rushd, considered the greatest Aristotelian philosopher in the Muslim tradition, was born in Cordova, Spain, and educated in jurisprudence, theology, medicine, and philosophy. A physician of note, he wrote a medical treatise called *al-Kulliyat* (The Compendium) and studied under the philosophers Ibn Bajjah and Ibn Tufayl. Ibn Tufayl introduced him to the caliph, Abu Ya'qub, and the meeting led to Ibn Rushd being named the chief judge of Seville as well as to a commission to comment on Aristotle's works. He then served as the chief judge in Cordova, after which he took up the post of the court physician in Marrakesh, Morocco, in 1182. In 1194 Ibn Rushd fell out of favor with the caliph al-Mansur, as a consequence of which he was banned from court, his works were ordered burned, and a general prohibition against the study of philosophy and science was effected. Although Ibn Rushd was restored to favor, he died shortly after, in 1198. He authored works on jurisprudence, medicine, and philosophy and is considered the foremost commentator on Aristotle next to al-Farabi and Ibn Sina. In addition to commentaries on all the works of Aristotle, he also wrote commentaries on Plato's *Republic* and the *Isagoge* of Porphyry. Many of these works were translated into Hebrew and Latin in the thirteenth and fourteenth centuries, and Ibn Rushd's influence on figures such as Maimonides, a key Jewish philosopher-theologian, and St. Thomas Aquinas, the leading Catholic theologian of his day, is well documented. In addition, Ibn Rushd wrote critiques of al-Farabi and Ibn Sina's treatment of Aristotle and some theological works as well.

A major issue preoccupying Ibn Rushd's mind was to demonstrate the harmony between philosophy and revelation, which can rightly be said to form the basis of his response to al-Ghazali's attack on the philosophers. This work, called the *Tahafut al-Tahafut* (The Incoherence of The Incoherence), was a careful rebuttal of each of al-Ghazali's criticisms against philosophic positions. While he acknowledged the truth of al-Ghazali's observation that there are some things that the human mind simply cannot know and for which it must therefore defer to scripture, essentially Ibn Rushd's argument in favor of the harmony between philosophy and revelation lay in showing that al-Ghazali had misunderstood the philosophers' position. That is not to say that he defends al-Farabi and Ibn Sina; rather, he turns his critique against them as well for having partly misunderstood Aristotle. He agreed with them that the soul continued in the afterlife in an immaterial form, in contrast to al-Ghazali's notion that the dead would be physically resurrected to experience the consequences of the final judgment.

## Ibn al-'Arabi ( 1165–1240)

The mystic philosopher Abu Bakr Muhammad ibn al-'Arabi was born in Murcia in Spain and had various titles: Muhyi al-Din (Enlivener of the Faith), al-Shaykh al-Akbar (the Teacher par excellence), and Ibn Aflatun (the Son of Plato). He studied in Seville, and early in his life began to experience visions, beginning during a severe illness at which the personification of the Qur'anic chapter (Ya Sin) recited close to the time of a person's death appeared to him in a vision. His most significant teachers were women, especially Fatima of Cordova, who schooled him on the spiritual path and whose disciple he remained for a number of years. Ibn al-'Arabi's father was acquainted with Ibn Rushd, the great Aristotelian philosopher, and he sent his young son to meet him. Their exchange, as reported by Ibn al-'Arabi, pointed to the necessity of experiencing reality in addition to reflecting on it philosophically.[14] A vision commanded him to journey eastward, and he traveled through Spain, North Africa, Mecca (in now Saudi Arabia), Iraq, Egypt, and finally settled in Damascus, Syria, where he died in 1240.

Ibn al-'Arabi authored more than 800 works, of which some 550 have survived. He reported that he was directed to write many of these by either the Prophet or divine command. His two major works were titled *Futuhat al-Makkiyah* (The Meccan Revelations) and *Fusus al-Hikam* (The Gems of Wisdom), in which he explored the idea that every prophet was the manifestation of one of God's divine names, each of which represented an aspect of divinity. In other works he explored the threefold path to spiritual self-realization: beginning with the exoteric following of the *shari'a* and proceeding through an investigation and practice of the inner meaning of rites and precepts to culminate in experiencing divine reality. Such reality was experienced in a manner that the mystic realized the unity of all being (*wahdat al-wujud*) and, hence, this was a doctrine associated with the name of Ibn al-'Arabi. He was considered to be an *uwaysi* Sufi—that is, one who was under the tutelage of the mysterious prophet Khidr, whom Ibn al-'Arabi met in his visions. Khidr is mentioned in the Qur'an as the guide of Moses who introduces the great lawgiving prophet to the realities of the hidden, inner, and spiritual meanings of rites and rituals—or the law, in other words. Ibn al-'Arabi's work was continued by 'Abd al-Karim al-Jili (d. 1428), a mystic who developed some of the themes found in Ibn al-'Arabi's writings.

### Rumi (1207–1273)

Mystic poet Mawlana Khodavandgar Jalal al-Din Mohammed b. Mohammed al-Balkhi al-Rumi was born possibly in Balkh, northern Afghanistan (hence the name al-Balkhi), in a region formerly part of the eastern Byzantine empire (hence the name al-Rumi, literally, "from Rome"). Early in his childhood he was given the title Jalal al-Din (Glory of the Faith) by his father. Mawlana ("Our Lord") and Khodavandgar ("Master") were also titles given to him. His family left Balkh, possibly fleeing from Mongol incursions. After traveling for 10 years, they settled in Konya, Turkey, in 1229. Rumi studied the Qur'an, *hadith,* theology, and law in Aleppo and Damascus, Syria (where he may possibly have heard the lectures of Ibn al-'Arabi), which he taught after his return to Konya in 1232. He commenced spiritual training and exercises under his father Baha al-Din and also under Borhan al-Din, and in 1244 he met the mysterious figure known as Shams al-Tabrez, who reportedly set Rumi's heart on fire and instructed him in *sama'*, the ecstatic ritual dance associated with the Mevlevi Sufi order later founded by Rumi. Shams disappeared in 1248, possibly murdered by Rumi's disciples who were jealous of the hold he had over Rumi. This loss initiated a dark period in Rumi's life. He composed the *Diwan-e Shams,* comprising some 35,000 lines; a collection of shorter lyrical poems; the *Masnavi*, comprising 25, 577 lines; the *Fihi ma fihi* (Discourses of Rumi); the *Majales-e Sab'e* (Seven Sermons); and the *Maktubat* (Letters). Rumi is significant in the history of Islamic mysticism, and his fame has spread through Europe and America as translators and seekers of a spiritual wisdom increasingly bring him to popular attention in a materialistic age. Although fully imbedded in Islamic spirituality, Rumi's ecumenical vision has struck a chord across religious boundaries as a humanist and mystic visionary.

### Ibn Taymiyah (1262–1328)

Legal scholar Ahmed b. Taymiyah was born in Harran, Syria, in 1262, where his family fled the Mongol invasions to settle in Damascus. He succeeded his father in teaching Hanbali law and lost his professorship after attacking other schools of Islamic law. He was sent to Cairo to drum up support in the wars against the Mongols, but was imprisoned soon after for his polemical opinions. He was reinstated as professor and imprisoned yet again, a pattern that continued throughout his life until, deprived of ink and paper in prison, he died in 1328 in Damascus. More than 200,000 people are thought to have attended his funeral.

Ibn Taymiyah took a firm stance against what he considered to be religious innovations such as pilgrimages to the tombs of persons considered holy by Muslims, including the tomb of the Prophet. An avowed literalist, he interpreted all the Qur'anic passages pertaining to God as meaning exactly what they said, lacking any metaphoric significance. He disputed the positions of all communities of interpretation among Muslims, including the positions of major schools of law and theology such as al-Ash'ari's. He leveled attacks against philosophers as well as mystics, accusing the philosophers of leading Muslims into disbelief and causing schisms. In his view, since Islam was revealed after Judaism and Christianity, adherents of those traditions should convert to Islam, a position contrary to the general Islamic tolerance toward "people of the book." Ibn Taymiyah's views, while contested in his own day by other Muslims, gained favor with the eighteenth-century founder of the Wahhabi school in Saudi Arabia, 'Abd al-Wahhab. As a consequence, Ibn Taymiyah's views found new life in a modern context.

### Ibn Khaldun (1332–1406)

Historian 'Abd al-Rahman b. Khaldun was born in Tunis into an Arab-Spanish family of scholars and was educated in the traditional sciences

comprising the study of the Qur'an, linguistics, the *hadith*, and jurisprudence, before taking up employment at the court of the sultan Abu 'Inan in
Fez, Morocco. There he was introduced to the writings of Ibn Sina and Ibn
Rushd. He then moved to Granada, Spain, and was sent to Seville, the home
of his ancestors, on a mission to broker a peace treaty between Muhammad
V, the ruler of Muslim Spain, and Pedro I, the king of Castile and Leon. He
instructed Muhammad V in philosophy, mathematics, logic, and the law
for a while before political exigencies necessitated his return to North Africa. Once there, he decided to retreat from political life and found seclusion in the castle of Ibn Salama, where he spent four years reflecting on the
causes of historical events. This reflection led to his writing a work that laid
out how history might be explained. Ultimately, he was appointed a professor of Maliki law at al-Azhar in Cairo and the chief Maliki judge in Egypt,
a post he held until his death. He is known chiefly for his *al-Muqaddimah*
or Introduction to his history of the world. The *Muqaddimah,* translated
as *The Philosophy of History,*[15] has established Ibn Khaldun not only as an
astute observer of human characteristics and affairs, but also granted him
the honor of being called one of the fathers "of modern social science and
history."[16] He also authored a summary of Fakhr al-Din Razi's theological
doctrines and a mystical treatise.

## Mulla Sadra (ca. 1571–1641)

The foremost Iranian philosophical and mystical thinker of the Early
Modern Period, Sadr al-Din Shirazi, known as Mulla Sadra, was born in
Shiraz, Iran, and moved to Isfahan where he studied with the renowned
philosophical and mystical Shi'i teachers, Mir Damad (d. 1631), Baha' al-
Din 'Amili (d. 1621), and Mir Fendereski (d. 1640). He assumed a teaching
position at a religious school in Shiraz and died on his way walking back
from his seventh pilgrimage to Mecca in 1641. He wrote many important
commentaries, including on al-Suhrawardi's and Ibn Sina's works. Of his
own works, the major ones are titled *Transcendental Wisdom* and *Four
Journeys.* Plagued by depression at the deplorable state of philosophy in
his day, he withdrew into performing spiritual exercises, resulting in experiences during which, he said, "the light of the divine world shone forth
upon me...and I was able to unravel mysteries which I had not previously
suspected."[17] For him, philosophy had two main divisions: the theoretical,
aimed at knowledge of things as they really were; and the practical, aimed
at realizing the perfections of the soul. Mulla Sadra sought to harmonize
the fruits of philosophical investigation with the aims of a religiously ob-

served life, seeing both as necessary for the soul's attainment of perfection within itself in recognition and emulation of the eternal, spiritual world. Indeed, for him the light of wisdom evident in the Greek sages was continued in the mystics or Sufis and in the Shi'ite *imams.*

## 'Abd al-Wahhab (1703–1787)

Founder of the Wahhabi movement, Muhammad b. 'Abd al-Wahhab was born at 'Uyaina in present-day Saudi Arabia in 1703 and educated in Medina. He traveled to Basra, Baghdad, Kurdistan, Isfahan, and Qumm, where he studied philosophy, mysticism, and finally settled on theology in the vein of Ibn Hanbal and Ibn Taymiyah. Upon his return to the Arabian Peninsula, he wrote the Book on Unity or Oneness (*Kitab al-Tawhid*), his most famous work and which led to his expulsion from 'Uyaina. He went to Dar'iya, where he was welcomed by the clan chief, Muhammad b. Sa'ud. The latter accepted his doctrines and undertook to defend them, thereby commencing a long relationship between the House of Sa'ud and Wahhabi (properly, *muwahhid*—that is, unified) doctrine. In addition to providing training in what 'Abd al-Wahhab considered to be the true doctrines of Islam, he also trained Sa'ud's men in the use of firearms, enabling Sa'ud to gradually increase his power through raids on surrounding towns. Eventually, Wahhabi control spread through much of the peninsula; Medina was captured in 1804 and Mecca in 1806. The Ottoman empire authorized Muhammad 'Ali Pasha, the ruler of Egypt, to deal with the Wahhabi threat, leading to a Wahhabi setback, which was regained a century later. Wahhabi doctrines were similarly spread in India through the military efforts of Sayyid Ahmed (b. 1786) from his center at Patna.

'Abd al-Wahhab's doctrines consisted of doing away with all innovations after the third Islamic century—that is, practices instituted after the ninth century of the common era. He declared that unbelief consisted of believing in anything except the one God, for which the penalty was death; that tomb visitations were a sign of heresy, including visitations to the tomb of the Prophet; that introducing the name of a prophet, saint, or angel into prayer was heresy; that intercession was to be sought from none but God (a polemic against Shi'ites and Sufis); that it was unbelief to accept any knowledge not based on the Qur'an or the six (Sunni) canonical books of *hadith;* that God's predestination must be acknowledged in all acts; and that the Qur'an should not be interpreted allegorically (thereby assuming a position against the philosophers, the mystics, and all other communities of interpretation that saw Qur'anic verses in a metaphorical light). He also required that all Muslims perform the ritual prayer (*salat*) in congregation, publicly; that men not shave their beards; that smoking be forbidden; and that a person's character be investigated to determine whether the person was indeed a Muslim. The use of prayer beads was forbidden, as were minarets or architectural ornaments, leading to the destruction of pre-Wahhabi architectural remains not only in Mecca and Medina but, more recently, in places such as Bosnia.

## Al-Afghani (1839–1897)

Jamal al-Din al-Afghani was born in 1839 in Asadabad, Afghanistan, and moved with his family to Teheran, Iran, where he studied under the leading Shi'ite theologian of the time, Aqasid Sadiq. He then went on to study under another important scholar, Murtada al-Ansari, in Najaf in Iraq, before leaving in 1853 for India, where he was introduced to European thought. After traveling through the Hijaz, Egypt, Yemen, Turkey, Russia, England, and France, he settled in Cairo, Egypt, in 1871 for eight years, where his ideas began to influence the leading Egyptian intellectuals of the day, notably Adib Ishaq, 'Arabi Pasha, and Muhammad 'Abduh. In his writings, he called for the unity of all Muslims and the restoration of the institution of the caliphate free from European interference, as well as a call to return to rationalist ways of understanding Islam.

His travels through Europe incited within him a deep desire to improve the conditions of Muslims and rescue Muslims from tradition-bound forms of thought. Although a modernist, he was not secular in his outlook, as revealed in his attack against naturalists and materialists, whom he considered godless. Rather, for al-Afghani civilization progressed in accordance with three fundamentals taught by religion: (1) the angelic or spiritual aspect of human, which led them to control their bestial impulses and strive to live in peace and harmony; (2) the belief in each religion's superiority over others, which led the faithful in that community to foster the pursuit of knowledge and excel in the arts; and (3) the realization that human life was simply preparatory for an eternal life free from sorrow, leading to the ethical desire to free oneself from malice and other egotistical impurities and to defend peace, love, and justice.[18] He undertook a purview of human history and traced the role of religion in the rise and fall of nations, ending with a critique of socialism and communism as undermining religion while continuing to shed blood under the pretext of championing the poor.

For al-Afghani, Islam was the most superior religion because it refused to accept anything without proof, thereby drawing attention to the need to rationalize religion at all times. Thus, he also criticized Muslims who he thought held blindly to a cultic expression of faith, such as the Hanbalites, the Ash'arites, and the Sufis. Al-Afghani is credited with fostering a nationalist and intellectual revival in Egypt, and his work has had an impact elsewhere, for instance, in Turkey.

### Muhammad 'Abduh (1849–1905)

The leading student of al-Afghani, Muhammad 'Abduh was born in 1849 in Mahallat Nasr in Egypt and was educated in Tanta in the religious sciences. There he met Shaykh Darwish, a Sufi teacher who profoundly influenced his life and who later encouraged his decision to study philosophy and science with al-Afghani.[19] 'Abduh entered the premier academy for the training of *'ulama,'* al-Azhar in Cairo, in 1866 C.E., but soon left it, disenchanted with the traditionalist modes of learning he encountered there. He became a student of al-Afghani, who was offering public classes. With al-Afghani, he explored studies in the Islamic sciences of logic, theology, astronomy, metaphysics, and Ishraqi thought. Through al-Afghani's influence, 'Abduh became interested in a career of public service. He then began teaching at al-Azhar, drawing large numbers of students to his classes and arousing the ire of the traditional theologians who faulted him for teaching courses on philosophy and theology, while also applying Ibn Khaldun's observations on human societies to contemporary Egypt. He held the editorship of various key periodicals and ultimately held the position of the Grand Mufti in Egypt, while also teaching at Beirut for a short while. He firmly upheld the importance of reason as the ultimate arbiter of truth, guided by revelation and its moral principles, and inveighed against the blind acceptance of any dogma. Like al-Afghani, 'Abduh did much to foster an intellectual revival in Egypt and elsewhere, and his most important student was Rashid Rida (d. 1935), who, however, took 'Abduh's teachings to mean that Muslims had to return to the path of the early Muslim community, guided solely by the Qur'an and the *hadith.* Rida's position was akin to that proposed by the later followers of Ibn Taymiya and 'Abd al-Wahhab.

### Muhammad Iqbal (1877–1938)

Poet Muhammad Iqbal stands in the liberal tradition of Muslim thinkers in India who emerged from the colonial encounter to consider how

Islam might be understood in ways compatible with Western discourse. One of Muhammad Iqbal's intellectual forebears included Sayyid Ahmad Khan of Bahadur (d. 1898), who founded the Aligarh movement in 1875 and established, with Sir Sultan Mohammed Shah (Aga Khan III), the Muhammadan Anglo-Oriental College, which later became the University of Aligarh. Iqbal also was influenced by Sayyid Ameer Ali (d. 1928), who argued that Islamic values lay at the core of Western liberal values. A poet of great distinction and a student of the Western intellectual tradition, Iqbal drew on the philosophers Hegel, Whitehead, and Bergson to make the case for the *Reconstruction of Religious Thought in Islam,* the title of one of his most well known works. Born in 1877 in Sialkot in Punjab, he received his early education in Sialkot and Lahore. He went to England and Germany in 1905 for higher studies in philosophy, and he returned to India in 1908 to practice law.

Iqbal considered religion to be one of the most important arenas upon which philosophic thought must reflect; in his view, religion "is an expression of the whole man."[20] Creation was not a process that has reached completion; rather, for him, the universe was something that is continually drawing out its potential, and humans are agents who continually assist God in realizing the innate potential of the universe. Religious experience, therefore, allowed people to encounter this dynamic reality that was continually unfolding, both outwardly and inwardly.[21] Iqbal further sought to remove the body-soul dualism inherent in Greek and some Muslim thought to advance the view, building on Ash'arite atomism, that each element of reality was spiritual, thereby making a case for an inherent connection between the finite and the infinite. Iqbal also took great pains to draw attention to the Islamic roots of modern Western scientific empiricism. Thus, although all three modernist and liberal Muslim thinkers in India (Iqbal, Khan, and Ali) sought to think about Islam using Westernized categories, they also firmly held the view that Islam could make a spiritual and ethical contribution to thinking about the place and mandate of humans in the world.

## Sayyid Qutb (1906–1966)

Author and educator Sayyid Qutb was virulently opposed to Western culture and ideas. He was born in 1906, educated in Cairo, and appointed inspector for the ministry of education, a post he held for a number of years before devoting himself full-time to writing. He wrote 24 books and innumerable articles. In the late 1940s, Qutb underwent a transformation during which he perceived the establishment of the state of Israel as a Western denial of the Arab right to self-determination, and his subsequent studies in the United States in educational administration led him to a rejection of all things Western because of the racial prejudice he witnessed there. On his return to Egypt, he joined the Muslim Brotherhood, and, inspired by the writings of an Indian revivalist thinker, Abu al-'Ala Mawdudi (d. 1979), he argued that there could be no compromise between Islam and modernity. Rather, he noted: "If it becomes evident that Islam possesses or is capable of solving our basic problems, of granting us a comprehensive social justice, of restoring for us justice in government, in economics, in opportunities, and in punishment...then without doubt, it will be more capable, than any other system we may seek to borrow or imitate, to work in our nation."[22]

Critiquing capitalism and communism, Qutb sought to formulate an Islamic ideology that would be an alternative to both and that would address the social and economic problems facing Muslims on the basis of the *shari'a* (Islamic law). He held to the notion that *shari'a* law was eternal and unchanging, but he identified jurisprudence as the arena within which the interpretation of the law could be granted the flexibility of taking contemporary circumstances into account. This Islamic ideology was worked out in several books written around the time of the Egyptian revolution in 1952. In 1954, Qutb was arrested on charges of conspiring against Gamal Abdel Nasser, the president of Egypt, and sentenced to 15 years of incarceration and hard labor. During his imprisonment, Qutb completed 13 volumes of his interpretation of the Qur'an in addition to writing two books, all of which argued that Islam applied to all areas of one's life. He was released after 10 years and wrote another work that led to his arrest in 1965 and his subsequent execution in 1966. He was buried in an unmarked grave, and his death raised him to the status of a martyr. His writings continue to inspire Muslim youth looking for a radicalized Islamic vision of society.

### Aga Khan IV (b. 1936)

Philanthropist His Royal Highness Prince Karim Aga Khan IV, leader of the Shi'ah Isma'ili Muslims, was born in 1936, educated in Kenya and France and at Harvard University in the United States. He was declared leader of the small Ismaili community (population estimates vary from 10 to 15 million worldwide) in 1957, after the death of his grandfather, Sir Sultan Muhammad Shah Aga Khan III, whose modernization efforts were far-reaching. Famed equally for his horses and for his philanthropic efforts through the Aga Khan Foundation, the Aga Khan has emerged as a thinker who views God's creation as continuous; the human soul as eternal; and the human mandate, based on the Qur'an, as one guided by the ethic of caring and compassion for others, regardless of race, class, gender, or creed. As a result, he has focused his considerable resources on development issues in five major areas: education as a means for the underprivileged to better their circumstances; medical care to manage the health crisis in developing countries; industrialization using local materials to enable developing countries to become self-sufficient; sustainable tourism that least damages the environment while providing a source of national income; and architecture as an arena in which humans, using local materials, can express an ethos that is mindful of humility before God as it recognizes the place of humanity in harmony with nature in keeping with Islamic aesthetics and ethics. His call for enabling and enhancing civil societies as well as calling for tolerance and the acknowledgement of pluralism within Islamic societies goes hand in hand with his conceptualization of Islam as a message of peace rather than conflict, and he is a vocal critic of the political use of Islam and its concomitant acts of violence as being unworthy of the spirit of Islam.

## NOTES

1. Majid Fakhry, *A History of Islamic Philosophy*, 2nd edition (New York: Columbia University Press, 1983), 235–36.
2. Fakhry, 67–68.
3. Fakhry, 71.
4. Fakhry, 243.
5. Fakhry, 207–8, 204–17.
6. Fakhry, 154.
7. Howard R. Turner, *Science in Medieval Islam* (New York: Oxford University Press, 1999), 136–37.
8. Fakhry, 164–81.
9. M. Arkoun, "Miskawayh" in *Encyclopedia of Islam*, CD-ROM, v.1.1.
10. Fakhry, 186–92.
11. Fakhry, 248.
12. Fakhry, 293ff.
13. Suhrawardi, *The Mystical and Visionary Treatises of Shihabuddin Yahya Suharawardi*, trans. by W. M. Thackston, Jr. (London: Octagon Press, 1982).
14. For an account of this meeting, see Henry Corbin, *Creative Imagination in the Sufism of Ibn 'Arabi* (Princeton, NJ: Princeton University Press, 1969), 41–42.

15. See Muhsin Mahdi, *Ibn Khaldun's Philosophy of History* (Chicago: University of Chicago Press, 1957). This has been reprinted several times.

16. Ibid., 5.

17. Fakhry, 306ff.

18. Fakhry, 334ff.

19. Fakhry, 338ff.

20. From *Reconstruction*, quoted in Fakhry, 350.

21. Fakhry, 351ff.

22. Yvonne Y. Haddad, "Sayyid Qutb: Ideologue of Islamic Revival" in John L. Esposito, ed., *Voices of Resurgent Islam* (New York: Oxford University Press, 1983), 70.

# GLOSSARY

**Abd:** One who serves.
**Allah:** God.
**Ayat:** Signs.
**Caliph:** Political ruler; head of all lands under his control.
**Dey:** Local governors.
**Dhimmi:** Non-Muslim.
**Din:** Religion.
**Faqr:** State of poverty.
**Fatwas:** Legal rulings.
**Fiqh:** Works written on legal understanding.
**Hadith:** Traditions.
**Hajj:** Pilgrimage to Mecca, in Saudi Arabia.
**Halim:** One who shows self-control.
**Hanif:** A non-Jewish, non-Christian monotheist; for example the original muslim: that is, Abraham.
**Hilm:** Self-control.
**Ibadat:** Acts of worship.
**Iblis:** Satan.
**Ibn:** Son of.
**Id:** Festival.
**Ijtihad:** Intellectual effort.
**Imam:** Prayer leader for Sunnis, chief spiritual authority for Shi'is.
**Jahil:** Ignorant one.
**Jihad:** Holy war.
**Jinn:** Spirit.

**Ka'aba:** House of worship in Mecca thought to have been built by Abraham and Ishmael.

**Kahin:** Seer.

**Khanqah:** Sufi house of worship.

**Madrasa:** Islamic religious school.

**Matam:** Acts of mourning.

**Millah:** Community of faith.

**Mujtahid:** Legal scholar who engage in ijtihad.

**Musnad:** Chain of transmission for a hadith.

**Ribat:** Sufi lodge.

**Salat:** Prayer.

**Sawm:** Fasting.

**Sha'ir:** Poet.

**Shari'a:** Divine law.

**Shaykh:** Master.

**Shia:** Branch of Islam considering 'Ali the legitimate spiritual successor to the Prophet Muhammad.

**Sufism:** Mystical branch of Islam.

**Sunni:** Branch of Islam that follows the sunnah or example of the Prophet Muhammad.

**Sura:** Chapter of the Qu'ran, Islam's holy book.

**Tajwid:** Recitation.

**Tawaf:** Circumambulation of the Ka'aba during pilgrimage.

**Ummah:** Community.

**Wird:** Supplicating prayer.

**Zakat:** Almsgiving.

# SELECTED BIBLIOGRAPHY

Ahmed, Leila. *Women and Gender in Islam.* New Haven, CT: Yale University Press, 1992.

Berg, C. C. "Sawm." In *Shorter Encyclopedia of Islam,* ed. H.A.R. Gibb and J. H. Kramers. Leiden: E. J. Brill, 1974.

Bloom, Jonathan and Sheila Blair. *Islam: A Thousand Years of Faith and Power.* New Haven, CT: Yale University Press, 2002.

Craig, Kenneth and Martin Speight. *Islam from Within: Anthology of a Religion.* Belmont, CA: Wadsworth, 1980.

Denny, Frederick Mathewson. *An Introduction to Islam.* New York: Macmillan, 1994.

*Encyclopedia of Islam,* CD-ROM, Edition v.1.1. Leiden: E. J. Brill, 2001.

Ernst, Carl. *Sufism.* Boston: Shambhala, 1997.

Ernst, Carl W. *Words of Ecstasy in Sufism.* Albany: State University of New York Press, 1985.

Esposito, John. *Islam: The Straight Path.* New York: Oxford University Press, 1992.

Fakhry, Majid. *A Short Introduction to Islamic Philosophy, Theology and Mysticism.* New York: Oneworld, 1997.

Farah, Caesar E. *Islam.* New York: Barron's, 1987.

Guillaume, Alfred. *Islam.* Harmondsworth, England: Penguin Books, 1971 (1956).

Halm, Heinz. *Shiism.* Edinburgh: Edinburgh University Press, 1991.

Hodgson, Marshall G. S. *The Venture of Islam: Conscience and History in a World Civilization*, 3 vols. Chicago: University of Chicago Press, 1974.

Hoffman, Valerie J. "An Islamic Activist: Zeinab al-Ghazali," in *Women and the Family in the Middle East*, ed. Elizabeth Warnock Fernea. Austin: University of Texas Press, 1985.

Ibn Hisham, Abd al-Malik. *The Life of Muhammad.* A translation of Ishaq's *Sirat Rasul Allah.* London: Oxford University Press, 1955.

Izutsu, Toshihiko. *God and Man in the Koran: Semantics of the Koranic Weltanschauung.* Tokyo: Keio Institute of Cultural and Linguistic Studies, 1964.

Kassam, Tazim R. "The Daily Prayer (Du'a) of Shi'a Isma'ili Muslims." In *Religions of the United States in Practice*, ed. Colleen McDannell. Vol. 2. Princeton, NJ: Princeton University Press, 2001.

Khusraw, Nasir. *Six Chapters or Shish Fasl by Nasir-i Khusraw.* W. Ivanow, trans. Bombay: Ismaili Society, 1949.

Lawrence, Bruce B. *Shattering the Myth: Islam Beyond Violence.* Princeton, NJ: Princeton University Press, 1998.

Madelung, Wilferd. *The Succession to Muhammad: A Study of the Early Caliphate.* Cambridge, England: Cambridge University Press, 1997.

Mernissi, Fatima. *Women and Islam: An Historical and Theological Enquiry.* Oxford, England: Basil Blackwell, 1991.

Michon, Jean Louis. "The Spiritual Practices of Sufism." In *Islamic Spirituality: Foundations*, ed. Seyyed Hossein Nasr. New York: Crossroad, 1997.

Moghadam, Valentine M. *Modernizing Women: Gender and Social Change in the Middle East*, 2nd ed. Boulder, CO: Lynne Rienner, 2003.

Momen, Moojan. *An Introduction to Shi'i Islam.* New Haven, CT: Yale University Press, 1985.

Nanji, Azim A., ed. *The Muslim Almanac: A Reference Work on the History, Faith, Culture, and Peoples of Islam.* Farmington Hills, MI: Gale Research, 1996.

Nicholson, Reynold A. *The Mystics of Islam.* London: Routledge and Kegan Paul, 1914, 1963.

Pinault, David. *The Shiites: Ritual and Popular Piety in a Muslim Community.* New York: St. Martin's Press, 1992.

Rahman, Fazlur. *Islam.* New York: Holt, Rinehart and Winston, 1966.

Rahman, Fazlur. *Major Themes of the Qur'an.* Minneapolis: Bibliotheca Islamica, 1980.

Sachiko Murata and William C. Chittick. *The Vision of Islam.* New York: Paragon House, 1994.

Schimmel, Annemarie. *And Muhammad Is His Messenger: The Veneration of the Prophet in Islamic Piety.* Chapel Hill: University of North Carolina Press, 1985.

Schimmel, Annemarie. *Islam: An Introduction.* Albany: State University of New York Press, 1992.

Schimmel, Annemarie. *Make a Shield from Wisdom.* New York: Kegan Paul International, 1993.

Schimmel, Annemarie. *Mystical Dimensions of Islam.* Chapel Hill: University of North Carolina Press, 1975.

Schubel, Vernon James. *Religious Performance in Contemporary Islam: Shi'i Devotional Rituals in South Asia.* Columbia: University of South Carolina Press, 1993.

Stowasser, Barbara Freyer. *Women in the Qur'an, Traditions, and Interpretation.* New York: Oxford University Press, 1994.

Walzer, R. *Greek into Arabic.* Cambridge, MA: Harvard University Press, 1962.

# INDEX

*Boldface numbers refer to volume numbers: 1: Judaism; 2: Confucianism and Taoism; 3: Buddhism; 4: Christianity; 5: Islam; 6: Hinduism.*

marriage, **1:**97–98; marriage
contract *(ketubbah)*, **1:**98–100;
redemption of firstborn, **1:**93–
94; wedding ceremony, **1:**100–
102
*Li Ji (The Book of Rights)*, **2:**31, 38
Lineages: Vaishnavism
*(sampradayas)*, **6:**47
*Lingam*, **6:**54–55
Lingayats, **6:**53–55
*Ling-bao*, **2:**20–21
Linji, Master, **3:**84
Linji school of Chan Buddhism, **3:**82;
meditation, **3:**105
Lithuania: Ashkenazi Jews, **1:**42
Liturgical (priestly) Taoism, **2:**20–22,
26–27, 104–6
Liturgy, **4:**97; Anglican Church,
**4:**118–19; Divine (Eastern
Orthodox), **4:**97–101;
Lutheranism, **4:**68; Roman
Catholic, **4:**103–8
Liturgy of St. Basil, **4:**100
Liturgy of the Catechumens, **4:**99
Liturgy of the Eucharist. *See*
Eucharist (Communion)
Liturgy of the Faithful, **4:**99
Liturgy of the Word, **4:**105
Livelihood, right, **3:**51
Logicians, **2:**13
Loi Krathong, **3:**145–46
Lombards, **4:**15
Lord on High, **2:**6
Lord's Prayer: Eastern Orthodox
Church, **4:**100
Lord's Supper, **4:**96, 105–6;
Pentecostal Church, **4:**124. *See also*
Eucharist (Communion)
Losar, **3:**154–55
Lotus Sutra, **3:**25, 40–41, 73;
Nichiren, **3:**186
Love: ecstatic, **6:**32
Lü, Zhang, **2:**174

Lubavitcher Movement, **1:**45–46;
United States, **1:**65
Lubavitcher Rebbe (Menachem
Schneerson), **1:**46, 162–64
Lulav, **1:**114
Lumbini, **3:**113, 140, 142
Lunar New Year (Chinese), **3:**149
*Lun-yü (The Analects)*, **2:**32–33, 37,
39, 43, 45–46
Luria, Rabbi Isaac, **1:**73, 145–46
Luther, Martin, **4:**65, 66–69
Lutheran Church, **4:**66–69; calendar,
**4:**166; church organization,
**4:**116–17; history and statistics,
**4:**115; practices, **4:**115–17; rituals,
**4:**160; worship, **4:**115–16. *See also*
Christian; Christianity
Lutheran Church–Missouri Synod,
**4:**116–17

Maccabees, **1:**7, 8, 35–36; **4:**5;
Hanukkah and, **1:**123–24. *See also*
Judah Maccabee
Ma-cig, **3:**190
Macrobiotics, **2:**98
Macy, Joanna, **3:**134
Madagascar: early Islam, **5:**21
*Madhhab*, **5:**62
Madhva (Madhva Acharya), **6:**5, 47,
112–13
Madhyamika, **3:**57–58; Atisha, **3:**
189
Magen David, **1:**79
Magha Mela, **6:**97–98
Magi, Zoroastrian, **4:**6–7
Mahabarata, **6:**3, 15–16; *ahimsa*,
**6:**28–29, 87; Bhagavad Gita,
**6:**16–18
Mahadeva, **6:**52
Mahakashyapa, **3:**81, 166
Mahamaya, **3:**4, 5
Maha-Maya, **6:**57–59
Mahapajapati, **3:**166–67

## About the Authors

**EMILY TAITZ** is an independent scholar and author of *The Jews of Medieval France: The Community of Champagne* (Greenwood, 1994) and numerous essays on Judaism and the coauthor of *Remarkable Jewish Women: Rebels, Rabbis and Other Women from Biblical Times to the Present* (2002), among other works.

**RANDALL L. NADEAU** is Associate Professor of East Asian Religions at Trinity University, San Antonio, Texas.

**JOHN M. THOMPSON** teaches in the Department of Philosophy and Religious Studies, Christopher Newport University, Newport News, Virginia.

**LEE W. BAILEY** is Associate Professor of Philosophy and Religion at Ithaca College.

**ZAYN R. KASSAM** is Associate Professor of Religious Studies and Chair of the Religious Studies Department, Pomona College.

**STEVEN J. ROSEN** is an independent scholar and prolific writer on Hinduism.